SINGING THE CHURCH'S SONG

SINGING THE CHURCH'S SONG

Essays and Occasional Writings on Church Music

CARL SCHALK

Lutheran University Press
Minneapolis, Minnesota

Singing the Church's Song
Essays and Occasional Writings
by Carl Schalk

Copyright © 2015 Carl Schalk except as indicated. All rights reserved. Published by Lutheran University Press, an imprint of 1517 Media. No part of this book may be reproduced or transmitted in any form by any means, electronic, mechanical, recording, or otherwise, without the express permission of the author. For information or permissions or excerpts, please contact the author.

> Published under the auspices of:
> Center for Church Music
> Concordia University Chicago
> River Forest, Ill. 60305-1402

ISBN 978-1-942304-06-7
eISBN 978-1-942304-78-4

Every attempt has been made to track down sources of quotations and contact copyright holders. In the event there is an omission, please contact the Center for Church Music.

About the Center for Church Music

The Center for Church Music was established in 2010 on the campus of Concordia University Chicago. Its purpose is to provide ongoing research and educational resources in Lutheran church music especially in the areas of congregational song and composition for the Church. It is intended to be of interest to pastors, musicians, and laity alike.

The Center maintains a continually expanding resource room which houses the Schalk American Lutheran Hymnal Collection, the manuscript collections of prominent Lutheran composers and hymn writers, and a broad array of reference works and resources in church music. To create a global awareness and facilitate online research, efforts are underway to digitize the hymnal collection, the manuscript archives, and the hymn festival recordings.

The Center publishes monographs and books covering various aspects of Lutheran church music.

The Center maintains a dynamic website whose features include devotions, presentations, oral histories, biographical essays, resource recommendations, and conversations on various topics in worship and church music.

The Center's Founders Group includes Linda and Robert Kempke, Nancy and Bill Raabe, and Waldemar B. Seefeldt, whose significant monetary gifts initiated the Center and have, along with the gifts of others, sustained its momentum.

The Center's Advisory Board includes James Freese, Scott Hyslop, Linda Kempke, Jonathan Kohrs, Nancy Raabe, Carl Schalk, Steven Wente, and Paul Westermeyer.

Barry L. Bobb serves as its volunteer director.

You can follow news about the Center on Facebook. Learn more about the Center and subscribe to its free e-newsletter at http://cuchicago.edu/about-concordia/center-for-church-music.

To my students,
as together we explored
the history and practice of church music
in the Lutheran tradition.

Contents

Foreword (Martin E. Marty) 11
Preface (Barry L. Bobb) 15
Introduction (Carl Schalk) 17

I. Music as the Church's Song

Why Christians Sing: Paradigms and Proposals 21
Celebrating Music 37
The Church's Song: Proclamation, Pedagogy, and Praise 43

II. Music in Liturgical Worship

Music in Lutheran Worship 57
Luther on Music Revisited 71
The Pastor and the Church Musician: Thoughts on
Aspects of a Common Ministry 89
The Church Musician as Steward of the Mysteries 99
Learning from the Past: What the Lutheran Tradition
Can Teach Church Musicians of Today 111
A Primer for Lutheran Music and Worship 129

III. The Lutheran Heritage of Hymnody

The Roots of Lutheran Hymnody in America 155

Paul Gerhardt: Some Thoughts on His Hymnody............................. 175

Friedrich Layriz: Forgotten Influence on
Congregational Singing in American Lutheranism 183

IV. The Role of the Composer

The Dilemma of the Contemporary Composer of Church Music 199

Some Thoughts on the Writing of Hymn Tunes 211

The Church and the Composer 221

V. Meditations and Homilies

A Lament for Resounding Praise 235

A Song for Silent Praise 241

Meditations on the "Great O Antiphons" 245

Mary and the Pound of Spikenard 251

Member, Dismember, and Remember 255

New Year: It's about Time 259

Now Thank We All Our God . . . with Hands.................................. 263

St. Michael and All Angels 267

Foreword

Those who know author and musician Carl Schalk personally will not be surprised to find me introducing this life-collection of his writings with a lighthearted story. After a funeral at Grace Lutheran Church in River Forest, Ill., my wife complimented the professor on a short song he had composed for the occasion. It had been sung by the children's choir of Grace. Moved by the work she said, "Oh, Carl, that is so beautiful. Can the congregation hear it at my own funeral?" Schalk flipped open his appointment book and with an ornery smile asked, "And what date did you have in mind?"

He and we hope it will not need to be scheduled for some years, but we both are in the vast company of people who have been moved by his compositions, his choirs, his organ-playing, even sometimes when he stands by or is the focus at Grace Church. I first came to hear him decades ago over the radio when, in St. Louis, he was in charge of music for the international program *The Lutheran Hour*. I could not have anticipated the fact that for a half century and more we would be privileged regularly to hear from him and hear his music as he developed his own "Schalkian voice" in music and in prose. So why commend *this* book, as I enthusiastically do, in a world in which so many experiences of music in church or for the church beckon and also offer much?

First, Schalk deserves notice because his church music is *church* music, boldly and consistently so. It is not first of all concert-performance music that happens to work in church, though Schalk has written anthems for choruses and works that are in the mode of Bach's "secular cantatas." His main creative energies have gone into writing, directing, and performing for worshippers, whether in congregations, on campuses, or through media. In a day of individualized and idiosyncratic "spiritual" music, often sensational in character, his music echoes a great line of Dietrich Bonhoeffer, "*Christus existiert als Gemeinde*"—Christ exists *as* congregation, not simply *in* congregation. This says not only that Christ exists *in* the gathering, but *as* the gathering. Schalk's music reflects deep pondering on the reality of the singing church as an expression of the Body of Christ, and Schalk will always be responsible to its community and message.

Second, his music is singularly focused in praise of God. Isn't everybody's? One hopes so, but his compositions, complex though some of them may be, are very simply and focally directed to God. When Martin Luther preached for the first-ever church built for Lutherans, at Torgau Castle—the building still exists and awaits your visit—he stipulated: "Nothing should ever happen here except that our dear Lord speaks to us through his holy word, and we, in turn, respond with prayer and songs of praise." "Praise" here is not the shallow but loud repetition of God-ward phrases, but is the response—in this case in music—to the "holy word." Again, heard beyond and above so much egocentric "I-talk" in church and culture, Schalk's music is seen and heard as support for and re-articulation of God's holy word.

That sentence leads me to a third to-be-noticed item in the collection which follows, this time in the essays and less directly in the music itself. Schalk is as much educator as he is composer or director. He has spoken to and written for teachers of the Church but has done so without being didactic. He never seeks a jazzy little adornment for his prose. He trusts the serious intent of readers and listeners, here in virtual dialogue with him, even when Carl does most of the talking, as one must when one is the lecturer. Since this is a collection, inevitably there are occasional repetitions or, I prefer here, repeatings of some themes. Such exceptional moments or paragraphs on these pages are not boring but rather enhancing: we get to regard a theme through many approaches, from many angles. Composers do that all the time, as in "variations on a theme," knowing that the repeated lines do change just as we, the hearers, change. Schalk assumes that such change can mean growth, and he writes to stimulate it.

P.S.: Schalk writes for the Church catholic, but his music and his essay themes are consistently Lutheran. That does not mean that there is a sectarian, in-house cast to it all. In the ecumenical era he knows and shows that when we reach into the particular vocabularies and emphases of our part of the Church, we can bring our best to the attention of others, and we will have been trained to listen more intently to the voices, choruses, and lectures of others. Bonhoeffer, again, liked to speak of the basics of the faith as providing the *cantus firmus* for our existence, experience, and expressions. Depending and drawing on it, we can take risks and even soar, as Schalk's writing and music help readers and musicians do, and for which we are grateful to him.

Martin E. Marty

Preface

In 1965 Concordia University Chicago (then Concordia Teachers College) called Carl Schalk to a new faculty position and a new venture. The administration wished to expand the academic program to include church music as its own discipline.

Schalk was uniquely qualified to take on this exciting challenge. He was an alumnus of Concordia; he had recently received his master's degree at the prestigious Eastman School of Music at the University of Rochester, N.Y., and was completing a second master's degree in religion at Concordia Seminary, St. Louis. He had served as a church musician in Wisconsin and was then director of music for the radio broadcasts of *The Lutheran Hour*.

Schalk accepted the challenge and set about the task quickly. In short order there were both undergraduate and graduate degrees in church music at Concordia. He helped found the journal *Church Music* and instituted an annual fall event—the Lectures in Church Music—which continues to this day, all the while teaching classes, directing the Chapel Choir, and serving as an organ instructor. He also began assisting Paul Bouman with organist and choir directing duties at Grace Lutheran Church (on the corner of the campus).

He was an avid reader in Lutheran theology and a diligent student of the Church's history, especially as it relates to worship and church music. He studied not only the Lutheran tradition but conversed with church music leaders in many faith traditions. He was also developing as a composer of church music (especially for his choir at the college and the adult choir at Grace), carving out a special reputation for practical settings and showing a gift for writing new hymn tunes, many of which have found an abiding place in the body of congregational song. Over time he amassed one of the best collections of Lutheran hymnals (of both German and Scandinavian origins) in the United States.

As his career blossomed he was called to serve on many committees both within and outside Lutheranism. With his practical bent, winsome manner, and a sly sense of humor, Schalk steadily gained a reputation as a thinker, speaker, and writer on many topics related to the Church's song.

His legacy is truly enduring and exemplary and has been recognized through several honorary degrees and awards.

It is for this reason that the Center for Church Music is pleased to offer this compilation of some of Schalk's most important essays, papers, and addresses spanning the course of his career. The best outcome of this publication would be that many church musicians, pastors, and laity would come to understand more fully the foundational ideas and values which continue to shape the Church's song, and further, that they be moved to carry this legacy to the coming generations.

>Barry L. Bobb
>Director, Center for Church Music
>Concordia University Chicago

Introduction

The essays in this collection are gathered from presentations made over the years to various groups interested in the worship and music of the Church. Some essays have previously appeared in print but are in a variety of publications no longer generally available.

While these essays were written at different times and for widely different occasions over an entire career, they are grouped here for convenience in five categories: three are general essays on the tradition of the Church's song; six deal specifically with the Lutheran tradition of worship and church music; three essays discuss different aspects of Lutheran hymnody; three essays are on the composer of church music in the Lutheran tradition; and several miscellaneous items address acoustics in worship, appearing together with several brief homilies and other devotional writings.

At the root of these writings is the simple proposition that church musicians need to be *both* theologically informed and musically skilled—that they are simultaneously *church* musicians and church *musicians*. It should also be evident that several underlying themes form the background of these essays. Sometimes explicitly stated, more frequently they are implicit in the argument. These include the central importance of the great tradition of the Church's worship and song and the central role of proclamation and teaching in the Church's worship, its music, and its congregational song.

My thanking and appreciation go to all those who have heard aspects of these presentations in the variety of circumstances from classroom to public forums where these were first presented.

Special thanks to the Center for Church Music at Concordia University Chicago and its director Barry Bobb, and to Karen Walhof of

Lutheran University Press for making this material more generally available to a wider audience through this collection.

Carl Schalk
Ash Wednesday 2015

I

Music as the Church's Song

Why Christians Sing: Paradigms and Proposals

Whenever Christians gather to worship and praise God, we sing songs—songs of confidence and faith, songs of confession and contrition, songs of exile and rebirth, songs of sin and salvation. Our music is a *cantus firmus* ("a fixed melody"). It extols God's glory and praise for rescuing his chosen people, and it sings the great central action of God in Jesus Christ, the love we celebrate with special emphasis each paschal season.

This theme of the Church's song has been clear and constant from the beginning. Ps. 118, the psalm appointed for the Feast of the Resurrection, was the song of the earliest Christians:

> Give thanks to the Lord for he is good; and his mercy endures forever.
>
> Let Israel now proclaim: his mercy endures forever.
>
> The right hand of the Lord has triumphed! The right hand of the Lord is exalted! The right hand of the Lord has triumphed!
>
> I shall not die but live, and declare the works of the Lord.
>
> I will give thanks to you for you have answered me and have become my salvation.
>
> The same stone which the builders rejected has become the chief cornerstone.
>
> This is the Lord's doing, and it is marvelous in our eyes.
>
> On this day the Lord has acted; we will rejoice and be glad in it.
>
> (Ps. 118; translation unknown)

This essay was first published in *Liturgy: Journal of the Liturgical Conference* 3, no. 3 (1983):7–15. Reprinted by permission.

Today this psalm is still the heart and center of the Church's teaching and proclamation, the reason for its celebration of the liturgy, and the content of its song.

Music in Christian Worship

The joining of music with Christian worship is not the result of historical accident. It is rather the deliberate result of the Church's concern for the faith joined together with an understanding of the power of music to move our minds and hearts. In theory, the wedding of music and worship appears to be a wedding of convenience; in practice, it is the unavoidable result of the new life in Christ. In theory, it may be possible to imagine Christian worship devoid of song; in practice, the Christian community fills its gatherings with psalms, hymns, and spiritual songs. As Martin Luther once remarked,

> God has made our hearts and spirits happy through His dear Son.... He who believes this sincerely and earnestly cannot help but be happy; he *must* cheerfully sing (emphasis mine). (Introduction to Valentin Babst, *Geistliche Lieder* [1545])

The history of the Christian community is the history of a singing and music-making community. We cannot imagine it otherwise.

In the corporate worship of the Church, music that celebrates the goodness of God in Jesus Christ is carried out in a variety of ways. Always, however, celebration in song should be disciplined and instructed by the liturgy. Congregations, celebrants, assisting ministers, choirs, soloists, and instrumentalists in their respective roles are guided, informed, shaped, and instructed by the liturgy of the Church. Without this basic understanding of the role of music in worship, distortions and misunderstandings easily arise that can prevent a fully communal celebration of God's great gift of self and salvation in the Son.

At the center of our music-making stand the church musicians, the latter-day psalmists who carry forward the Church's musical tradition. They teach, encourage, nurture, and help congregations—sometimes even recalcitrant congregations—to fuller understanding and celebration of the faith. Such respect for church musicians has not always been the norm. In the view of some parishes, church musicians are "an affliction sent by God, that those who have never suffered for their faith may not be denied the opportunity to do so." Countless other parishes, however, can testify to the rich blessings that church musicians bring to the prayer life of the parish community. Through their winsome and persistent example, they lead Christians to a fuller and richer understanding and practice of the mysteries of faith that are celebrated in the corporate worship of God's people.

The Church has never in its history held to a single and consistent view of the role of music in worship. Rather, at different times, the Church has recognized a variety of often-conflicting views on the role of music in worship; and, as our models or paradigms for understanding music change, so do our emphases and intentions. Each of the paradigms of the past, taken singly, builds on a point of truth. The Christian community is always a singing and music-making community. But, should any one model become the final arbiter of the place and function of music in worship, an impoverished experience of music in the life and worship of God's people easily results.

Thus, music can be understood to teach, to exhort, to edify, and to entertain, but the boundaries of Christian song are too tightly drawn in places that limit the functions of music to any one of these. Theological presuppositions, the piety of the assembly, and the musicians' art interact with other factors to define the paradigms of Christian song in any given age. Past and limited though some views are, they are also the path to new viewpoints.

1. Music as Educator

One of the persistent models that has shaped the relationship between music and worship presents music as a Christian teacher or pedagogue. Closely tied to this paradigm is the didactic view that turns songs into weapons of argument. Virtually from the beginning Christians have recognized that psalms, hymns, and spiritual songs can be enlisted in the battle to refute heresies. The early Church faced a largely hostile, pagan culture that threatened it from within. Education, indoctrination, and teaching became the crucial means for carrying on the Church's mission. The song of the Church was an important tool in that task.

Basil, in the fourth century, rhapsodized "the wise invention of the teacher who devised how we might at the same time sing and learn profitable things" (*Homily* 10). Basil also suggested that it was the Holy Spirit itself who "blended the delights of melody with doctrines in order that through the softness of the sound we might unawares receive what is useful in the words."

Christians readily perceived that truth more easily impresses itself upon the hearts of the faithful when it is sung. And heretical groups quickly made use of the same device. Thus, it is both instructive and ironic to note that the development of Christian hymnody received its greatest impetus from the rise of heresy. In the East, Gnosticism was the catalyst; in the West, the Arian controversy.

In the sixteenth century, Luther did not hesitate to "correct and improve" certain medieval Latin hymns to correspond more clearly to the Reformation's understanding of the Gospel. The strongly doctrinal hymns of that time reflect the Church's concern for teaching the faith in a manner easily accessible to the people. Luther's battles with the pope are present, for example, in the hymn "Lord, Keep Us Steadfast in Your Word." But, as Luther was also concerned with the errors of the "enthusiasts," his conflict with them is equally apparent in the hymnody of the time.

The confessional revivals of the nineteenth century—both in Germany and the United States— promoted a return to the unaltered tunes and texts of the Reformation. Music revived in the name of orthodoxy was a tool against the hegemony of rationalism. Revivalism in the expanding American frontier, the awakening of social consciousness at the end of the nineteenth and beginning of the twentieth centuries, the temperance movement, the mid-twentieth-century religious emphasis on community, spontaneity, and celebration—each of these movements sought in its own way to reach for acceptance and to spread its message through the medium of the Church's song.

2. Music as a Shaper of Morals

Another paradigm of the relationship between music and the Church's song sees music as a guardian and shaper of the moral condition. This view of music is part of the philosophical framework inherited by the early Church. On the one hand, the ancient Greeks viewed music as part of a larger moral concern, as a reflection of the stability and continuity of an ordered universe. They spoke of the "harmony of the spheres" and of "celestial music." Music that undergirded such a view was good; music that threatened it was dangerous.

In a narrower sense, the Greeks ascribed to music the power to soothe or to inflame the senses and the passions, to strengthen of weaken the moral fiber. The Church, in the midst of a pagan culture, was quick to adopt this view. Thus Basil admonished "Christians not [to] be drawn down by the pleasantness of the melody to the passions of the flesh" (*Homily* 10). And Augustine, in his *Confessions* (XXXIII:49), noted that "the several affections of our spirit, have their moods answerable to their variety in the voice and singing, and by some secret association therewith they be stirred up."

This theme reappears with particular force in the thought of the sixteenth-century reformer John Calvin, himself greatly influenced by Augustine. According to Calvin,

> There is hardly anything in the world with more power to turn or bend, this way and that, the morals of men. . . . [Music] has a secret and almost incredible power to move our hearts in one way or another. (*La forme des prières ecclésiastiques* [1542])

Calvin's conclusion was simple: "Wherefore we must be the more diligent in ruling (music) in such a manner that it may be useful to us and in no way pernicious." The result was a closely regulated church music of the simplest possible kind. Ulrich Zwingli, Calvin's somewhat earlier contemporary, had carried this view to its logical conclusion. He made no place at all for music in his worship order, and replaced it instead with a holy silence.

Whenever this essentially platonic view of music prevails in the Church, as it does in many protestant churches in America, music becomes a tool of human behavior and motivation. From such a viewpoint music is always potentially troublesome, a medium that seeks to entice and to attract attention to itself. It calls for close supervision and control. Thus popular songs that are attractive to young people inevitably call forth warnings that they are endangering the morals of the young. This was so in the early Church, in the sixteenth century, and in our own time. Church music in popular styles stirs so much controversy in some sectors of the Church that it is condemned. Whenever zealous preachers organize record burnings of popular music, or hold earnest discussions about "Christian rock music," they are using this paradigm of music as shaper of morals, of music consequently in need of careful control and direction.

3. Music as Edification

Edification, or spiritual improvement and instruction, is always a concern of the Church. In the relationship between music and the worship life of the Christian community, however, the paradigm of music as edifier is sometimes more problematic. The authors of the New Testament understood edification in a corporate sense and applied it to the upbuilding of the local community. But by the seventeenth century for many Christians, edification had become a purely private matter. Long before Philip Spener's *Pia desideria* of 1675, in which he coined the phrase "edification of the inner man," a new and personal piety had begun to develop which not only characterized the period of Pietism, but also had significant consequences for both worship and the music of worship.

As this new piety developed, music was valued increasingly as a means to stir up feelings of devotion in the hearer. Edification was valid if the hearers' feelings were moved, if, that is, they *felt* themselves being edified. Music that helped to achieve this end was favored; music that did not was scorned. "Learned" or contrapuntal music soon fell into disfavor, and the simple hymn style became the most important musical vehicle for this kind of edification. The stately, somber, and slow execution of the music enabled the hearer to absorb what was useful in the text.

The lively rhythms of the sixteenth-century chorales were altered gradually. They became the flattened out, even-note melodies that characterized congregational singing throughout the eighteenth century and which, by the nineteenth century, had almost destroyed it. This was the period of the *Geistliche Arien* and the melodies of Georg Schemelli's *Musikalisches Gesangbuch* of 1736. J. S. Bach himself had a part in the latter. Edification in a personalistic and privatistic sense pervaded both the texts and music of the Church's song.

Such a view of edification was effected at the cost of a rupture with the general musical culture of the day. In a culture highly receptive to the arts, Pietism advocated an ascetic, fundamentally reactionary rejection of "secular" intrusions into the musical culture of the Church. The controversies between J. S. Bach and the Pietists of his day are an example.

Rationalism, a somewhat later development, sought to edify its hearers also, but along different lines. For the rationalist, edification meant being filled with a useful knowledge of God. As this knowledge was often available apart from the liturgy and the worship life of the Church, this view was an ethico-humanitarian ideal rather than a churchly one. In its musical expression it favored biblical texts; therefore, it was connected with religion. Handel's sacred oratorios are good examples of this newer ideal; they had religious content, but they were not really church music.

As the concept of edification developed in both Pietism and Rationalism, texts were required to incite hearers to feelings of devotion. That they did this in ways increasingly divorced from the historic liturgy of the Church mattered little. Music was simply a means to achieve a personal and private devotion. Ultimately this view shifted the focus of one's praise and adoration from Jesus Christ and the good news of the Gospel to the subjective feelings and judgments of individuals as to whether they indeed had been edified. For thoroughgoing pietists, praise and edification were subjective realities.

4. Music as Entertainer

Rarely is entertainment publicly announced as a model for music in the Church. Yet the view is pervasive that whatever else music does, it entertains. Accordingly, music in worship functions as a momentary diversion, a psychological change of pace, a pleasure to titillate our ears in new and exciting ways. Nowhere is this view expressed in so frank and direct a manner, but the typical modern emphases in North America on consumerism and voluntarism combine to ensure that the church with an "attractive" music program is a "successful" church. One certain way to attract an audience in a competitive situation is to entertain.

Such an attitude is nourished and fed by a related problem. Members of the worshipping community too often see themselves as spectators. We come to church to listen, to watch, to be entertained. Woe to the preacher or church musician who does not measure up to this typical, though unspoken, attitude, namely: "We came to worship to be entertained (religiously entertained), and either you fulfilled or you fell short of our expectation." Even churches of long liturgical tradition are not exempt from the possibility that the paradigm of music as entertainment has worked its way into their midst.

Each of these four paradigms or models for understanding the role of music in the church's life and worship is faulty or incomplete. We must search for a paradigm that will more adequately reflect all sides of the relationship between music and worship. New understandings must be found in order to tap the whole range and power of music in community prayer. The question, however, is where to look for such a paradigm. If it is not in our current practice, is it, perhaps, in our past?

Music as God's Gift

Luther provides us with a starting point precisely because his view of music in the life of the worshipping community transcended all of these limiting views and placed them in a larger and more useful perspective.

In Luther's view, music is a good and gracious gift of the Creator, a gift that is ours for the praise of God and the Gospel of Christ. Thus, Luther, alone among the sixteenth-century reformers, unhesitatingly commended the use of music in the nourishment of the Christian life. In contrast to Calvin, who only grudgingly permitted music a place in corporate worship, and to Zwingli, who banished it entirely from corporate worship, Luther accorded to music the highest place next to theology. Luther's understanding of music as God's gift made possible its cultivation at high levels of artistic excellence and freed the Church to use all kinds of music without fear:

> when man's natural musical ability is whetted and polished to the extent that it becomes an art, then do we note with great surprise the great and perfect wisdom of God in music, which is after all, His product and His gift. (*Luther's Works*, American ed., foreword to Georg Rhau's *Symphoniae iucundae*)

Luther's view encouraged the teaching and singing of chant and polyphony—the most sophisticated musical forms—as well as simpler congregational hymns. The Latin Renaissance tradition had developed a sophisticated art music for the Church with little, if any, music for the people. The Calvinist tradition had excluded art music entirely, allowing only a simple congregational psalmody. In contrast to both, the Lutheran Reformation tradition encouraged a reciprocal action between art music of the most sophisticated kind and simple congregational song. The result was a flourishing tradition of church music of great richness and depth.

By emphasizing music as God's creation and God's gift, Luther set the stage for a situation in which composers, congregations, choirs, and instrumentalists were free to develop their talents and abilities to the highest reaches. The development of music in the Lutheran tradition is eloquent testimony that people and church musicians found in Luther's views a healthy and wholesome environment in which to work, to sing, and to make music in praise of God and God's good works. At the root of this flourishing tradition was the paradigm of music as God's good gift to all creatures.

Reshaping Church Music

The question remains, "How can the paradigm of music as God's good gift be realized more faithfully and adequately in the circumstances of the present?" The suggestions that follow are directions for using this gift in our time. Put into practice, they can help the Church to reshape the role of music in its life and worship.

Church music is the gift of God and the living voice of the Gospel. Its greatest function is to praise God and to proclaim God's word to the Christian faithful.

Music functions as proclamation when it is associated with texts that speak clearly and directly of Law and Gospel, of sin and salvation, with texts that speak not only the stern words of judgment, but also the comforting words of assurance and grace. From such a perspective, music in the Church is never only a teacher, an edifier, or an entertainer. Nor is it merely a way of filling the Christian community with useful information. It is, rather, the living Gospel. Music lays bare our utter alienation from God; it is, at its best, always accusing, yet always reconciling, always bringing words of promise. Texts, therefore, are of crucial importance, just as is the music itself with which the texts are associated.

Music participates in the proclamation of the Word. It faithfully reflects the honesty, integrity, and truthfulness of the Gospel message itself. Thus, the ideas that music relates to worship as "the perfect setting for the perfect jewel of the Gospel," and that the role of music is "to beautify" the service, or to be as the wrapping enclosing the gift, a wrapping that can be cast aside once the gift is revealed, miss the mark. Church music can never be simply a part of the wrapping; rather, it is part of the unwrapping. Either music contributes to faithful proclamation and witness or it detracts from it.

Music in worship is part of the ministry of the Word. Whether one speaks from the pulpit, choir loft, or organ bench, whether the Gospel is being proclaimed in word or tone, it is always the same Gospel that we speak with faithfulness and hear with contrite and trusting hearts.

Church music as the gift of God proclaims and praises God in ways that are disciplined by the liturgy.

Church music finds its most comfortable and appropriate place in the liturgy, in all its fullness and richness. Liturgy, as the gathering of God's people, is a living tradition of communal praise, proclamation, prayer, and mutual edification. It is the best focus from which to determine how music is used, what its spirit and mood and discipline should be, and the appropriateness of specific music for particular occasions.

Church musicians must give primary attention to two kinds of texts: (1) those that follow the church year and the lectionary, and (2) those that are designed to enhance specific liturgical moments in the celebration of particular feasts. Texts in the first category call for a more serious search for music to underscore the specificity of particular celebrations, while those in the second category demand a radical realignment of the priorities enjoyed by various segments of our present musical repertoires.

Accepting the discipline of the liturgy points also to the need for a radical reordering of congregational expectations. Congregations that view music as "a beautiful addition to the service" must be brought slowly and carefully to see the organic relation between the liturgy and the Church's song. The discipline of the liturgy can make available to the worshipping community the wealth and experience of the Church at worship throughout the centuries. Without discipline, the community is always at the mercy of the musician's individual experiences and unprotected from the faddishness that passes for relevance. Finally, to place oneself and one's musical or preaching ministry under the discipline of the liturgy may require from some musicians and some pastors the courage to begin anew. But without such courage and discipline, richness and depth in worship are not possible.

Church music needs to find its way back to a more radical simplicity.

"Radical" music, by definition, is music that arises from or goes to a root or source; it is fundamental and basic. "Simple" music is unaffected, unassuming, and unpretentious; it is not guileful or deceitful, but sincere.

Such a radical simplicity in church music will stem, first of all, from a greater understanding of what liturgy is, from the musical priorities inherent in the flow of the liturgical action, and from the use of music as doxological proclamation. Music should be chosen to underscore particular liturgical actions in ways that quietly and appropriately relate the action to the particular celebration. Liturgical music need not be pretentious to be effective. Music that strives for a "big effect" (even from meager materials) or places a premium on winning acceptance from the hearer with a superficial attractiveness does not add anything to Christian worship.

In some instances church musicians have viewed music in worship as a means for personal or congregational aggrandizement. More often, perhaps, their lapses result from a lack of understanding or sensitivity to the specific demands of particular celebrations. A commitment to the discipline of a radical simplicity will enable them to forgo the pretentious, bombastic music which panders to the hearer, exploits the easily achieved effect, and seeks to please everyone at all costs. It will also free them to apply to music these architectural principles: "form follows function," and "less is more." This is not a recommendation for some kind of austere musical spartanism. It does suggest, however, that music should not be used in worship if it reflects an ostentation that is either irrelevant to or unjustified by liturgical circumstances, or both.

The involvement of congregations in the singing of psalms is one of the elements in recent liturgical reform that reflects this thrust. To continue to concentrate the musical resources of the parish on those basic involvements in the liturgy that are the particular province of people, choir, or organ is a step in the right direction. Eventually we may even prefer the simplicity and directness of a liturgical Passion setting by Victoria or Hillert to the pretentious bombast of Du Bois's "Seven Last Words." And we may learn to use a simple hymn alternation or a choral Kyrie at times instead of some old choral chestnut which might better have been retired. In brief, the return to a more radical simplicity is a return to liturgical roots and to liturgically appropriate music.

Church music as a gift of God is for participation, primarily, rather than for listening only.

The participatory nature of church music emphasizes that the liturgy is never simply a high drama we have come to observe, nor an event that we hope will entertain us. We do not come to the liturgy to be spectators but to be involved participants in communal song. We come to liturgy to praise in song the same Lord whose Word we hear in the lessons and preaching, whom we confess in the creed, and whose gift of self is communicated to us in the sacrament of the altar.

Recent events among Lutherans have emphasized the participatory nature of church music. For the first time, two musical settings of the liturgy have been written specifically for congregational singing. The new emphasis on singing the psalms is also a major thrust in helping congregations participate musically in the liturgy. That a significant place has been given to the hymn of the day in the liturgy is yet another example of the sensitive use of congregational song in the prayer of the church.

Church musicians have discovered new responsibilities in the implications for teaching and learning that participation in music inevitably brings. We can no longer simply teach others "to sing the liturgy" or a new hymn, but teaching and learning must also increase one's actual understanding of the Church's worship. Only in this way can congregations avoid using an ever-diminishing circle of "favorite hymns," singing endlessly only what they already know.

Church music as a participatory medium does not merely give people something to do. Music involves people in more effective and faithful singing of the liturgy, and it expands their understanding of and participation in the total prayer life of the Church. Music that is a trip down some nostalgic trail is demeaning not only to music and the liturgy, but also to the congregation whose unique role in the priesthood of all believers is to sing the Church's song.

Music as a gift of God necessitates a clearer view of music as craft.

Music, like other human actions, must be well made. It must be fit for its purpose and suitable for its function.

Music as craft has given rise to at least two misleading views. One is the still-popular nineteenth-century view that music is basically artistic inspiration. This is exemplified by the popular story of Handel, who retired to his garret, only to emerge a few weeks later with the score of *Messiah* in his hand, the result of a blinding flash of inspiration. The other misreading of music as craft results in the "stories of favorite hymns." While such stories are often interesting and instructive, they tend to suggest a direct correspondence between the worth of a hymn and the poignancy of its origin.

Although music is a craft, the goal of music in worship is not beauty. To "worship the Lord in the beauty of holiness," as Eric Routley and others have said, means no more than to "worship the Lord with decent or appropriate ornaments." Aside from the fact that two people can seldom agree on what actually constitutes beauty—there is no "mawkish anthem or organ voluntary, no spiritually depressing piece of church furniture, but somebody has thought it beautiful"—to seek beauty as the goal is to stress the effect of sound rather than its rightness.

If music is indeed God's good gift to be used in praise and adoration of the Creator—if, that is, it finds its ultimate purpose in the proclamation of the Gospel—then to proclaim the Gospel in texts and music that are cheap, superficial, banal, shoddy, and perhaps worst of all, pretentious is to contradict in our art the truth, honesty, and integrity of the

Gospel itself. Much of the music heard in churches today can be characterized by its trite rhythm and treacly harmony, and by its striving for the easy effect. A combination of large and impressive size combined with cheap materials implies contempt for craftsmanship. The materials of music are so often overlaid with a patina of surface gloss and superficial attractiveness that they do a disservice to the liturgy. As we readily decry this lack of integrity in church architecture, it is time to listen seriously to similar criticisms of church music—particularly from those who fashion the songs of faith.

Church music as gift of God must reflect both an external and an internal balance.

Much of church music in parishes is out of balance. The first kind of imbalance is *external*. Such imbalance occurs when parts of the liturgy that are the special province of the choir are given scant attention in preference to other parts of the service of lesser importance. In both Lutheran service books now in use in America, choirs should be giving their primary attention to the psalms, verses, offertories, and hymn of the day as they prepare for their role in worship. These are the texts the choirmaster must use to begin his or her preparation and planning. For such an attitude to establish itself, however, a major reordering of priorities is required of choirmasters and singers, as well as congregations. To give these parts of the liturgy first priority in rehearsal and in the choir's participation in worship is possible only if church musicians, singers, and congregations participate in an ongoing educational effort. This imbalance, where it exists, is external.

A second level of imbalance is *internal*. It requires equal attention. No portion of the liturgy, be it in the choir's province or not, ought to be given greater musical importance than it actually has in the totality of the liturgical action. Large-scale musical settings of the verse, for example, coupled with minimum attention to the Gospel acclamations that follow, can easily give a false impression of their relative importance. Elaborate processionals or recessionals, if not balanced by equal or greater attention to more significant liturgical actions, create equally false impressions as to what is truly important in the liturgy. If the *Sanctus*, surely a climactic moment in the liturgy, is accompanied in a listless fashion with anemic organ registration, while the full resources of the organ are reserved for the prelude or postlude, something is certainly out of balance.

Church musicians will need to be sensitive to such internal balance in the musical portion of the liturgy as they plan and prepare music for corporate worship. Such sensitivity, modeled for congregations over longer periods of time, will do more than anything else to help parishes sense the action and flow of the liturgy, and to discern its inner dynamics.

To accept and use music to praise the Creator and to proclaim God's good news to the world is to hold up a paradigm that includes and surpasses all lesser views of music in the life, witness, and worship of the Church. Music as gift frees us to use all music without fear, because it encompasses both the simple communal song of the people of God and the most sophisticated art music that the Church has or will yet develop. As our view of music in the totality of the prayer life of the Church deepens, so does our focus broaden and settle where it always should be, on the good news of God in Jesus Christ. This is the focus that all preachers, church musicians, and congregations earnestly desire, the center that unites us in a common ministry and prayer.

Celebrating Music

The trumpet shall be heard on high, / The dead shall live, the living die, / And music shall untune the sky.

—Dryden, *Song for St. Cecelia's Day*

To be asked to speak on this distinguished occasion of the inauguration of a newly established chair of music is not only a great honor, it also presents one rather immediately with a particular problem. It is not unlike being asked to speak about food. One can discuss its color, its texture, its aroma, its nutritional value—but all that ultimately misses the point. For in the last analysis, food is not meant to be talked about; it is meant to be tasted, savored, eaten, and enjoyed. Even the most ingenious television commercial can show us the sizzle of the hamburger and the crispiness of the French fries; but what they cannot show—and what we really want to know—is how do they taste? "Where's the beef?" is more than a question of quantity. It is ultimately a question of quality.

It is no different with music, for music is an art which comes to fruition not by speaking about its beauty, proportion, or craftsmanship, but only in the performance itself and in the listener's personal engagement with this art of sound. This presents a particular problem today since the one we honor in this newly established chair is not one who primarily talks about music, but one who performs, one who stimulates our hearing, engages our listening, and who ultimately attempts to involve us in the sound of music itself. And for that words are hardly adequate.

Nevertheless, we can and we should speak about this day and its importance in our lives, and especially in the life of this community. For

---

Presentation at the convocation for the introduction of Philip Gehring as the Frederick A. and Mazie N. Reddel Professor of Music, Valparaiso University, Valparaiso, Ind., October 25, 1985.

it is important. And the impact of the generosity of the gift which makes this day possible will certainly be reflected in the lives of all of us here today, and in the lives of many yet to come.

It is a day for celebrating. And especially in this community it is a day for celebrating the gift of music: music, that gift which so often permeates our lives in trivial and inconsequential ways, our too-constant companion in elevators, supermarkets, student unions, and automobiles; music, that gift which is also with us in the more particularly profound and significant events and experiences of life; music, which gives us wings in times of joy, which buoys us up in times of sadness, which gives us delight and hope in times of both promise and despair. It is that gift of music which we celebrate today.

Moreover, it is a day for everyone to celebrate. The celebration is for all: whether we have trouble keeping the beat, or can tap out a double paradiddle with ease; whether we have difficulty singing a simple tune, or can join in the most complex of polyphonic motets; whether our musical training has been rich and varied, or whether it has consisted largely of once-a-week piano lessons in the fifth grade in which the teacher's challenge was somehow to attempt to bridge the gap between Chopin and us. It is a day for each of us—and all of us together—to celebrate this marvelous gift of music. On pitch or off, the celebration includes us all. It does not exclude a single one.

It is a day for celebrating precisely because music is God's good creation and God's good gift to us all. It is God's creation. It is God's gift. And it is God's *good* creation and gift. As such, it is to be received and enjoyed by his people in praise of the Creator who has graciously given this good gift to us. Martin Luther understood this simple fact as clearly as anyone:

> I would certainly like to praise music with all my heart as the excellent gift of God which it is and to commend it to everyone. But I am so overwhelmed by the diversity and magnitude of its benefits that . . . as much as I want to commend it, my praise is bound to be wanting.[1]

Nothing here of Augustine's scruples at having received pleasure from this wonderful gift. Nothing here of Augustine's "floating between peril and pleasure" as far as God's good gift was concerned. "Augustine," Luther pointed out on one occasion, "was a fine and pious man. However, if he were living today," Luther gently reminded his hearers, "he would agree with us." For Luther, music understood first of all as God's good creation and as God's good gift to man made music next in importance to theology, made possible its cultivation and enjoyment at the highest levels of artistic excellence, and gave man the freedom to use all of music without fear.

Whether Stravinsky or Springsteen, Gibbons, Gershwin, or Gehring, music is God's good gift to us all. Whether Mozart or Beethoven, Bach or Buxtehude, it is first and last a song of praise to the Creator of music, a song of praise to him who has given man this good and gracious gift.

But music is always a gift for us to use. It is never simply a gift to be acknowledged and then hung in the closet like an unwanted Christmas tie. It is a gift to be used in praise of music's and our Creator. If music was indeed God's gracious gift, it was so in order that man might in turn use it in God's praise.

> Use the gift of music to praise God and him alone, since he has given us this gift.
>
> And you, my young friend, let this noble, wholesome, and cheerful creation of God be commended to you. . . . At the same time you may by this creation accustom yourself to recognize and praise the Creator.[2]

The words of the morning office underscore as clearly as possible this creator/creature relationship. God is Creator, we are his creatures. So we are called to worship with the words "O come, let us worship the Lord." Why? Our simple and direct response: "For he is our maker." Therefore, in the words of Ps. 95, "Come, let us sing unto the Lord. . . . Let us shout for joy. . . . O come let us bow down and bend the knee, and kneel before the Lord, our Maker."

But there is still another dimension to be explored.

Music is God's good gift in order that his name might be praised and his Word proclaimed to all the world.

No one spoke so clearly and forthrightly about the union of word and tone to the end that God might be praised and his Word proclaimed as did Martin Luther. For Luther, to sing and praise the Triune God for all he has done for mankind, especially for his goodness revealed to us in Christ Jesus, was for Luther to proclaim the good and gracious will of God. The gift of language combined with the gift of music, said Luther in his preface to Rhau's *Symphoniae iucundae*, "was only given to man to let him know that he should praise God with both word and music, namely, by proclaiming [the Word of God] through music by providing sweet melodies with words." For Luther, as for us today, to "say and sing" was a single concept erupting from the joyful heart of the redeemed.

> From heaven above to earth I come, / To bear good news to every home. / Glad tidings of great joy I bring / Whereof I now will *say and sing* (emphasis mine).[3]

Not say, and then sing; but *say and sing*! In contrast to other reformers who saw music as potentially troublesome and in need of careful direction and control, Luther—and we—in the freedom of the Gospel can exult in the power of music to proclaim the Gospel and to touch the heart and mind of man, and exult as well in our opportunity to "say and sing."

Today we celebrate the gift of music in yet another way.

It helps us celebrate our lives together in the community of the Church.

It needs to be said again that the Church, before it is anything else, is a worshipping community. One may disagree about the priorities of the tasks the Church is always about—mission, education, evangelism— but about what the Church is, first and foremost, there should be no question. It is first and foremost a worshipping community centered, in Gordon Lathrop's words, around "bath, Word, and table."

In this worshipping community music holds a place of the highest esteem. In this community, music—properly used—always unites, bringing together our individual concerns and uniting them in the prayer and praise of all. In a very practical sense, music is the glue which holds together the actions of the liturgy. It unites us into one community as it helps focus attention where it really belongs: on Christ and what he has done for us. Music divides when it becomes mere entertainment or when its focus is on lesser or peripheral concerns.

As music unites us and brings us together in praise and prayer, it addresses in a most direct way the alienation and selfishness of our fallen world. One may well ponder Dietrich Bonhoeffer's observation in his "After Ten Years: A Reckoning Made at New Year 1943"[4] concerning the hopelessness and frustration he saw all around him. "One may ask," Bonhoeffer remarked, "whether there have ever been people with so little ground under their feet—people to whom every available alternative seemed equally intolerable, repugnant, and futile." It is especially here, in the discordant polyphony of our lives and times, that music as God's good and gracious gift helps us see the strong and firm cantus firmus about which all else revolves, that enduring melody, that song which is Jesus Christ himself.

In this connection I am reminded of the story of the farmer walking down a path and encountering a little bird lying on its back with its feet sticking up in the air. "You stupid bird," the farmer said, "what are you doing lying on your back with your feet sticking up in the air?" "Haven't you heard?" the little bird replied. "The sky is falling." "Well," said the farmer, "do you think you can prevent the sky from falling by lying on your back with your feet sticking up in the air?" "Well," the bird replied, "we all do what we can." In our world in which the sky seems so often to be falling all around us, God's good gift of music helps to remind us that we are not, as the world may think, shouting forlornly into the bitter wind. For it is music which helps us to sing the triumphant song of faith in the face of all doubt, and to sing a song of confidence and trust in the face of all despair and seeming futility.

Finally, today is a day to celebrate the gift of music as it helps us sing and dance the faith.

We celebrate today the special joy in the hearts of the redeemed as through the song of faith we confidently affirm the goodness of all of God's creation. To sing and dance the faith with great exuberance is to save us from the false sobriety and pretentious somberness which characterizes so much of the Church today. To sing and dance the faith is to bring us into the presence of the morning stars which sang together for joy before the foundation of the world, and into the company of all the saints with whom we sing, "Holy, holy, holy, heaven and earth are full of your glory."

To sing that song in confidence and faith even now as a worshipping community can be done only as we hold together the two words which signify what our song and our music-making are all about: the *dogma* or the teaching, and the *doxa* or the praise. We need to be reminded again that "orthodoxy" means, first of all, "right praise," and that the *dogma* and the *doxa* are best held together when we see ourselves first of all as a worshipping community.

Music and music-making is always a sign. It should be a sign of God's continuing goodness, a sign of God who gives us songs to sing, and a sign of the One who gives art and music to his people that we might glimpse his beauty, that we might see in this good gift our Creator, delight in his gracious gift, praise his name, and proclaim his Word to the world.

To be a part of that endeavor is a high and noble calling indeed. It is a calling which reaches its final and glorious culmination as one day we join in the music-making of the song of the Lamb at that final feast of victory:

> Worthy is Christ, the Lamb who was slain, whose blood set us free to be people of God. Sing with all the people of God, and join in the hymn of all creation: blessing, honor, glory, and might be to God and the Lamb forever. Alleluia! Alleluia![5]

Amen!

Notes

[1] Martin Luther, *Luther's Works*, American edition, vol. 53, *Liturgy and Hymns*, ed. Ulrich S. Leupold (Philadelphia: Fortress, 1965), 321–22 (preface to Georg Rhau's *Symphoniae iucundae*).

[2] Ibid., 324.

[3] *Lutheran Service Book* #358, st. 1.

[4] Dietrich Bonhoeffer, *Letters and Papers from Prison* (New York: Macmillan, 1953).

[5] Liturgical song text by John W. Arthur based on Rev. 5:12-13.

The Church's Song: Proclamation, Pedagogy, and Praise

The song of the Church is a response of faith to what God has done in Jesus Christ. It is a song from the heart of the Church to the heart of God, from the heart of the Church to the heart of each believer, and from the heart of the Church to the world.

As God's people gathered around Word and Sacrament, we sing. But the song is not, first and foremost, our song, but rather the Church's song. Of course it is we who sing, but in worship we sing as a community of faith, joining together with angels, archangels, and all the company of heaven. It is a song sung by all the faithful who have gone before us, and a song which will continue after we are gone. It is a song that, in our own time and place, we are privileged to join. It is a song in which proclamation, teaching, and praise interweave in a tapestry of song unique to the Church. At the heart and center of that song is the proclamation of the good news of the Gospel of Jesus Christ.

The Song of the Old Testament

The song of the Old Testament provides the pattern. In the Old Testament God identifies himself through his actions on behalf of his chosen people: God is the God who acts to save us. The very first song recorded in the Old Testament, the Song of Miriam, celebrated God's saving act in rescuing the children of Israel from the armies of Pharaoh. "Sing to the Lord, for he has triumphed gloriously, the horse and his rider he has thrown into the sea" (Exod. 15:20-21). Miriam and the women gave voice to their thanks and praise

---

This article is set to appear in the forthcoming handbook to *Lutheran Service Book* (Concordia).

by singing from their heart of how God had acted in bringing them out of Egypt and freeing them from slavery. For ancient Israel the deeds of the Lord revealed God as the God who saves, who was "glorious in power," "majestic in holiness," "terrible in glorious deeds," "doing wonders."

Israel's song of praise and thanks to God consisted of rehearing what God had done to rescue them. What drove their praise and thanksgiving was the story of God's mighty acts on their behalf. *To sing God's praise meant, for ancient Israel, to tell again and again in song the story of how God had acted to save them,* how God had brought them up out of Egypt, led them through the wilderness, and brought them to the Promised Land. That was their song.

The constant refrain in the book of Psalms, the "hymn book" of the Old Testament, is Israel's response of praise described by such phrases as declaring God's mighty acts (Psalm 145:4), making known God's mighty deeds (Ps. 105:12), calling to remembrance God's wonderful works (Ps. 105:5), recounting God's wondrous deeds (Ps. 75:1). *To sing and praise God in the Old Testament was to "sing and praise the God who . . . ,"* the ellipsis being filled with the particular story of God's delivering his people. The exhortation of Ps. 98 to "Sing unto the Lord a new song" is incomplete without the second half of the phrase: "for he has done marvelous things! His right hand and his holy arm have gotten him the victory." Ps. 96:2-3 exhorts: "O sing unto the Lord. . . . Declare his glory among the nations, his marvelous works among all the peoples." For the psalmist "to declare his glory" was to declare "his marvelous works."

It was in the telling, over and over, again and again, remembering and recalling God's promise and covenant, that God was praised and thanked in song. Israel was to remember what God had done for them, to recount God's glorious deeds, and to speak and sing of them in the assembly. The "good news" for God's people in the Old Testament was not simply *who God was,* but *how God had acted* on their behalf to rescue them from their sin. This was the content of their song.

The Song of the New Testament

The song of the New Testament maintained the pattern of the Old, continuing to rehearse and celebrate the mighty acts of God. But it added to the Old Testament song the good news celebrating the ultimate revelation of God's goodness revealed in his Son Jesus Christ. The New Testament celebrates the good news that at a particular time and in a particular place God sent his Son to be born of a virgin, to fulfill the Law for us, to suffer death on a cross, to be raised from the dead by the glory of the Father, to ascend to heaven and to now sit at the right hand of God, and to come again at the end of time, in fulfillment of his promise, to judge the world.

It was this good news that was the heart and center of such psalm-like New Testament songs as young Mary's *Magnificat*, Zechariah's *Benedictus*, and the *Nunc dimittis* from the heart of the aged Simeon. Each testifies to God's new act of deliverance in his Son Jesus Christ.

This story about Jesus the Christ and the hope he brings for the future is what Christians call the Gospel, the Good News, the *kerygma* ("message" or "proclamation"). It is not a set of moral or ethical standards, not the Golden Rule, not a set of rules for a successful life, not a religious philosophy. It is not any kind of good news that is healing, positive, helpful, or that seems good to me. It is a specific story which is both history and promise.[1] It became the basic content of the songs of the New Testament and the early church. It became the essential content of the Church's liturgy and song in succeeding centuries. Apart from that story of Jesus' death and resurrection the Church's song ceases to be the *Church's* song.

The Church's Song in the Middle Ages

As the Church moved into the early Middle Ages, the structures within which it worshipped and which provided the context for the Church's song grew to embrace a more richly developing Church Year, the gradual establishing of the basic structure of the Mass, and the development of the Daily Office, celebrated largely, though not exclusively, in the many monastic communities which were beginning to develop across Europe and the British Isles at that time.

While there was a prodigious outpouring of new hymnody by such writers as Ambrose of Milan, Gregory the Great, Sedulius, Prudentius, and later Thomas Aquinas and many others, its use was largely confined to the monastic communities. It was this particular repertoire of early medieval hymns that centuries later Martin Luther would commend for use as a sign of continuity with the whole Church.

> St. Ambrose composed many hymns of the church. They are often called church hymns because the church accepted them and sings them just as though the church had written them and as though they were the church's songs. Therefore it is not customary to say "Thus sang Ambrose, Gregory, Prudentius, Sedulius, but thus sings the Christian church." For these songs are now the songs of the church.[2]

Yet while, for a variety of reasons, the voice of the people in the church's worship was largely stilled during the medieval period, popular religious song flourished in many places, however, outside the celebration of the Mass and the Daily Office. The medieval *Leisen*, the *Cantios*, and macaronic songs of the pre-Reformation period, the popular religious songs of the Minnesingers and Meistersingers, some of which influenced the church, the songs of the Flagellants, and similar groups, all contributed in their own way to the context facing the reformers of the sixteenth century. So by the sixteenth century there was available to the Reformers a variety of popular religious song which served as one, though not the main, source for the people's song in the early years of the Reformation. The main source of the people's song in the early years of the Reformation would be the treasury of Gregorian hymnody which was born in the early Middle Ages and nurtured by the Church and adapted in a variety of ways by the Lutheran church of the Reformation.

The Song of the Reformation

Martin Luther (1483–1546) saw the "telling of the story" of how God had acted to save us as the central role of the song of the church. He wrote in the introduction to Georg Rhau's *Symphoniae iucundae* (52 choral motets for the Sundays of the church year),

> the gift of language combined with the gift of song was only given to man to let him know *that he should praise God with both words and music, namely, by proclaiming the Word of God through music* and by providing sweet melodies with words[3] (emphasis mine).

Johann Walter, Luther's friend and the first Lutheran cantor, said that the purpose of Christian song was that God's promise of free and unmerited grace "might be kept fresh in human memory" and to "move the heart to high delight in praising God both day and night."[4] It was in the telling and retelling of the story of God's salvation that God's promises were kept fresh in human memory and so delighted the heart.

The very first hymn in the earliest Lutheran collection of 1524, Luther's hymn "Dear Christians, One and All, Rejoice," underscores this point:

> Dear Christians, one and all, rejoice,
> With exaltation springing,
> And with united heart and voice
> And holy rapture singing,
> *Proclaim the wonders God has done,*
> *How His right arm the vict'ry won.*
> *What price our ransom cost Him!*[5] (emphasis mine)

The succeeding stanzas tell the story in great detail.

Paul Speratus, Luther's contemporary and leader in the Reformation, echoed Luther's concern for proclaiming the good news.

> Salvation unto us has come
> By God's free grace and favor;
> Good works cannot avert our doom,
> They help and save us never.
> Faith looks to Jesus Christ alone,
> Who did for all the world atone;
> He is our one Redeemer.[6]

It is hardly a coincidence that Luther's one musical composition (*Non moriar sed vivam*) was based on a verse from Ps. 118 which states simply: "I shall not die, but live, and *declare the words of the Lord*" (emphasis mine). Such examples could be multiplied. The central point is that this hymnody speaks Law and Gospel, proclaiming the good news in direct, clear, and unequivocal terms.

The expanding repertoire of Lutheran hymns in the sixteenth and eighteenth centuries centered on the proclaiming of the story of salvation. Christopher Boyd Brown's description of how the new Reformation hymnody penetrated every facet of life of the early Lutherans is instructive. It describes how in a typical city in Germany ordinary people learned these songs from memory, singing them "by heart" at home, at school, in church.[7] These hymns, centered on the church year and on their value for teaching the faith, told the story of how God had acted to save his people, proclaiming what the faith taught and teaching what the faith proclaimed.

In the seventeenth century Paul Gerhardt's (1607–76) hymns continued this emphasis, though with a warmth not seen in earlier Lutheran hymnody. His familiar texts such as "O Lord, How Shall I Meet You," "Evening and Morning," "If God Himself Be for Me," and his translation of a medieval Latin text which we know as "O Sacred Head, Now Wounded," have worked their way into the hearts and minds of Lutherans everywhere. Born of the trials and tribulations of the Thirty Years' War and the personal, professional, and ecclesiastical difficulties which affected his life, Gerhardt's hymns struck a responsive note in those who sang them precisely because they proclaimed the Gospel clearly and unambiguously. Gerhardt's great Easter hymn "Awake, My Heart, with Gladness," is a case in point:

> The foe in triumph shouted when Christ lay in the tomb;
> But lo, he now is routed, his boast is turned to gloom.
> For Christ again is free; in glorious victory
> He who is strong to save has triumphed o'er the grave.[8]

Gerhardt's texts move us because they reach beneath the shallow surface of human emotion, reaching into the depths of the human condition, touching us at the root of our being with the good news of what Christ has done for us.

The Song of Pietism and the Enlightenment

The story of the gradual loss of emphasis on proclaiming the good news of the Gospel in the Church's song during the periods of Pietism and the Enlightenment has been told at length elsewhere. Suffice it to say that throughout the latter seventeenth and eighteenth centuries Lutheran hymnody was gradually inundated in a Pietism which sought to bring a deeper personal piety to a faith often seen as mired in abstract intellectualism. Instead, with a few exceptions, it produced a hymnody increasingly and more intensely personal, subjective, individualistic, less suited for corporate worship, and focusing more on the feelings of the individual than on the actions of God in Christ.

Rationalism, which sought to bring the Christian faith more in line with human reason, produced a hymnody which was arid and undercut the very faith it hoped to rescue.[9] Ultimately, and unfortunately, both lost any connection with a confessional Lutheran foundation.

Recovering the Song

The nineteenth century saw the beginnings of a confessional revival which recovered many earlier treasures of Greek, Latin, German, and Scandinavian hymnody translated into English. The translations of John Mason Neale brought into common use such favorite hymns as "Of the Father's Love Begotten," "O Wondrous Type, O Vision Fair," "O Come, O Come, Emmanuel," "All Glory, Laud and Honor," and "Ye Sons and Daughters of the King." Likewise, the translations of Catherine Winkworth gave us such hymns as "Now Thank We All Our God," "All Glory Be to God on High," and "Praise to the Lord, the Almighty." What these hymns, and others like them, have in common is a clear focus on the proclamation of the good news of God in Christ.

Similarly, mid-twentieth-century Lutheranism saw a significant revival of hymn writing. Among the more prominent text writers to achieve widespread use are Martin Franzmann (1907–76): "In Adam We Have All Been One" and "Thy Strong Word Did Cleave the Darkness"; Jaroslav J. Vajda (1919–2008): "Now the Silence," "Before the Marvel of This Night," and "Go, My Children, with My Blessing"; Susan Palo Cherwien (b. 1953): "O Blessed Spring" and "As the Dark Awaits the Dawn"; Stephen Starke (b. 1955): "In the Shattered Bliss of Eden" and "Light of Light, O Sole-Begotten"; and Herbert Brokering (b. 1926): "Thine the Amen Thine the Praise" and "Earth and All Stars." Each in its own way resonated with countless singers as they explored new images and poetic devices in telling the story of salvation.

The Song of the Church and Teaching the Faith

If the church sings what it confesses and confesses what it sings, it is only natural that the Church's song would play an important role in teaching of the faith. Early in its history the song of the Church also became a vehicle for combating error and heresy as it developed in both East and West.

In the early centuries two heretical views arose to threaten the church. In the East it was Gnosticism, a complex movement which held that there was a secret knowledge (*gnosis*) given only to some Christians. Bardesanes (154-222) and his son Harmonius, for example, wrote a large collection of hymns in Syriac, a kind of Gnostic psalter, to promulgate his views. In the West the Arian heresy denied the true divinity of Christ and Arius (c. 250-336) attacked Christ's divinity in song. Western Latin hymnody, particularly the hymns of St. Ambrose (c. 339-97) which were clearly Trinitarian, arose largely in reaction to Arianism.

The early church fathers also emphasized the teaching function of Christian song. St. Basil (fourth century) wrote in his *Homily on the First Psalm* that the Holy Spirit "blended the delight of melody with doctrines in order that through the pleasantness and softness of the sound we might unawares receive what was useful in words." And in a similar vein, those who sing the psalms while "in appearance they sing, may in reality be educating their souls." "Oh, the wise invention of the teacher," Basil wrote, "who devised how we might at the same time sing and learn profitable things."[10] St. Chrysostom (347?-407) and others wrote in a similar vein.

Martin Luther also saw hymnody as a vehicle for teaching the faith. His hymns continue the Old Testament pattern by rehearsing the story of salvation in his hymns by "telling the story" of how God has acted to save his people. Ulrich Leupold remarks that "Luther's hymns were not meant to create a mood, but to convey a message. They were a confession of faith, not of personal feelings."[11] This is most clearly reflected in his catechetical hymns, but especially also in his hymns for the Mass and for the church year. They were to "proclaim the wonders God has wrought." In contrast to the many "love ballads and carnal songs" to which many youth were attracted, Luther suggests in the preface to the very first collection of Lutheran hymns in 1524 that such should be replaced with hymns which would "*teach* [the young] something of value" (emphasis mine).

Those who suggest that the Church's song should be simply "devotional" in contrast to "didactic or homiletical" overlook an important part of the Church's historical view of the church song. They have forgotten that, in Richard R. Caemmerer's words, "If the hymn is to fulfill its task, it must actually sing the Gospel."[12] Throughout the Church's history there has been a constant concern that the faith of the Church be reflected in its song, and that the Church's songs reverberate with the Church's faith. In those periods when the Church flirted with heterodoxy, evidence of its dalliance could usually be found in the church's song.

A Note on Praise

While a variety of words describe what Christians do in liturgy and song at worship—"pray," "praise," "adore," "give thanks," among others—at the heart and center of them all is the proclamation of the good news of the Gospel of Jesus Christ. We pray to "the God who . . . "; we praise "the God who . . . "; we adore "the God who . . . "; we give thanks to "the God who . . . ." The rest of the clause "the God who . . ." is ultimately "*raised Jesus Christ from the dead.*" Christ's death and resurrection are at the heart of what is proclaimed in worship. We dare never let it go unsaid. It is not something to be tacked on as an afterthought, but something which is part of the very fabric, the very warp and woof (underlying structure) of the tapestry we call the Church's song.

In recent years the word "praise" has enjoyed great popularity as songs designated as "praise songs" or "praise bands" have come to be familiar terms in many churches. They have been utilized by congregations attempting to reach people they believe are not attracted by the so-called "traditional" worship of many congregations. Characterized by simple, repetitive lyrics, they are normally led by a soloist or small group of amplified singers and band.

"Praise songs," developed in the worship of a variety of evangelistic and charismatic churches, too often embrace a musical idiom identified with commercial pop music. Even admirers acknowledge their texts are often weak, simplistic in theology, and many are borrowed from traditions which are non- or antiliturgical and which have theological presuppositions often contrary to the Church's historic understanding of the faith. Most praise songs tend to emphasize God's *attributes* rather than his actions to save us, often emphasizing a subtle decision theology, and rather than employing music as a vehicle for proclamation use music as a means of stirring up religious feelings. Such concerns have contributed toward a lively conversation as to their appropriateness for corporate worship.

Whatever the outcome of that conversation may be, one thing is certain. The song which truly touches the heart is ultimately the song that gets to the heart of the matter. Many songs skim the surface of religiosity. They may have religious, even scriptural, words; they may be thought of as "spiritual." Such songs come and go, attracting momentary interest but quickly fading away. Much in our culture tempts the Church to substitute for song which speaks the Gospel, a song that simply entertains, makes us feel good, or only superficially engages the emotions. Where that occurs, the Church's song is transformed from a confession and proclamation of faith to something that confuses what we truly need with what we, for the moment, think we want.

But the song which truly touches the heart and reaches to the depths of our human condition, offering the word of hope and comfort, is always the song that speaks the good news of the Gospel clearly and directly. It is the song that rehearses the story of what God has done and who we are as a redeemed community.

Throughout its history the song of the Church has been a guardian of the proclamation of the Gospel. It is the Church's song which has often had to carry the story of salvation in spite of bad preaching or no preaching at all, in spite of bad liturgy or no liturgy at all. It is a dis-spiriting fact that it is usually in congregations where the liturgical tradition of the church is weak that one finds the greatest impetus to use a repertoire of song that is musically simplistic and theologically questionable, if not often erroneous, all in the name of a distorted understanding of both worship and evangelism.

One of the Church's greatest gifts to itself is its rich heritage of song. All talk of diversity and inclusiveness is disingenuous if we neglect to "include" and "welcome" this great gift of the Church's song—old and new. When that song, sung to God, to each other, and to the world, is centered in God's saving act at the cross and at the empty tomb, it is the only song that truly touches the heart. It is the only song that moves us to genuine thanks and profound praise. We can sing no other.

Notes

[1] See Robert Jenson, *Story and Promise: A Brief Theology of the Gospel about Jesus* (Philadelphia: Fortress, 1973), 3ff. See also Paul W. F. Harms, "The Gospel as Preaching," in *The Lively Function of the Gospel*, ed. Robert W. Bertram (St. Louis: Concordia, 1966), 43-44.

[2] Martin Luther, *Luther's Works* (hereafter *LW*), American edition, vol.15 (Ecclesiastes; Song of Solomon; Last Words of David), ed. Jaroslav Pelikan (Philadelphia: Fortress, 1972), 274.

[3] *LW* 53:319-24. The *Symphoniae iucundae* was the first volume of 12 collections offering a complete repertory of Masses, Vespers, antiphons, responsories, and hymns in both Latin and German.

[4] Johann Walter, "In Praise of the Noble Art of Music," tr. by F. S. Janzow, quoted in Carl Schalk, *Music in Early Lutheranism: Shaping the Tradition (1524-1672)* (St. Louis: Concordia Academic Press, 2001), 188.

[5] *Lutheran Service Book* #556.

[6] *Lutheran Service Book* #555.

[7] Christopher Boyd Brown, *Singing the Gospel: Lutheran Hymns and the Success of the Reformation* (Cambridge: Harvard University Press, 2005).

[8] *Lutheran Service Book* #467.

[9] Christian Gellert's (1715-69) "Jesus Lives! The Victory's Won!" (*Lutheran Service Book* #490) is an exception for its forthright affirmation of the resurrection.

[10] Oliver Strunk, *Source Readings in Music History* (New York: Norton, 1950), 65.

[11] Luther, 53:197.

[12] Richard R. Caemmerer, "The Congregational Hymn as the Living Voice of the Gospel," in *The Musical Heritage of the Lutheran Church*, ed. Theodore Hoelty-Nickel, vol. 5 (St. Louis: Concordia, 1959), 170.

II

Music in Liturgical Worship

Music in Lutheran Worship

Ecclesia cantans ["the singing church"] is a particularly apt phrase to characterize the importance of music in Lutheran worship. Lutherans, following the example of the Church of the first 15 centuries, have always believed that music is an important part of corporate worship, and have attempted throughout their history to put this conviction into practice. It was interesting to observe the suspicion humorously voiced by the Very Reverend Francis P. Schmitt that "when Protestants do sing well as a congregation, it is because the people who go to church are precisely the people who like to sing," It is rather—we might hope—that congregations which have learned to sing in a liturgical context have found a direction and focus for their efforts not attainable in any other way. While the popular designation of the Lutheran Church as "the singing Church" has given rise to a certain smugness on the part of that Church, there are many within the Lutheran tradition who are concerned over whether or not Lutherans are doing enough to retain the designation justifiably.

Nevertheless, the fact remains that with the sixteenth-century Reformation there began a flowering of Christian music which has added immeasurably to the treasury of the Church's song and which has placed Christians of all succeeding ages in its debt. It is significant to note for the purpose of our discussion here that the Church of the sixteenth-century Reformation, under the impetus of Martin Luther's thought and its development and refinement in the succeeding centuries, developed a consensus on three important points which have continued to inform

---

This lecture was first given at the 1966 meeting of the Liturgical Conference and the Church Music Association of America in Washington D. C. It was later published in *Crisis in Church Music?* (Washington, D.C.: Liturgical Conference, 1967). Reprinted with permission.]

Lutheran thought and practice regarding the role of music in worship. From its earliest days to the present, the Church of the Augsburg Confession has held that:

1) Lutheran worship is liturgical worship. Therefore music which is a part of this worship must always be seen in its liturgical context and function.

2) Lutheran worship regards vital congregational participation in its music as one valid expression of its belief in the doctrine of the priesthood of all believers.

3) Lutheran worship has a continuing concern for the development of a rich palette of attendant music for the service, a concern which in no way dilutes its commitment to vital congregational participation.

That music in Lutheran worship was in fact guided by these three concerns may be readily demonstrated by even a cursory look at the tremendous musical output, which had as its goal usefulness in Lutheran corporate worship, particularly the music from Luther to Bach, and the resurgence of church music composition in the twentieth century. That this consensus is still a vital influence in the music of Lutheran worship today may be seen particularly from the direction and work of a whole new generation of young Lutheran composers.

While the entire scope of music in Lutheran worship is broader than the time we have at our disposal, the particular thrust of this paper is to suggest some ways in which this consensus was influential in the Church of the Reformation and to indicate some of the musical forms and practices which were developed in or adapted by Lutheran worship in an attempt to reflect this consensus. The ideas, forms, and practices which developed in the musical worship life of Lutheran congregations, particularly from Luther to Bach—reflected in the German *Kirchenordnungen* (church orders) of the sixteenth and seventeenth centuries and in the musical work of such giants as Michael Praetorius, Hans Leo Hassler, Johann Hermann Schein, Samuel Scheidt, and Heinrich Schütz, together with a host of lesser figures—determined in large measure the shape and direction which Lutheran worship and its music would take in the centuries following. That these forms, practices, and ideas have remained a continuing and vital influence in contemporary Lutheran worship music at the level of the local parish to the present day is a testimony to their vitality and usefulness.

I

Lutheran worship is liturgical worship. Therefore music which is a part of this worship must always be seen in its liturgical context and function.

Luther's thought regarding the place of music in worship grew out of his general concern for worship itself. Music in Lutheran worship developed in, grew out of, and nourished the corporate liturgical life of this part of the Christian community. For Luther, therefore, Lutheran worship is liturgical worship, rooted in Scripture and ordered in accordance with those historic forms which were a part of his particular heritage.

Luther's liturgical reform in the sixteenth century showed him to be just that—a reformer, not a rebel. Thus in the course of his liturgical writing and reform, Luther's entire thrust was to maintain a vital contact with the Church of Rome, deviating only where his conscience demanded. Recognizing much that was good in the Roman mass, his approach was that of a conservative: retain the basic order; excise only that which was doctrinally unsound. Luther's interest was not in a new service, but in a newly ordered service in which the congregation might take a direct, vital, and leading part.

Luther's own writing clearly demonstrates that his emphasis was on corporate worship which maintained a strong link with the Church's past and in which Word and Sacrament were simply two parts of a single thrust. While Lutheranism must recognize times in its own history when an emphasis on the Word nearly overshadowed the importance of the Sacrament, at its best, Lutheranism has always maintained a healthy balance between the two.

In Luther's first reform of the Mass, the *Formula missae et communionis pro ecclesia Vuittembergensi* of 1523, the Office of the Word was left virtually intact with only minor alterations.

The sermon might be preached either before the introit or after the creed. The offertory and canon, however, "reeked of sacrifice" and were omitted totally. After the creed, the bread and wine were merely brought to the altar, the preface was sung, and the *verba* ("consecration") followed. The Office of the Eucharist then continued with *sanctus* (with elevation), the Lord's Prayer, *pax*, Communion (with *Agnus Dei*), post-Communion, collect, *benedicamus*, and Aaronic benediction. The language of the order was Latin, but Luther encouraged the singing of German hymns. The Sacrament was distributed in both kinds.

It was but a short step from the *Formula missae* of 1523 to the complete vernacular mass. Andreas Karlstadt had celebrated a German mass in Wittenberg in 1522. The following year an order similar to the *Formula missae*—except that it was in German—was celebrated by Thomas Müntzer. The experiments were multiplying. Luther was somewhat reticent to abandon the old partly because of the radical nature of some of the experiments, partly because of his love for the traditional plainsong melodies with which he was loath to part, and partly because of his awareness of the difficulties in setting German words to these melodies.

Finally, however, with the assistance of Johann Walter, Luther prepared his *Deutsche Messe und Ordnung Gottes Diensts* which was published in 1526 and which, though never regarded as binding upon the Church, was nevertheless highly influential in shaping Lutheran liturgical development. Though this was the more radical departure from the Roman rite than his *Formula missae*, it retained much of this former rite in a simpler fashion, particularly with its greater emphasis on the use of the German hymn. With the *Deutsche Messe* Lutheranism launched out into the vernacular. It might be noted that both the Latin and German orders were descriptive, not prescriptive. Lutheran congregations were free to develop their own orders, yet always within the limits of proper liturgical practice and liturgical good sense.

Of particular importance for our concern here, it should be noted that music for the worship of Lutheran congregations remained within the context of liturgical worship. It was always the liturgical context in which Lutheran music developed, grew, and was nourished. Music in this context was to be servant to the Word, a "handmaiden to the Gospel." Yet it was to be such, not by abasing music as an art form, but by utilizing it at its best and by placing it in the service of the Word and in the service of the Christian people.

II

Lutheran worship regards vital congregational participation in its music as one valid expression of its belief in the doctrine of the priesthood of all believers.

Luther's concern for vital congregational participation is nowhere seen as clearly as in his concern for a living vernacular hymnody. His concern for hymnody was not primarily in that it finally "gave the congregation something to do," but in the specific orientation which Luther intended for the new vernacular hymnody. Luther's intent was clearly not that hymnody become an intrusion in the liturgical action, an intrusion which could be justified in that it gave the assembled congregation an excuse to "participate." Rather Luther's hymns were specifically and directly oriented to the liturgical action itself. They were hymns conceived as a specific part of liturgical worship and so constructed that the congregation might once again participate directly in liturgical actions which had previously either been denied them or in which their participation was at best only indirect.

The liturgical focus of Lutheran hymnody is nowhere seen as clearly as in the development of five classic Lutheran hymns which were in essence versifications of the five parts of the ordinary of the Mass. (At least two of these hymns are generally ascribed to Luther himself; the others developed in the early years of the Reformation.) They are (1) the *Kyrie, Gott Vater in Ewigkeit*, in its original text a paraphrase of the Latin sequence *Kyrie, Fons bonitatis*; (2) *Allein Gott in der Höh' sei Ehr'*, a version of the *Gloria in excelsis*, very likely by Nikolaus Decius (1525) whose tune is derived from the ancient *gloria* tune used in the *Kyrie maius dominicale*; (3) *Wir glauben all' an einen Gott*, Luther's own metrical paraphrase of the Nicene Creed; (4) *Jesaia, dem Propheten, das geschah*, Luther's famous German *sanctus*, first published in his *Deutsche Messe* of 1526 together with its traditional melody, a free adaptation by Luther of a plainchant *sanctus* from the *Graduale Romanum*; and (5) the *Christe, du Lamm Gottes*, a metrical *Agnus Dei* which first seems to have appeared in its German form together with the tune with which it is associated in Johann Bugenhagen's *Kirchenordnung* of Braunschweig in 1528. These hymns offered a unique opportunity for the congregation to participate in song in these parts of the service in a way never before possible. The real significance of these hymns, especially in the context of liturgical renewal, is the kind of participation which they encouraged, a participation predicated on a direct relation to the liturgical momentum and action of the service.

When in 1524 Luther set about to create his own hymnbook for the young church, he wrote and gathered together seven paraphrases on seven psalms. These hymns—*Ach Gott vom Himmel sieh darein* ("O God, Look Down from Heaven, Behold"), Ps. 12; *Es woll' uns Gott genädig sein* ("May God Bestow on Us His Grace"). Ps. 67; *Aus tiefer Not* ("From Depths of Woe I Cry to Thee"), Ps. 130; *Wohl dem der in Gottes furcht* ("Blessed Is He That Fears His Lord"), Ps. 128; *Wär Gott nicht mit uns dieser Zeit* ("If God Had Not Been on Our Side"), Ps. 124; *Es spricht der unweisen Mund* ("The Fool Now in His Heart Doth Say"), Ps. 14; and *Ein feste Burg ist unser Gott* ("A Mighty Fortress Is Our God"), Ps. 46—made psalms the focus of much of later hymn writing so that the term "Little Wittenberg Psalms" was used to describe the entire field of evangelical church songs. The liturgical uses of such paraphrased psalms were obvious, not only as introit hymns but especially in Matins and Vespers, the two offices which Lutheranism retained. By 1602 Cornelius Becker supplemented the seven paraphrases of Luther with the remaining 143 psalms.

The importance of such metrical psalmody or psalm paraphrases in the Reformed Church is well known. In the Netherlands, the *Souterliedekens* (Little Psalm Songs set to already existing folk tunes) was a significant collection. The rhymed psalms of the French Huguenots and the Swiss Calvinists by Clement Marot and Theodore Beza were also important developments which ultimately have their roots in Luther's example.

Paraphrases of other portions of Scripture such as the paraphrases of the *Nunc dimittis* (*Mit Fried und Freud ich fahr dahin*) or the Lord's Prayer (*Vater unser im Himmelreich*) suggest their most obvious usage. The transcriptive translations into the German or Latin office hymns and antiphons such as "Come Holy Ghost, God and Lord," based on the *Veni Sancte Spiritus* and "Now Praise We Christ the Holy One" based on *A solis ortus cardine*, demonstrate Luther's interest in retaining the best of the treasury of the Church's song from the past and effectively bringing it into the vernacular of his day.

The pre-Reformation *Leisen* such as "God the Father Be Our Stay" (*Gott der Vater wohn uns bei*) and "We Now Implore God, the Holy Ghost" (*Nun bitten wir den heiligen Geist*) were recast by Luther and their use encouraged in corporate worship. Not every hymn which derives from these early years of the Lutheran Reformation fits so neatly into the above categories. Yet whatever their particular emphasis, it is clear that the overriding intent of early Lutheran hymnody was that it be suited for inclusion in a liturgical framework as an essential part of the corporate action, not as an effort set apart from the action and movement of worship.

Of particular interest is the development of the *de tempore* hymn. It was the practice of Lutheranism well into the eighteenth century that the text of the gradual for each Sunday was replaced with a hymn for the congregation, a hymn reflecting the liturgical concerns of the particular day or special feast. Thus, for example, on the first Sunday in Advent, Lutheran congregations would join together in singing as the *Hauptlied* (or main hymn of the service) *Nun komm, der Heiden Heiland*, Luther's German version of the Latin *Veni, Redemptor gentium* which appeared as early as the Erfurter Enchiridion of 1524 and for which polyphonic settings were provided in Johann Walter's *Geystliche gesangk Buchleyn* of the same year. In similar fashion there developed in Lutheran worship a corpus of hymns, one for each Sunday of the church year, which reflected the particular liturgical concerns for that day. The current status and use of the *de tempore* hymn in American Lutheranism today may be seen in Ralph Gehrke's *Planning the Service* (St. Louis: Concordia Theological Seminary Press, 1961). a workbook for pastors and musicians.

The use and importance of the *de tempore* hymn in Lutheran worship as a direct way of involving congregational participation in the liturgical action of the service itself cannot be overestimated. This, by the way, was in direct opposition to the use of hymnody in much of later Protestantism which saw the hymn merely as a device to underscore a sermon otherwise unrelated to the church year, or as is so frequently the case today, to utilize the hymn as a psychological device to guarantee some sort of "participation": when in doubt sing "Onward Christian Soldiers" or "Abide with Me, Fast Falls the Eventide." Properly employed, the *de tempore* hymn was a didactic, homiletic, liturgical action underscoring the changing themes of the church year.

Textually, early Lutheran hymnody was marked by a strong didactic, doctrinal, yet always vitally doxological note. Musically and melodically, it was marked by a strong rhythmic character which served to encourage spirited singing rather than to hinder it, and by unison singing—a unison which in the early years of the Reformation was unaccompanied.

That Lutheranism at its best has preserved these characteristics of congregational singing, particularly its liturgical orientation, is a tribute to the vitality and correctness of the path which Lutheranism set for itself in its early years. As Lutheranism in each new age recaptures these aspects of its original genius, it can properly offer its unique musical gift to the whole treasury of the Church's song.

III

Lutheran worship has a continuing concern for the development of a rich palette of attendant music for the service, a concern which in no way dilutes its commitment to vital congregational participation.

As Lutheran composers began to develop a corpus of attendant music—more elaborate "art music" if you will—for the liturgical service, it was never a question as to which would ultimately predominate, simple music for congregational participation or more sophisticated "art music." The creative tension in which these two poles interacted never resulted in an either/or; it was always both/and. It was a matter of constant interaction between the two, each strengthening and reinforcing the other. To this developing coalition the congregation brought its simple sturdy hymn melodies which were in turn utilized by the composer as the basic raw material for much of the attendant music which was developed for the Lutheran mass.

One important factor which facilitated the development of a climate in which a rich treasury of such attendant music was a distinct probability was Luther's personal attitude. Not only was Luther well acquainted with the musical culture of his day, encouraging and guiding the church in its proper use, but his admiration for the works of Ludwig Senfl, the ablest German composer of his time, as well as for Josquin des Prez,

Pierre de la Rue, and others is well known. Luther himself was an accomplished musician on the lute; at least one motet based on the text *Non moriar sed vivam* is attributed to him. His appreciation for the polyphony of his day is represented in the following quotation from the preface to a collection of part-songs published in 1538:

> Outstanding in this art is this, that while one voice continues to sing its *cantus firmus*, other voices at the same time cavort about the principal voice in a most wonderful manner with praise and jubilation, adorning the *cantus firmus* with most lovely movement.... Those who are not moved by this, are, indeed unmusical and deserve to hear some dunghill poet or the music of swine. (*Luther's Works*, vol. 53, preface to Rhau's *Symphoniae iucundae*)

Another factor in the development of the attendant music for Lutheran worship was the importance of the *Kantorei* (singing groups) and the critical role they played in nourishing this music's continued performance. Three types of *Kantorei* were especially important in this regard: the *Hofkantorei* ("court choir"), which gained particular splendor at the courts of German princes until the story of its fame was cut short by the outbreak of the Thirty Years' War; the *Schulkantorei* ("school choir"), which functioned as a church choir and in which musical education was entrusted to the schools which in turn presented the fruits of its musical education to the church; and the *Kantoreigesellschaft* (sometimes called a "society of choir singers"), which were regular gatherings of the burghers of the city together with some of the pupils from the schools to study and practice the music to by sung in the regular services. The importance of these organizations for the performance of much of this attendant music for the Lutheran mass cannot be overemphasized.

Specifically, how did the attendant music for the Lutheran Mass take shape? Let us mention four ways. The first was in connection with the *de tempore* hymn already mentioned and was related to the *alternatim-praxis*, the practice of having the congregation sing alternate stanzas of the *de tempore* hymn while the choir, organ, or other forces would present the remaining stanzas, occasionally in more elaborate polyphonic musical settings. Thus, in Paul Gerhardt's "O Sacred Head, Now Wounded" the congregation might sing stanzas 1, 3, 5, 7, etc., while the choir, organ, instruments, or other musical forces would present the even-numbered stanzas. This practice not only allowed the congregation opportunity to reflect devotionally on those stanzas presented by the choir, organ, or instruments but also took into consideration that many German chorales were blessed with a multiplicity of stanzas which, if they were all sung by the congregation, simply tended to induce physical fatigue. Many of the magnificent settings of the Lutheran chorales by Michael Praetorius, Seth Calvisius, Johann Jeep, Johann Hermann Schein, and a host of others were utilized in just such a manner as that described. Here was "art music" not apart from the congregation but an organic part of the Lutheran worship, drawing the congregation into the music-making, yet—through its connection and close association with the *cantus firmus*—demonstrating that the choir was not a lord over the congregation and the liturgy, but rather its servant.

A second way in which the attendant music for the Lutheran Mass took shape was in the development of a rich treasury of organ music. In the sixteenth century the organ was used chiefly to present alternate stanzas of hymns in the manner of the *alternatim-praxis*, the congregation singing their stanzas without any accompaniment. Likewise, alternate verses of the *Magnificat, Benedictus, Te Deum,* and other canticles were presented by the organ alone, a practice which Lutheranism simply took over from the contemporary practice of the Roman Church. As the Church of the Reformation moved into the seventeenth century, the organ was called upon to accompany congregational singing more or less in a manner reflecting today's customary practice, a practice which necessitated the development of collections of organ chorales such as Samuel Scheidt's Görlitz *Tablaturbuch*. Much of the great chorale-based organ literature from Luther to Bach arose as a direct response to the specifically practical demands of the Mass that the chorales be intoned by the organ immediately prior to congregational singing, and that simple settings be available for use in *alternatim-praxis*. Pachelbel's *Magnificat Fugues*, Johann Walter's chorales preludes, and the organ works of Dietrich Buxtehude, Johann Sebastian Bach, and a host of other composers all testify to the significant involvement of their compositions in the liturgical context of the Lutheran mass.

Thirdly, in contrast to the post-Tridentine restrictions which Rome placed on church music in an effort to retain the Palestrinian ideal of pure a cappella choral music (which was the most recent attempt by Roman Catholicism to define music as either "sacred" or "secular" in contrast to Lutheranism's usual reference simply to "church music"), the Church of the Reformation turned instead to the development of liturgical music in which instruments and concerted groups of many kinds were common. The effect of this development may be seen as most Lutheran congregations today accept as a matter of course the frequent use of string, brass, woodwind, percussion, or other instruments in their corporate worship.

A fourth way in which the attendant music for Lutheran worship took shape was in the development of a rich treasury of *figural* music. This was chiefly polyphonic music for choir in the form of gospel motets, antiphons, canticles, cantus firmus-based selections, etc., by such men as Hans Leo Hassler, Heinrich Schütz, Michael Praetorius, and Johann Hermann Schein which firmly rooted Lutheran practice in the past without thereby restricting it or preventing it from a continuing development within the musical framework and musical vocabulary of succeeding ages. Those who feel that the sixteenth-century Reformation necessarily reduced Lutheran music to simplistic congregational singing, a feature unfortunately characteristic of much of later Protestantism, need only look at Johann Walter's *Geistliches Gesangbüchlein* of 1524, a collection of five-part music for choir in Latin and German based largely on the German chorale *cantus firmus*, or at the present-day work of such contemporary Lutheran composers as Richard Hillert, whose current work on a complete series of motets based on the gospels for each Sunday, will be a significant addition to contemporary liturgical polyphony in the idiom of the twentieth century.

In these ways, the music for Lutheran worship has developed in the context of corporate liturgical worship, maintaining at the same time a healthy and fruitful relationship between the music of the congregation and that of more specialized choral and instrumental groups. The genesis of Lutheran service music as basically *Gebrauchsmusik* ("music for use") has been and continues to be its real strength. It is music with a specific use: the praising and glorifying of God in corporate worship, yet so oriented that it can be effectively employed even in parishes with modest musical resources.

In conclusion, three points might yet be made to characterize briefly the continuing development of music in Lutheran worship.

First, music in Lutheran worship has remained close to its congregational hymnody, particularly the chorale, as the basic raw material for its continuing creativity. Lutheranism has chosen this road freely, not restrictively, because it realizes the congregational hymn and particularly the chorale in its liturgical context as a gracious gift of God.

Second, the development of music for Lutheran worship has always related itself closely to the musical forces available in the local parish. From Heinrich Schütz's *Kleine Geistliche Konzerte* to contemporary settings for unison choir, the shape of the local musical resources of the parish have largely determined the shape of most Lutheran worship music. And at its best, Lutheran worship music has clearly demonstrated that simple, direct, yet artful music, within the capability of modest musical forces in the parish, will accomplish the goals of music in worship more effectively than intricate musical bombast even when skillfully and impressively presented.

Third, Lutheran worship music has never been afraid to reflect the changing musical vocabularies of succeeding eras. It has attempted to avoid attachment to any one musical style as being particularly "sacred," not out of an attempt for a superficial relevance, but out of the firm conviction that *all* music is a gift of God and has the possibility of redemption and recreation for the worship of its Creator. The changes in musical style from Luther to Bach are hardly greater than from Bach to the present time. If we accept the one, how can we in principle necessarily reject the other?

The exciting story of music for the liturgical service which is being written in our time by composers who are rooted both in the liturgy and in the music of the twentieth century is one which needs telling. We see only an occasional glimpse now and then. But that story is for another time.

As Roman Catholicism looks toward an even greater musical participation in the celebration of Word and Sacrament, Lutheranism can only wish you well and offer whatever help may be useful in what may temporarily be a frightfully traumatic experience for some, but which will ultimately and surely be a joyous experience for all.

As Lutheranism did not abandon the rich musical heritage of the Roman Church, but moved forward on its foundations, so Lutherans might hope that as Roman Catholicism moves into the unchartered waters of the vernacular and increased congregational participation, she will do so most faithfully by building upon her heritage new forms and practices which are most faithful to the genius of her original vision and which at the same time can speak meaningfully and faithfully to her people in these days.

As such a vision comes to reality, the words *ecclesia cantans* will cease to be a slogan designating (properly or improperly) a particular segment of the Church. They will become instead a vital and living mark of the entire body of Christ.

Luther on Music Revisited: Reassessing Luther's Thoughts for Today

Some years ago—18 to be exact—Concordia Publishing House published a small monograph[1] in which I attempted to draw out of Luther's scattered comments on music, found in a variety of his writings, several basic themes which illustrate his orientation and viewpoint on music, especially but not exclusively as it relates to the worship life of the Church. These themes included (1) Luther's view of music as a gracious gift of God, a gift to be used in the praise of God and in the proclamation of the Gospel; (2) music as liturgical song; (3) music as the song of royal priests; and (4) music as a sign of continuity with the whole Church. These patterns in Luther's thought about music are, in my opinion, as viable and important today as when Luther first gave prominence to them in the sixteenth century.

However, events in the now almost two decades since that monograph was written have, in my opinion, given greater urgency to several of these emphases in Luther's writings about music in the worship life of the Church. These would certainly include (1) the dramatic rise of the evangelical movement in the United States and its impact on the worship and musical practices of many churches, (2) the impact of the church growth movement and its vigorous promotion among Lutheran congregations, and (3) the effect of religious television and Christian

---

Originally presented at the Good Shepherd Institute, Concordia Theological Seminary, Ft. Wayne, Ind., November 6-9, 2005, and subsequently published in *Luther on Liturgy and Hymns*, ed. Daniel Zager (Ft. Wayne, Ind.: Concordia Theological Seminary Press, 2006). Reprinted by permission.

radio and their influence on congregational expectations of what might or should occur when they gather for Sunday morning worship.

While each of these trends is important in itself, these are penultimate matters, related to more basic movements which have had and continue to have a profound effect, not always for the better, on the worship and musical life of the Church. These include, to name only a few: (1) the rise of a radical individualism which, as it manifests itself in the Church and its worship, makes each individual the ultimate arbiter of all things musical and liturgical; (2) the gradual abandonment of any kind of theological, musical, or liturgical standards in assessing current movements and practices; (3) the increasing loss of faith and trust in church bureaucracies; and (4) the escalating adoption by many local congregations and denominational churches of a business model for organizing their life together with the emphasis on bottom line strategies and numbers. (Remember—as a rule of thumb—when they say that it's not about the numbers, it's about the numbers.)

To suggest that none of these developments have any impact on what Lutherans believe, how they worship, and the songs they sing is to live in Alice's Wonderland. To suggest that these trends swirling around us need not concern us or do not affect us, or that all is well as long as "it's all about Jesus," is to be oblivious to the fact that in worship, while what we believe certainly affects what we do and how we do it, the obverse is equally true: what we do and how we do it in worship affects—more deeply than some care to admit—how and what we believe.

Let me mention then three aspects of Luther's thought that I believe need particular reaffirming and emphasis in our day when turmoil continues to roil the worship scene. They are (1) the understanding of both liturgy and music in worship as a sign of continuity with the historic faith, (2) the role of music as praise and proclamation of the good news of the Gospel, and (3) the particular role of the church musician in all of this.

Liturgy and Music as a Sign of Continuity with the Historic Faith

Martin Luther valued both liturgy and music as an important sign of continuity with the whole Church and with the historic faith. It is a commonplace, but nevertheless true, that according to the Lutheran confessions the Lutheran rites of the Reformation period reflect the fact that "the Church of the Augsburg Confession is consciously and determinedly a part of the Catholic Church of the West."[2] As far as worship is concerned, in essence the Lutheran reformers were saying:

> We recognize an obligation, born of our historic past and our historic situation, not to exercise the liberty that we could theoretically invoke. As little as [the reformers] felt that they could dispense with the doctrinal categories, formulations, and terminology which they had inherited, so little did they feel themselves privileged to dispense with their inherited worship categories and formulations. Both comprised symbols. Absolutely these symbols were only the vehicles, the shells, the husks, the masks, the *larvae* of the divine truth; their theology used *verbal* symbols, their worship used *ceremonial* symbols. But in both areas the symbol and the-thing-symbolized —when considered concretely, actually, and historically—coalesced and could not without great peril be separated.[3]

Luther understood that external ceremonies are necessary conditions of corporate worship,[4] and that, except where it acted contrary to his understanding of the Gospel, the great tradition of the Church was to be treasured as a rich and reliable guide for worship.

In both his Latin Mass (1523) and German Mass (1526), the continuity with the Western catholic tradition is clearly evident. And in both writings, Luther's contempt for those who would precipitously change an old and accustomed order of worship for a new and less usual one is clear. In the preface to his Latin Mass, he refers to those who "rush in like unclean swine without faith or reason, and who delight only in novelty and tire of it as quickly, when it has worn off. Such people are a nuisance even in other affairs, but in spiritual matters they are absolutely unbearable."[5] But his most scathing criticism is in the preface to his German Mass where he speaks of "the general dissatisfaction and offense that has been caused by the great variety of new masses. . . . Some have the best of intentions, but others have no more than an itch to produce something novel so that they may shine before men as leading lights, rather than being ordinary teachers."[6]

Likewise his statement that "it is not now nor ever been our intention to abolish the liturgical service of God completely, but rather to purify the one that is now in use"[7] and his comments that the old practice should continue and that the Mass should be "celebrated with consecrated vestments, with chants and all the usual ceremonies in Latin"[8] hardly suggest a liturgical or musical iconoclast. Rather, they reflect the thoughts of one who sought to affirm the continuity of the Reformation with the Church catholic and to reflect that unity of liturgical and musical forms and practices.

In the Augsburg Confession of 1530, which sought to "restore unity,"[9] and the Book of Concord, which some 50 years later affirmed that it was based "on the ancient consensus which the universal church of Christ has believed, fought for against many heresies and errors, and repeatedly affirmed"[10] and which placed at its very beginning the three ecumenical creeds confessed and accepted by the whole Church, one has ample evidence of Luther's view of the Reformation as a confessing and reforming movement within the Church catholic. It clearly affirms the importance he and the early reformers gave to the matter of continuity with the tradition of the whole Church. The basic ceremonial and ritual principle of the Reformation, reflected not only in their writings but also in the liturgical and musical practice of the time, is that a maximum of traditional rite and ceremonial is to be retained, except where it was in conflict with their understanding of the Gospel. Among the many traditional elements which were retained by the reformers and which are specifically mentioned and recommended in the Symbolical Books (and use of which would cause many pastors today to blanch) are, to name a few: the pericopal system, sermons, the Ordinary of the Mass and other chants, Sunday, the ecclesiastical year, the dignity of feasts, the ancient collects, the Pentecost sequence, Eucharistic and other vestments, altar ware of gold, the use of Latin (on account of those who understand or are learning the language), chanting of the psalms, the sign of the Holy Cross, the customary ceremonial of the Mass, kneeling for prayer, and folded hands.[11] All of this will come as news to some.

What of Today?

Much of American culture today suggests that the past has nothing to teach us, that we live in a time when the past is irrelevant, and it is only the present that matters. While we quote Santayana's comment that "those who cannot learn from the past are doomed to repeat it," many act as if the lessons of the past have no bearing on the present, that we live in a time that is unique, facing challenges and situations never faced before, and that, for all practical purposes, there is nothing the past has to teach us. Not only are the lessons of the past summarily dismissed, any knowledge of the past is absent, is either unknown, or, where some knowledge remains, it is distorted beyond belief. The words of the writer of Ecclesiastes have come to haunt us: "There is no remembrance of former things."[12]

It is no different in the Church. Even if those who claim an interest in the music and worship of the Church are aware of its history, there seems to be a basic disconnect between the present and the past. With much of the Church and virtually all of the culture focused almost exclusively on the present, the tacit understanding seems to be that whatever the theological significance and musical glory of our liturgical and musical heritage may be, or may have been, while we honor it in the abstract, it is for all practical purposes inapplicable, no longer germane to our currently felt needs, and ultimately immaterial to our present situation as we seek to reach out with the good news of the Gospel.

That this is indeed the case is painfully obvious if one merely observes what happens on Sunday mornings in too many Lutheran churches throughout this country. The continuity of our churches today with that of the great Western Christian—let alone Lutheran—tradition is not only conspicuous by its absence, anyone brash enough to mention the obvious is met with disdain, if not outright hostility. To honor the liturgical and musical treasures of the church's tradition means, in Gilbert K. Chesterton's words, "giving votes to the most obscure of all classes, our ancestors. . . . Tradition refuses to submit to the small and arrogant oligarchy of those who merely happen to be walking about."

Much of what I, at least, see happening in congregations throughout the Church seems to be dictated by just such "small and arrogant oligarchies which merely happen to be walking about." This is to recommend neither antiquarianism nor repristination. It is to suggest that a healthy regard for the liturgical and musical tradition of the Church is a vital step on the road to recovering a living worship for our time. It is those who, having adopted an attitude toward tradition, liturgy, music and the rites of the church quite in opposition to that of the Lutheran Confessions, have brought us to our present state.

Music as Proclamation and Praise

Luther's view of music was that it is God's good and gracious gift to be used for his praise and in the proclamation of the Gospel. This viewpoint must necessarily be seen against the background of the history of God's dealing with his chosen people.

In the Old Testament when people offered their praise and thanks to God, they did so by telling and singing what God had done for them. What drove the praise and thanksgiving of Israel was the story of God's mighty acts on their behalf. To praise God meant, for ancient Israel, to tell the story of how God had acted on their behalf. In what is perhaps one of the earliest poetic couplets in the Old Testament, we are told that following the Exodus from Egypt, Miriam took a timbrel in her hand and all the women went out after her with timbrels and dancing. And Miriam sang to them:

> Sing to the Lord, for he has triumphed gloriously; the horse and its rider he has thrown into the sea.[13]

Miriam gives voice to her praise and thanks by telling of the deeds of the Lord which had brought God's people to their present situation, and which demonstrated that he is, in the subsequent words of Exod. 15, above all gods, that there is no god like unto him, majestic in holiness, terrible in glorious deeds, doing wonders. Likewise, when David brought back the Ark of the Covenant to Jerusalem and appointed that thanksgiving be sung to the Lord, his song was simply:

> Oh give thanks to the Lord, call on his name; *make known his deeds among the people!* Sing to him; sing praises to him; *tell of all his wondrous works!*[14] (emphasis mine)

The book of Psalms is replete with praising and thanking God by reciting his good and gracious deeds on behalf of his people. Ps. 136[15] is a prime example. After a brief summons to the people to give thanks (vv. 1-3), the psalmist extols God's goodness as creator of all (vv. 4-9), his work in the history of Israel (vv. 10-22), which comprised the story of the Exod. (vv. 10-15), the journey through the wilderness (v. 16), and the conquest of Canaan (vv. 17-22), followed by a brief recapitulation (vv. 23-25) and concluding summons to give thanks (v. 26). This basic pattern is repeated again and again in the psalms.

The constant refrain of the psalms is that praise and thanksgiving are always the declaring of God's mighty acts,[16] making known God's mighty deeds among the people,[17] calling to remembrance the wonderful works that God has done,[18] recounting God's wondrous deeds,[19] and similar phrases. What God did for his people was to bring them up out of slavery in Egypt, through the wilderness, and into the Promised Land. In response Israel gave voice to its thanks and praise by rehearsing God's wondrous deeds. To sing and praise God in the Old Testament was to "sing and praise the God who . . .," the sentence being completed with the particular story of God delivering his people.

If in the Old Testament "God spoke to our fathers by the prophets," the New Testament celebrates God's ultimate revelation in his Son Jesus Christ, and adds to the wondrous deeds of God celebrated in the Old Testament: the incarnation, suffering, death, and resurrection of the Savior, his ascension into heaven, and the assurance that he will come again at the end of time. These are God's wondrous deeds that Christians celebrate in word and song in "these last days."

As Christians gathered weekly to offer their worship and praise, they rehearsed the great and glorious works which God had done on their behalf. They spoke and sang their praise and thanksgiving first *to God* (pleading the Gospel before him and praising and thanking him for it), second *to one another* (as witness to the faith they held and in the building up of one another in the faith), and third *to the world* (by rehearsing what God had done as God's message of salvation to all people). The Church's liturgy and its song were central to this act of proclamation and praise.

All the New Testament songs such as the *Magnificat*, *Benedictus*, and such later songs as the *Te Deum* and *Gloria in excelsis*—all of which eventually found their way into the liturgy of the Church—clearly reveal how the Church continued to praise and celebrate God's goodness by recalling what he has done for us. One example from the hymnody of the early church, the sixth-century hymn of Venantius Fortunatus, "Sing, My Tongue, the Glorious Battle," must suffice. Appointed in *Lutheran Worship* as one of two possible hymns of the day for Good Friday, it clearly shows the importance of proclamation in the hymnody of the early church:

> Sing, my tongue, the glorious battle, sing the ending of the fray.
> Now above the cross, the trophy, sound the loud triumphant lay;
> Tell how Christ, the world's redeemer, as a victim won the day.
> (*Lutheran Worship* #117)

Even a superficial exegesis reveals that the "loud triumphant lay" we are to sing is to tell how the battle turned out, how Christ the world's redeemer, while apparently a victim, in reality won the day, won the battle between life and death, the cross standing as the ultimate sign, not of defeat, but of triumph. In succeeding stanzas the writer details how Christ came to fulfill the Law, how "like a lamb he humbly yielded on the cross his dying breath," and concluding in a grand doxological stanza of praise to Father, Son, and Holy Spirit. Even in the midst of Good Friday we are pointed to the victory of Christ's resurrection.

For the early church the very purpose of the liturgy, like that of hymnody, was to proclaim the wondrous works of God. To cite only one example, the second-century Apostolic Tradition of Hippolytus describes the work of God in Christ in a series of parenthetical phrases which occur before the Words of Institution. It bears quoting:

> We render thanks unto thee, O God, through Thy beloved Child Jesus Christ,
>
> > Whom in the last times Thou didst send to us (*to be*) a Saviour and Redeemer and the Messenger of Thy counsel;
> >
> > Who is Thy Word inseparable (*from Thee*), through Whom Thou madest all things and in Whom Thou wast well-pleased;

(*Whom*) Thou didst send from heaven into (*the*) Virgin's womb and Who conceived within her was made flesh and demonstrated to be Thy Son being born of the Holy Spirit and a Virgin;

Who fulfilling Thy will and preparing for Thee a holy people stretched forth His hands for suffering that He might release from suffering them who have believed in Thee;

Who when He was betrayed to voluntary suffering that He might abolish death and rend the bonds of the devil and tread down hell and enlighten the righteous and establish the ordinance and demonstrate the resurrection.[20]

That is the Christ who "taking bread (*and*) making eucharist [i.e., giving thanks]" they were praising. It is clear that the liturgy and hymns of the Church were, for the early Christians, vehicles for proclaiming the good news of the Gospel.

Luther also saw music, hymnody, and the liturgy as a vehicle for the praise of God and the proclamation of the good news of the Gospel. Two familiar hymns from the Reformation's early years illustrate the point that music's role is to proclaim the Gospel. The first, "Dear Christians, One and All, Rejoice" by Martin Luther, recounts in ten stanzas the saving act of God in Christ. The first stanza announces the purpose of the hymn and, by extension, the purpose of the Christian song generally.

> Dear Christians, one and all, rejoice,
> With exultation springing.
> And with united heart and voice
> And holy rapture singing
> *Proclaim the wonders God has done*
> *How his right arm the vict'ry won,*
> What price our ransom cost him (emphasis mine).
>
> (*Lutheran Worship* #353)

Succeeding stanzas fill in the details. A second example, the well-known hymn by Paul Speratus (1484-1531) "Salvation unto Us Has Come," tells the story of salvation: that none could render to God the demands of the Law, but God sent his Son to work for us full atonement, concluding with a doxology that identifies the triune God as "The God who saved us by his grace." These examples tell the story of salvation; they "proclaim the wonders God has done" simply and directly.

For Luther praise and proclamation were inextricably linked. To praise God meant to proclaim the Good News; conversely, when one proclaimed the good news of the Gospel, that was the way that God was properly praised. After all, said Luther in one of his most important statements on the role of music,

> The gift of language combined with the gift of song was only given to man to let him know that *he should praise God* with both words and music, namely, *by proclaiming* [*the Word of God*] through music[21] (emphasis mine).

Remember, Luther reminds us,

> the prophets did not make use of any art except music; when setting forth their theology they did it not as geometry, not as arithmetic, not as astronomy, but as music, so that they held theology and music most tightly connected.[22]

The content of the Christian's song was always, for Luther, the "victory that was not won or achieved in battle by us . . . but was presented and given to us by the mercy of God." But, Luther concludes, "*We must sing of this victory in Christ*"[23] (emphasis mine),

In the linkage of music and the proclamation of the Word of God, Luther suggests that music does not simply play a neural or instrumental role in conveying the Word. It is not simply an inert medium for carrying words. Rather, in the combining of the Word with music one is no longer dealing just with music or just with words, but with a third entity in which music and words combine to express in a richer and deeper way what neither words nor music alone can express. The Word brings substance to the music; the music enlivens the Word as the *viva vox evangelii*, the "living voice of the Gospel." Moreover, Luther suggests that this is especially the case when music is cultivated at the highest levels of artistic achievement.

> When [musical] learning is added to all this and artistic music which corrects, develops, and refines the natural music, then at last it is possible to taste with wonder (yet not to comprehend) God's absolute and perfect wisdom in his wondrous works of music.[24]

All this suggests a higher, deeper, and richer view of music in Luther than is commonly assumed and popularly acclaimed. Music is indeed a handmaiden to the Gospel, an art whose essential role is to serve and assist. But Luther's comments that theology and music are "most tightly connected" suggest a more complex view of their relationship, and especially his comment that "Music is . . . next to theology" might just as well be interpreted as not so much next *in importance* to theology, but rather as theology and music *standing next to each other*, side by side, each assisting the other in ways unique to their own form and structure toward the common end of the proclamation of the Gospel.

Luther's hymns, as well as those of his immediate followers, emphasized their role as proclaimer and, following the example of the early church fathers, also as teacher or pedagogue. St. Basil, an important fourth-century preacher and theologian, could exclaim, "O the wise invention of the teacher who devised how we might at the same time sing and learn profitable things."[25] Ulrich Leupold, the editor of volume 53 of *Luther's Works*, says that "Luther's hymns were meant not to create a mood, but to convey a message. They were a confession of faith, not of personal feelings."[26] They were didactic, homiletical, and occasionally hortatory. Luther's "catechism hymns"—written specifically to teach the chief parts of the Small Catechism—are a prime example.

In the century and a half following Luther's death, Lutheran hymnody took a turn from the confessional, proclamatory, and didactic and moved increasingly toward hymnody as an expression of individual feelings. In Johann Walter's rhymed homage to music, *In Praise of the Noble Art of Music*, he indicated the reasons God had given the art of music to mankind. It was that God's "unmerited free grace . . . might be kept fresh in human memory / And move the heart with high delight / In praising God both day and night."[27] It was precisely the move from hymnody as a confession of faith to statements of individual feelings of devotion, from *Erkenntnisslieder* to *Erbauungslieder*, which occurred in the latter seventeenth and early eighteenth centuries, which set Lutheran hymnody on a different path, a path from which it is still attempting to recover.[28]

What of Today?

Although few would acknowledge it, too few pastors and church musicians take seriously the Reformation axiom that the hymnody and liturgy of the Church are truly channels for the proclamation of the good news of the Gospel. Certainly music in the church is generally held in high regard. But the working assumption on the part of many, an assumption born of the spirit of American pragmatism, is that liturgy and hymnody are simply means to another end, ways to attract, entice, or engage the worshipper, psychological tools which serve only as a warm-up for the real proclamation which occurs solely in the preaching for the day. Certainly the words of the hymns and liturgy should be generally religious in some sense, but when push comes to shove, we can take them or leave them. Such a view, however popular it may be, hardly reflects the seriousness of the view of either Luther or early Lutheranism.

We live in a time when the concept of "story" is a current theme for both theological reflection and for homiletical purposes. Yet the story, in too many instances, is not the story of the Gospel, but rather "my story," or "whatever is 'justifying' or 'healing' or 'liberating' or whatever value the individual finds her- or himself affirming."[29] To praise God means to speak of *God's* mighty acts, to speak and sing the good news of the *Gospel*. And to speak and sing the good news of the Gospel does not mean to speak or sing *about* the Gospel, but to speak and sing it, clearly and unambiguously.

We live at a time when there has been an outpouring of new hymnody, unlike anything that has been seen for almost a century, that has been both a bane and a blessing. There is good material among this vast body of hymnody. And there is also much that is neither useful nor edifying, much of it offering theological perspectives at variance with and sometimes simply contrary to basic Christian understandings.

Yet few ask the simple question: is any of this material good or useful for corporate worship? Does this material actually proclaim the good news of the Gospel? It is easy enough to dismiss such favorites among some as "In the Garden," or "I Have Decided to Follow Jesus" as reflecting, in the first example, an exclusively individualistic or personalistic attitude toward the faith or, in the second example, an outright rejection of Luther's explanation of the Third Article that "I cannot by my own reason or strength believe in Jesus Christ, my Lord, or come to Him." The matter becomes more heated when one points to the deficiencies of some hymns in wide currency in some books widely circulated and used in our congregations.

Ours is a time when pastors and worship leaders see fit to write their own liturgies and hymns, or cut and paste together liturgies from a variety of often questionable and all too readily available "worship resources." Most such attempts are justified in the minds of their creators as being more relevant, creative, accessible, or meaningful to congregations. Most of these efforts are done with little knowledge of the structure of the liturgy or no awareness of the role of hymnody in the church's worship, often eroding the Gospel they purport to proclaim, is, it seems, largely irrelevant.

The Role of the Church Musician

In the sixteenth century and the centuries following the Reformation, the general title for the Lutheran church musicians was "cantor." The cantor was generally in charge of the vocal music at both the church and school, where there was one, and conducted the main polyphonic music that followed the Gospel reading on Sundays and holidays. In larger cities, such as Leipzig at the time of Bach, the cantor was required to supply music for at least the main churches of the city. Following the Reformation the cantor generally was a lay person, while prior to the Reformation the position was normally filed by clergy.

The cantor was expected to be a "learned companion and a good musician,"[30] trained not only in music but committed to the theological understandings of the Reformation. He served not only in his musical capacity but was involved as a teacher in the Latin school which was normally connected to the church. In that capacity he was second only to the rector of the school, since among his duties was to evaluate the school boys to determine their musical fitness, ability, and promise. The cantor was usually required to teach religion and/or Latin in the school, and teaching experience, religious beliefs, and personal conduct were carefully examined before being hired. In addition the cantor was required to commit himself to particular religious beliefs. He instructed the school boys in music and, frequently, in other subjects as well.

The hymns for the services were traditionally selected by the cantor, a principle strenuously upheld by Johann Sebastian Bach as late as the early eighteenth century in his dispute with Gottlieb Gaudlitz, subdeacon at the Nicholas church in Leipzig, who sought to usurp for himself the task of choosing hymns for the Vesper services, as well as introduce new hymns not contained in the Dresden hymn book.[31] But the life and work of the cantor went beyond merely providing music for the services. He was concerned also for the personal lives of those with whom he worked and he was usually involved in the community, especially as the leader of the *Stadtkantorei* ["city choir"].

Luther held the role of the church musicians of his day in high regard, reflected in his support of music in the schools; his view that teachers and pastors needed to be able to sing; his correspondence with some of the most notable musicians of his day, such as Ludwig Senfl, with whom he discussed the meaning and role of music in the church; and his letters of support for cantors who found themselves out of work and were seeking employment. His affection and regard for Johann Walter, the first Lutheran cantor, is well known, as was Luther's invitation to two church musicians, Johann Walter and Conrad Rupsch, to his home to help in preparing the music for his German Mass. The cantor was an important figure in the Reformation churches.

What of Today?

As at the time of the Reformation, church musicians today serve in what Martin Luther referred to as their station, their *Stand*, their "walk of life," their *Amt*, their "office," their vocation as church musician. That vocation is described by Paul Westermeyer as "leader of the people's song." To be sure, it is the people's song but, first and foremost, it is the *Church's* song which church musicians sing and lead.

Every Christian, whatever their vocation, serves by bringing the very best of their talent to their work and through it to serve the larger community in which they live. The same was and is true of the church musician today.

The church today needs to be reminded that Lutheran church musicians exercise their vocation by bringing three things to their work as leaders of the people's song:

(1) We bring our *musical skills*—skills which are always a work in progress, skills we are always working to improve, skills we are always honing and sharpening, whether it be playing the organ, directing a choir, or composing a new piece of music. Our vocation as church musicians is always to bring the very best of our skill and talent to the service of the praise of God and the proclamation of the Gospel. Just as the shoemaker serves in his vocation by making the very best shoes possible, not third-rate shoes with little crosses of them, church musicians serve by bringing our very best to the task at hand. We are not called to be third-rate musicians camouflaging a lack of skill behind a façade of piety. To be a good church musician is, first of all, to be the best musician of which we are capable.

(2) We bring a distinct *theological perspective*. Lutheran church musicians, and congregations, need to be reminded, although it should be self-evident, that we are not simply *musicians*, but *church* musicians. This means that a knowledge, understanding, and commitment to the Church's liturgy, the Church's year, and the Church's song are necessary ingredients of who we are and how we serve. And it means assuming the responsibility to help others understand the centrality of worship to the Christian life as the community gathers regularly around Word and Sacrament. It means that we understand the role of music in worship is to be the praise of God and proclamation of the good news of the Gospel. It means that the distinct theological perspective of the Lutheran church musician should be reflected not only in the music we sing and play, but also how we employ music in worship. This may come as news to some.

(3) We bring our *musical and theological judgment*. To exercise sound judgment requires the ability to make distinctions: to distinguish between music that is liturgically useful and that which is not; to distinguish between music that is appropriate for worship and that which is not; to distinguish between texts which give a clear witness of the Gospel and those which obscure or blur that witness; to distinguish between music which is shoddy, trite, and unfit for worship and music which possesses the character and qualities appropriate for corporate worship; to distinguish between music poorly written and that which demonstrates the skill, competence, and inspiration called for by our vocation as musicians and as leaders of the people's song.

To exercise musical and theological judgment means that we worship the Lord not only with heart and soul, but with our minds as well. It means that the judgments we make are not simply "practical," or "matters of taste," but are ultimately theological and moral judgments. To paraphrase Edmund Burke from another context, as church musicians we owe the church not only our musical skill but our theologically and musically informed judgment. And if we sacrifice our considered judgment to the passing opinions of that "small and arrogant oligarchy of those who merely happen to be walking around," we betray both the church and our vocation.

To faithfully fulfill our vocation as church musicians is often difficult in a time when for many the past is irrelevant; when the rise of a rampant individualism dictates that each person is the ultimate arbiter of all things; when a widespread relativism mandates that there are no objective standards except those I as an individual choose to observe; when the adoption of a business model for the church's life with its emphasis on bottom line strategies and numbers dictates how we ought to worship and chooses the music we sing; when the often soft conclusions of the social sciences are made determinative as to the course we are to take as musicians; and when those who know least about the Church's worship and the Church's song seem to want to determine both its shape and its direction.

What we seem to have forgotten in all the current discussion of the relationship of the Church and the culture is that the Church has a unique culture of its own, a new and larger vision of reality than the secular culture can ever offer. That unique culture—born in baptism and nurtured by Word and Sacrament—has, over the centuries, developed a unique musical and liturgical heritage and a dynamic and glorious body of song that has, in Fred Pratt Green's words, "borne witness to the truth in every age." It is a heritage we as Lutherans can rightfully call our own and to which we have made a significant contribution.

Perhaps what we needed today is a musical expression that is not wedded to the popular commercial musical culture of our time, but a musical expression which reflects that greater reality, a larger and greater vision of the Church. For the ever-present danger is that when the Church becomes captive to the culture it loses its voice, the Gospel itself is turned out, and we find ourselves on the road to a particular, and unbiblical, view of success.

What would such a musical culture sound like? That is the challenge before us in the years ahead as we seek to live out our vocation as church musicians. It is a challenge worthy of the best of each of us. And it is a challenge about which Martin Luther and early Lutheranism have much to teach us.

Notes

[1] Carl Schalk, *Luther on Music: Paradigms of Praise* (St. Louis: Concordia, 1988).

[2] Arthur Carl Piepkorn, *What the Symbolical Books of the Lutheran Church Have to Say about Worship and the Sacraments* (St. Louis: Concordia, 1952), 10.

[3] Ibid., 11.

[4] Martin Luther, *Large Catechism* I: 82, 94.

[5] Martin Luther, *Luther's Works* (hereafter *LW*), American edition, vol. 53, *Liturgy and Hymns*, ed. Ulrich S. Leupold (Philadelphia: Fortress, 1965), 19.

[6] *LW* 53:61.

[7] *LW* 53:20.

[8] *LW* 36:254.

[9] Theodore G. Tappert, ed., *The Book of Concord: The Confessions of the Evangelical Lutheran Church* (Philadelphia: Fortress), 25 (preface to the Augsburg Confession).

[10] Ibid., 3 (preface to the Book of Concord).

[11] Piepkorn, 12.

[12] Eccles. 1:11.

[13] Exod. 15:20-21. See also the parallel and lengthier account in Exod. 15:1-18, the so-called Song of Moses.

[14] 1 Chron. 16:8-9.

[15] See also the parallel in Ps. 135.

[16] Ps. 145:4.

[17] Ps. 105:1-2.

[18] Ps. 105:5.

[19] Ps. 75:1.

[20] Bard Thompson, ed., *Liturgies of the Western Church* (Cleveland: Meridian, 1961), 20.

[21] *LW* 53:323-24 (preface to Georg Rhau's *Symphoniae iucundae* [1538]).

[22] Ibid.

[23] *LW* 28:213. For a similar comment from Luther's sermons on the Gospel of St. John, see *LW* 24:421-22.

[24] *LW* 53:324 (preface to Georg Rhau's *Symphoniae iucundae* [1538]).

[25] Oliver Strunk, *Source Readings in Music History* (New York: Norton, 1950), 65.

[26] *LW* 53:197.

[27] See Carl Schalk, *Music in Early Lutheranism: Shaping the Tradition (1524-1672)* (St. Louis: Concordia Academic Press, 2001), 39.

[28] In the introduction to the Common Hymnal as part of the *Service Book and Hymnal* of 1958, for the first time to my knowledge an American Lutheran hymnal suggests that "hymns should be devotional rather than didactic or homiletical" (286), a marked departure from the understanding of the early Reformation.

[29] Robert Jenson, *Systematic Theology*, vol. 1, *The Triune God* (New York: Oxford University Press, 1997), 12.

[30] Herbert Nuechterlein, "Cantor," in *Key Words in Church Music*, ed. Carl Schalk (St. Louis: Concordia, 2004), 72.

[31] Christoph Wolff, *Johann Sebastian Bach: The Learned Musician* (New York: Norton, 2000), 258

The Pastor and the Church Musician: Thoughts on Aspects of a Common Ministry

Pastors and church musicians, more than any other persons, are the shapers of the worship life and church music practice in most congregations. To be sure, many others—hopefully—are also involved in the planning, preparation, and conduct of corporate worship in the local parish. Yet it is the skills, understandings, and breadth of vision of pastors and church musicians—or the lack of them—which exert the greatest influence in the worship life of most congregations.

For both, doxology is the name of the game. And as A. R. Kretzmann once reminded us, "If we [pastors and church musicians] are to rise to the heights of a constant doxology, we must rise together"[1] because in corporate worship we share a ministry of proclamation, praise, and nurture centered in the Gospel of Jesus Christ.

It is important, then, that pastors and church musicians look carefully at those aspects of their ministry which they share in order that they may be increasingly faithful and effective leaders in congregational worship. Where such shared concern already exists these words may be superfluous. Where it still needs to be cultivated—or where it has not yet even begun—these words may point the way to a continuing conversation.

From "The Pastor and the Church Musician" © 1984 by Concordia Publishing House. Used by permission. All rights reserved.

Introduction

Church musicians and pastors are always looking at each other. Some with admiration and appreciation for the other's concern for making worship a living, vital reality in the parish; others, perhaps, with something less. Some look across a great gulf of hostility; others enjoy a warm relationship of cooperation in a common task. Some look only for those attitudes or personality traits which will help them get their job done with the least fuss and bother.

In the Lutheran tradition, however, both pastors and church musicians have a responsibility to look beyond surface matters to more basic insights, understandings, and points of view concerning worship and the role of church music. As one working within the tradition of the Church of the Augsburg Confession let me attempt briefly to sketch some of the assumptions which many pastors and church musicians feel are central to their work as worship leaders and which they hope to see reflected in the understanding and activities of their co-workers.

What follows could be entitled "What Pastors Look for in Their Church Musician" or "What Church Musicians Look for in Their Pastor." Perhaps it might be better phrased "What Pastors Treasure in Their Church Musician" or "What Church Musicians Treasure in Their Pastor." In either case let what follows be the beginning of a conversation between those who occupy crucially important positions in the developing worship life of every congregation.

What do Lutheran Church Musicians Treasure in a Pastor?

They treasure a pastor who understands that the Church—before it is anything else—is a worshipping community.

They treasure pastors who see the church first of all as the community of the faithful gathered about Word and Sacrament to receive strength and nourishment for its life together, offering its sacrifice of praise and thanksgiving for what God has done on its behalf. One may argue about the priorities of the tasks the church has been given to do: mission, evangelism, education, stewardship. But about what the church is, first and foremost, there should be no argument. Basic to the church musician's task is the fundamental understanding that worship is the Christian's first response to what God has done in Christ. A pastor who shares that understanding is a rich blessing and treasure, not only to church musicians but to all the people he is privileged to serve.

In many parishes the worship life of the gathered community is often a peripheral concern, the priorities of time, energy, and resources being expended elsewhere. Yet the corporate worship of the congregation is for many people their one regular contact with the church. To understand the church as first of all a worshipping community gathered about Word and Sacrament may result in a realignment of priorities in congregational life. A pastor who understands this and attempts to put this insight into practice is a rich treasure for all with whom he comes into contact.

They treasure a pastor who understands that the Church of the Augsburg Confession is consciously a part of the Western Catholic tradition.

They treasure a pastor who understands that Lutherans see themselves in continuity with the Church of the preceding centuries. Sixteenth-century Lutherans did not reject their heritage of worship forms and music. For Luther and those who followed him it was the retention of that heritage which was at the heart and center of their liturgical reform. Their reform was essentially an affirmation of the tradition, an affirmation which rejected only that which was contrary to their understanding of the Gospel.

The implications of such an affirmation of tradition for the church musician are far-reaching. Lutherans did not and do not abandon their rich musical and liturgical heritage and become merely a hymn-singing sect. They were and continue to be part of the one, holy, catholic Church. They continue to make use of its rich experience in their worship. Even a cursory look at the symbolical books of the Lutheran church affirms that stance. Church musicians can only treasure a pastor who sees Lutheran worship as a continuing affirmation of the tradition and uses such a perspective to nourish people in a rich and varied worship life.

They treasure a pastor who understands and respects the integrity of the worship forms with which the Church offers its sacrifice of praise and thanksgiving.

They treasure a pastor who understands that the structures of worship are the result of the collective experience of the Church at worship throughout the centuries, a tradition which we accept, though not uncritically, with grateful thanks and appreciation. Church musicians treasure a pastor who realizes that it is the regular and recurring use of such forms—with all their attendant richness and variety—which gives continuity and stability to Christian worship. Such a view is not a plea for dull, unimaginative, boring worship; rather, it is a necessary correction in those places where traditional forms are violated, emasculated, or discarded with an impunity unbecoming a Lutheran view of worship and tradition.

In some places, for worshippers and church musicians alike, worship often seems to be a game of "Guess what's coming next!" Is time running short? Skip to the Benediction. Is the service running long? Omit the rest of the hymn—no matter what the damage to continuity of thought. Behind such examples of liturgical whimsy may lie a desire for creativity, originality, an ignorance of the structures themselves, or simply a failure to plan properly and adequately. Yet the implications of such an approach for those who are sensitive to the integrity of the rite, the flow of the liturgical action, or the balance between various parts of the service are far-reaching. Whimsical tampering with the structures of worship can be devastating to the church musician who has planned carefully. The pastor who practices respect for the integrity of the rite can perhaps do more than anything else to make the church musician's life a happy one. Such a pastor is surely treasured by those who work within the tradition of the Church of the Augsburg Confession.

They treasure a pastor who not only preaches the Gospel clearly and forthrightly, but who expects the music of worship to do no less.

They treasure pastors who insist that the same Gospel sound out loud and clear from both pulpit and choir loft. They treasure and respect pastors who help them understand that weak or vapid texts are not salvaged by treacly music, by the sincerity of those singing, or even by expert performances. Church musicians need and welcome the kind of firm, evangelical guidance from pastors who insist that the choir loft, no less than the pulpit, is no place for poor theology. Neither sentimentalism nor bombast—whether from one end of the church or the other—are replacements for the nourishing word which builds and sustains the faith. The only word which does that is the Word of the Gospel. Pastors and church musicians need constantly to remind each other of that simple fact.

They treasure pastors who understand the Reformation insight that music is a gift of God, the "living voice of the Gospel"—to be used in his praise and in the proclamation of his Word.

They treasure pastors who understand that it was Luther alone among the sixteenth-century reformers who warmly embraced music as God's good gift to us and enlisted it as an important part of the life of the worshipping community. They treasure pastors who—with Luther—understand that music is not merely part of the wrapping surrounding the gift, to be thrown away once the gift itself is revealed, but rather part of the unwrapping. They treasure pastors who understand that for Luther and Lutherans music in worship is doxological proclamation in which words and music join together to move the heart and mind of man in ways which words cannot always do. Such a view of music as doxological praise and proclamation integral to the people's work of liturgy stands at the heart and center of a Lutheran understanding of music in the life of the worshipping community.

They treasure pastors who understand the importance of their role in guiding, supporting, and furthering a properly focused liturgical-musical tradition in their parish.

It means pastors who give constant attention to their important role in singing the appropriate parts of the service. It means pastors who support the efforts of their church musicians in helping congregations, choirs, organists, instrumentalists, and composers see their unique roles in the worship of God's people. It means pastors who work together with church musicians in leading congregations into the richness and diversity of worship in the liturgical tradition. It means pastors who are willing to learn, study, and grow in their own understanding of their tradition.

Where pastors reflect such support, interest, and growth in the worship of God's people—and where they are willing to invest the time and effort required to make worship what it can be in the Lutheran tradition—such pastors are treasured not only by church musicians, but by all of God's people whom they serve.

They treasure pastors who plan for worship, who plan adequately and sufficiently ahead of time, and who plan for worship as part of a team.

They treasure pastors who look upon the time devoted to worship planning as a necessary, vital, and important part of their ministry. They treasure pastors who see the need to plan weeks, months, perhaps even a year ahead of time so that choirs, instrumentalists, and the congregation will have sufficient time to prepare to do their part most effectively. They treasure pastors who see team planning as an opportunity for greater richness and variety in worship, and not as an impertinent or intimidating encroachment on "their" domain.

Pastors who are secure in their understanding of the Church, worship, and ministry and who understand liturgy as the people's work will have little difficulty involving the talents and insights of many people in worship planning. Pastors who work toward the greater involvement of many within the congregation in worship planning are surely a treasure for which church musicians and parishes alike are thankful.

What Do Lutheran Pastors Treasure in a Church Musician?

They treasure a church musician who understands that music in corporate worship is a vehicle for the common praise and prayer of the entire worshipping community.

They treasure a church musician who understands that the church is a community called and gathered together by the Holy Spirit convinced that Jesus Christ is in their midst as his Word is preached, signed in the sacraments, and shared in the mutual conversation and song of the believers. Music, properly used, is a uniting force helping to bring together the various concerns of each individual and uniting them in the common prayer and praise of all. In a practical sense good church music is the glue which helps hold together the action of the liturgy, gives it more discernible shape and form, and projects in a unique way its varying moods and emphases. Music is a *uniting* force when it helps the Christian community focus attention where it belongs: on Christ and what he has done for us. Music is a *dividing* force when it becomes entertainment or when its focus is on lesser or peripheral concerns. The church musician who is sensitive to music's function of uniting God's people in common supplication, adoration, and thanksgiving, and who translates that insight into practice in the corporate worship of God's people is a treasure, not only to his or her pastor, but to the entire worshipping community.

They treasure church musicians who understand that music in Lutheran worship finds its most comfortable home in the liturgy.

It is the liturgy in all its richness and fullness in which God's people can best express their *common* worship and praise. For Lutherans, music in worship—whether congregational song or the music of choir, pastor, organ, or other instruments—is liturgical song. Lutheran pastors treasure a church musician who understands that it is the liturgy, the living tradition of praise, proclamation, prayer, and mutual edification, which determines how music is best used in worship, its spirit and mood, and the appropriateness of specific music for particular occasions.

For organists this means giving primary attention to playing the liturgy and hymns effectively, thereby enabling the congregation to sing with confidence and enthusiasm. For choirs it means giving primary attention to psalms, responses, Gospel motets, offertories, music to enrich congregational singing, and similar literature. Lutherans see all music in corporate worship as part of the people's work of liturgy. Church musicians who share this understanding and seek to put it into practice in the parish are a treasure not only to pastors but to all the people they serve as well.

They treasure a church musician who understands that God is praised and the faithful are edified when the Word is proclaimed through texts which speak the Gospel clearly and distinctly, and through music which in its honesty, integrity, and craftsmanship reflects the same Gospel.

Not to care enough about *what* is sung is to neglect the Church's concern for music as the "living voice of the Gospel." Not to care enough about the *musical* vehicle for that proclamation and praise is to forget that music is God's gift to us to be used to the best of our ability in his praise and for his glory. Our common praise and thanksgiving demands uncommon musical vehicles. The truly great songs of the Church share traits which make them simultaneously uncommon and truly popular:

texts which speak of the heart of our faith, and music which reflects the character of that faith in its simplicity, directness, suitability to its function, and in its careful craftsmanship.

A church musician's task in this regard is twofold. They must help people learn to make a distinction between texts which speak the Gospel with clarity and distinctness and those which blur its witness. They must also help people see the difference between music which reflects the character of the Gospel in the honest integrity of its craftsmanship and music which is too ready to sacrifice those characteristics for other more immediate goals. A church musician who understands this as part of their ministry is a treasure to any pastor with whom he or she may serve.

They treasure church musicians who value increasing competence and continued growth as essential to their ministry.

Pastors treasure church musicians who are not satisfied with merely getting by or with second-rate effort, whether with themselves or with those they lead. While an undue emphasis on skills and competence can easily lead to a professionalism detached from what worship is all about, the greater danger in most places is that pious intentions are too easily substituted for musical competence in leading the worship of God's people. Effective worship calls for competent church musicians who are always growing in their understanding and skills.

It is the firstfruits, the very best of our talents, skills, and abilities that we are called to offer God in praise and thanksgiving for what He has done for us. Pastors and congregations treasure church musicians who see their ministry in that light.

They treasure a church musician who understands that corporate worship calls for the best of the talents and efforts of every part of the worshipping community.

None of us is exempt from offering our very best in God's praise and adoration. Second best simply will not do. Every part of the worshipping community has its unique role to play according to its special ability. The genius of music in Lutheran worship is that it provides opportunity for each part of the worshipping community to bring to corporate worship its special talents and abilities for the mutual praise and upbuilding of all.

Congregation, choir, composer, organist, instrumentalist, each is able to offer their sacrifice of praise and thanksgiving in ways suited to their special talents and abilities. Each part of the community is challenged to offer their very best. And the church musician is the catalyst in this process.

It is always our best, our firstfruits, which we willingly bring as our reasonable sacrifice. Pastors and church musicians who see this as the goal in worship, and who also possess the abilities to elicit the best from every segment of the worshipping community, are a treasure to all they serve.

They treasure a church musician who understands that winsome examples of patient teaching are the best ways to help congregations grow into new or old worship and church practices.

The church musician is a servant of the worshipping congregation. The faithful and effective church musician can serve best by avoiding two extremes: arrogantly attempting to teach worshippers what is "good music" even "if it kills them" (it often does just that); or, meekly submitting to poor standards of worship and church music because that is what a congregation is used to or what it seems to like or want.

Pastors treasure a church musician who understands that one begins work with people where they are, but then moves with them to a fuller understanding and a more meaningful participation in the total action of worship in which music plays such a vital part. It may be the introduction of a new setting of the liturgy, a more exciting way of singing hymns, a fuller observance of the church year. But whatever the new musical idea or worship practice, pastors treasure a church musician who understands that it is best achieved by careful preparation, by a well-paced introduction (not everything is learned in a day, or a week, or year), and by constant repetition and reinforcement. When that process occurs, what was once new, different, and perhaps even threatening to some will soon become familiar, with the result that worship and the music of worship will be a richer and more meaningful experience for the entire congregation.

They treasure a church musician who understands that the church worships best with a living musical tradition.

The phrase "living musical tradition" suggests a responsibility to past, present, and future. The worshipping congregation has a responsibility to all three because the faith we hold now is rooted in a past event and will come to fulfillment in the future. Singing the songs of faith which we share with the saints of the past is a vivid reminder of our unity with the Church of past ages and emphasizes that fact in a way few other things can do. But our faith—and our song of faith—is ever new and the best of the songs of our own time may well become part of tomorrow's tradition. The church musician who cultivates the old and simultaneously nourishes the new is faithful to the vision of a living musical tradition in worship. To worship in that way is to have one's feet firmly rooted in the past experience of the Church yet with one's face looking to the future. A church musician who has that vision is a treasure and a blessing for those they serve.

Conclusion

Pastors and church musicians share a need—together with others in the parish involved in worship planning—to come together in order that they might work more effectively in the work of worship. Perhaps this is a propitious time for both to come out from behind the barriers which—in some places—both have perhaps contributed toward erecting.

The church has always struggled to maintain the connection between two terms which signify what pastors and church musicians, among others, are all about: the *dogma* or teaching, and the *doxa* or praise. Perhaps all of us need to remind each other that orthodoxy first of all means "right praise," and that the *dogma* and the *doxa* are best held together when the Church sees itself first of all as a worshipping community.

To realize this ever more faithfully and effectively in parish practice may require a realignment of priorities on the part of pastors and church musicians alike. But that is precisely what all of us—pastors and church musicians—are to be about. When this begins to happen in the local parish, then—and only then—will worship become the exciting and enriching experience all of us—pastors, church musicians, and people—know that it can and should be.

Notes

[1] A. R. Kretzmann. "The Pastor and Church Musician: A Constant Doxology," *Church Music* 70, no. 2 (1970): 8-11.

The Church Musician as Steward of the Mysteries

It hardly comes as a surprise to most that in the midst of the confusion generated, on the one hand, by proponents of a rigid repristination of worship practices or, on the other hand, by the downright liturgical stillness perpetuated by those determined to "sell" religion in the worst possible way, there is equal confusion as to the role of the musician in the life and worship of the church. Proponents on either side of this great divide have radically different understandings of the role of music in the Church. And if there is little agreement on the role of music in the life and worship of the church, it is hardly surprising that there should be so little agreement as to the role of the church musician.

Congregations are ambivalent as to what the church musician's role is or should be. Pastors— who are having their own identity problems—are not often too helpful. Schools that train church musicians are criticized for not producing the kind of musicians the church "needs," although any distinction between needs and wants seems to be irrelevant. And most of all, church musicians themselves find they are betwixt and between a variety of conflicting ideas and demands as to what they should be about.

Requests from parishes seeking church musicians, conversations with church committees wrestling with job descriptions for "directors of celebration," and visits with congregations trying to cope with the perennial problem of finding competent choir directors and organists all suggest that the confusion is widespread. Many pastors and congregations are adamant that the head of the list must be "flexibility." It is

---

This was first published in the Institute of Liturgical Studies (Valparaiso University) *Occasional Papers* (1996). Reprinted by permission.]

hardly surprising that under such circumstances there is confusion and frustration and, on the part of many conscientious musicians who see service in the church as part of this calling, a simple concern for survival.

Paraphrasing Humphrey Appleby from another context, it is axiomatic that for church musicians simply to survive in many parishes, "hornets nests should be left unstirred, cans of worms should remain unopened . . . boats [should remain] unlocked, nettles ungrasped, [one should] refrain from taking bulls by the horns, and [one must] resolutely turn [one's] back to the music."[1] Nor does one have to be completely cynical about the state of interpersonal relationships between many pastors and church musicians to resonate with the advice given by one battle-scarred church musician who suggested: "If you are not happy with a minister's decision, there is no need to argue him out of it. Accept it warmly, and then suggest that he leave it to you to work out the details."

What role should the church musician play in the life of the Church today? What god is he or she to serve? Is it the god of religious individualism, of congregational pragmatism, of musical dilettantism, or the god of religion as fun and games? What exactly is the role that the church musician is called upon to fill in a time when, as Martin Marty has remarked, those "who know least about the faith (seem to want to) determine the most about its expression."[2]

That the various answers to this question as they play themselves out in parishes and congregations have given rise to confusion and conflict in many places is a fact of contemporary church life. This is true whether the church musician's title is choir director, organist, minister of music, pastoral musician, director of celebration ministries, cantor, or hired hand. It remains true that, regardless of one's title, how one understands—and how one's pastor and congregation understand—what one is about as a church musician often plays a more significant part than any other factor in shaping one's understanding and misunderstanding of one's role. Some titles may direct that understanding in more fruitful paths; others may lead down ways that would be best avoided.

Among the welter of titles, let me suggest another, one with Biblical overtones. It is that of steward. The author of the First Epistle of Peter says it this way: "As each has received a gift, employ it for one another, as good stewards of God's varied grace . . . in order that in everything God may be glorified through Jesus Christ (1 Peter 4:10-11). My *Webster's Third New International Dictionary* suggests that a steward is "one called to exercise responsible care over possessions entrusted to him." Perhaps a little exegesis, or at least a gloss or two, might help here.

Called: Whatever the bureaucratic machinery is naming them these days, the work of the church musician is a "calling," a ministry. To be a latter-day psalmist—a leader of the people's song, a steward of the mysteries, standing in the succession of Heman, Asaph, Ethan, Azariah, Chenaniah, and all the Levites mentioned in 1 Chron. 15—is a calling worthy of our best efforts.

Responsible care: To be responsible implies that we are able to be trusted and depended upon, that we are personally accountable—accountable, that is, first to the one who has given us this great gift of music. Such "responsible care" includes both the conservation and the development of the gift. The church musician preserves the gift of the Church's musical heritage and at the same time moves it forward. Many present-day problems that church musicians encounter may be found exactly at this juncture. Where the emphasis is rather exclusively on one or the other of these—either on an exclusive preoccupation with preservation or repristination or, on the other hand, on a self-serving preoccupation with the present or movement toward the future apart from one's heritage—problems are sure to erupt.

Over possessions entrusted: Of all the gifts given to the Church, music should, according to Luther, be given the highest place next to theology: "music is an endowment of the gift of God, not a gift of men. . . . I place music next to theology and give it the highest praise."[3] Music is a great gift given to the Church for the praise of God and the proclamation of his Word to the world. As a gift entrusted to our care, we are called to use it with care and with responsibility. Responsible care certainly includes a knowledge of the art of this great gift. As the author of 1 Chron. reminds us, Chenaniah, leader of the Levites in music, was appointed to direct the music, "for he understood it."[4]

How does all this work its way out in the daily calling of the church musician? How is one a careful and responsible steward in the course of one's daily work as a parish church musician? Let me make four tentative suggestions for the church musician as responsible steward of the mysteries.

As a church musician, one is a responsible steward of the mysteries when one understands that the Church—before it is anything else—is a worshipping community.

We begin with what should be rather self-evident. The church is first of all a community of the faithful gathered about Word and Sacrament to receive strength and nourishment for its life together and for the sake of the world. But in many parishes worship is a peripheral—or at best, penultimate—activity, as the priorities of time, talent, and energy are given over to a host of important, but secondary, matters. Too many parishes with sanctuaries now designated as "Worship Centers" are, in reality, centered in activities other than worship. One may argue about the priorities of the tasks the Church has been given to do—education, mission, evangelism, stewardship—but about what the Church is, first and foremost, there should be no argument. It is a worshipping community gathered around Word and Sacrament.

In that worshipping community music plays an important part in its corporate proclamation and praise. And at the center of its music-making stands the church musician, the latter-day psalmist who nurtures and carries forward the church's musical tradition. Church musicians are faithful and responsible stewards as they teach, encourage, nurture, and help congregations—sometimes even reluctant congregations—to a fuller, richer, and deeper celebration and understanding of the faith. The joining of music with Christian worship was hardly the result of historical concern for the faith, joined together with an understanding of the power of music to move our minds and hearts. In theory, the wedding of music and worship appears to be a wedding of convenience; in practice it is the unavoidable result of the new life in Christ. In theory, it may be possible to imagine Christian worship devoid of song; in practice the Christian community fills its gatherings with psalms, hymns, and spiritual songs. As Luther once remarked, "God has cheered our hearts and minds through His dear Son. . . . He who believes this earnestly cannot be quiet about it. But he *must* gladly and willingly sings"[5] (emphasis mine). The history of the worshipping Christian community is the history of a singing and music-making community. We cannot imagine it otherwise.

The church musician is a responsible steward of the mysteries when she understands that music in corporate worship is a vehicle for the common praise and prayer of the entire worshipping assembly.

The Church is a community gathered by the Spirit and convinced that Jesus Christ is in its midst as his Word is preached and as the sacraments are celebrated and shared in the mutual conversation and song of the faithful. In a very practical sense, music is the glue that helps hold together the action of the liturgy, that gives it more discernible shape and form, and that projects in a unique way its varying moods and emphases. Music is a uniting force when it helps the Christian community focus its attention where it belongs—on Christ and what he has done for us. Music becomes a dividing force when its focus is on lesser or secondary concerns—or on musicians as performers, or on the congregation as a group to be entertained or manipulated.

Music for the *common* praise and prayer of the community involves both the music the congregation actually sings, as well as—for want of a better term—the art music of choir and organ. As to congregational song, be it settings of the liturgy, hymnody, or psalmody, music for the congregation must, on the one hand, be capable of being sung. But, on the other hand, congregations are generally more capable musically than we tend to give them credit for. To be sure, music exists in worship not for the sake of the musicians, but for the sake of the people; at the same time to affirm that music in worship is for the sake of the people does not imply a license or an excuse for the perpetuation of inanely simplistic music just because it is supposedly "singable" by a congregation. One goal of a good congregational melody—whether liturgical or hymnic—is to help stretch the congregation beyond what they thought might be possible, and in so doing help them to achieve and embrace a richness and depth of Christian experience and expression they never thought possible. Successful settings of the liturgy, hymnody, and psalmody do just that.

The music of so many "new" liturgies seems to perpetuate the notion that congregations are incapable of anything beyond the simplest and most boring snippets of melody. On the other hand, some musical settings seem to suggest that the composer has had little ongoing contact with singing congregations and has written choir or concert music in which the congregation is assigned a role, but, because of its complexity, has little chance of achieving successful participation. Exactly where one draws the line between the inanely simplistic and stretching people too far is a matter of experience and informed judgment. But that is part of the task of the church musician, part of his stewardship, and those whose eyes are focused on the common prayer of the people will be on the way to making the right judgments.

The church musician is a responsible steward of the mysteries when he understands that music in the Lutheran tradition finds its most comfortable home in the liturgy.

It is in the liturgy in all its richness and fullness that God's people can best express their common worship and praise. For Luther, certainly, and for Lutherans at their best, music in worship is liturgical song. The church musician understands that it is the liturgy—that living tradition of praise, proclamation, prayer, and mutual edification—that disciplines our use of music and best determines how it is used in worship and for specific occasions.

For organists this means giving greater attention to playing the liturgy and hymnody with care and confidence in order that the people might sing with greater understanding, vitality, and enthusiasm. For choirs it means giving primary attention to psalmody, hymnody, responses, verses and offertories, Gospel motets, music to enrich congregational singing, and less attention to so-called "special music," which generally interrupts and intrudes into the liturgy. For this to happen where presently it does not will necessitate a dramatic change of attitudes and priorities—first of all, perhaps, a change of attitudes and priorities in the thinking of many church musicians who sometimes come with other agendas, and certainly a change of attitudes and priorities among pastors and congregations where they have come to expect music in worship to serve a variety of other concerns. Patiently and winsomely helping that change to occur is part of the faithful stewardship of the church musician.

As the sixteenth-century church of the Reformation dealt with the matter of the relationship between congregational song and art music in worship, it found a middle way. The Lutheran church was the heir of a Western Catholic tradition, which had placed great emphasis on art music and had little, if any, place for simple congregational song. It also existed in the midst of a developing Reformed tradition, which placed great emphasis on simple congregational song and had essentially no place for art music of any kind. Luther's genius was to welcome both—simple congregational song and art music of the most sophisticated kind—to the liturgy, and to unite them on the basis of the Lutheran chorale, the people's song of the Reformation, which provided the link and was the unifying factor in so much of the music that flourished in the centuries following the Reformation. Here was music for the liturgy, which provided opportunity for participation by people at every level of their ability: congregation, choir, organist, instrumentalist, composer.

This uniting of simple congregational song and art music was not simply a practical solution to an immediate problem. Rather, it was a practice that emerged from a distinctive theological understanding of music as a gift, music as doxological proclamation and praise, music as liturgical song, and music as the song of royal priests, as those ideas worked out their way in the regular worship of God's people. A confessional faith does not simply result in generalized abstractions as it deals with matters of worship; rather, it has practical ramifications in terms of what we do when we worship. A closer acquaintance with our rich musical heritage and practice as Lutherans might well help guide church musicians today through the treacherous waters of contemporary church life and musical practice where the luring calls of contemporary Loreleis too frequently lead only to liturgical and musical shipwreck.

The church musician is a responsible steward of the mysteries when she understands that God is praised and people are edified when the Word is proclaimed through texts, which speak the Gospel clearly and distinctly, and through music, which in its honesty, integrity, and craftsmanship reflects that same Gospel.

Not to care enough about what is sung is to neglect the Church's concern for music as *viva vox evangelii*, as the "living voice of the Gospel." Not to care enough about the musical vehicle for that proclamation and praise is to forget that music is God's gift to us to be used to the best of our ability in his praise and for his glory. Our common praise demands uncommon musical vehicles. Uncommon musical vehicles must not be confused or equated with either complexity or difficulty. The truly great songs of the Church share traits that make them simultaneously uncommon and truly popular: texts that speak of the heart of our faith, and music that reflects the character of faith in its simplicity, directness, suitability to its function, and in its careful craftsmanship.

The church musician's task is twofold. She must help people to see the difference between texts that speak the Gospel clearly and distinctively, and those that blur its witness. And she must also help people see the difference between music that reflects the character of the Gospel in the honesty and integrity of its craftsmanship, and music that is too ready to sacrifice those characteristics for other more immediate goals.

For a church musician to see no significant theological difference between such a rich text as Jaroslav Vajda's "Christ Goes Before" and "I Have Decided to Be a Christian," a blatant contradiction of Luther's explanation of the Third Article of the Creed in his Small Catechism, is to avoid the first of these two tasks. For church musicians to suggest that there is no real musical difference between, for example, *Sine Nomine*, and many of this week's favorites in the "contemporary Christian music" category, is to avoid the second task and indulge in our own kind of musical deconstruction, which ultimately concludes that there are no objective standards at all. This is not to set up a false choice between a populist view and an elitist view, between music for its own sake and music for the people's sake; rather, it is a concern for music and words for the Gospel's sake.

We live in a time when an unprecedented number of new texts, both liturgical and hymnic, are being written and are readily and easily available for congregational use. Many such texts come out of traditions or have developed from causes with presuppositions often at variance with confessional Lutheranism, and in some cases, with the stance of historic Christianity. In some cases their authors are among the most heralded in our day. Where texts are in fact at variance with the historic faith of the Church, the church musician must be ready to say clearly and forthrightly that—despite their popularity or their politically correct stance—such texts are wanting, that the emperor, so to speak, has no clothes. To see—and help others to see—that some texts speak the Gospel clearly and distinctly, and that others blur its witness, is part of the stewardship of the church musician.

But there must also be a concern for the music of worship. Not every piece of "religious" music may be suitable for use in the liturgy. Here it is the liturgy that must discipline our choices and ultimately determine use and suitability. Where church musicians begin to make a distinction between generally "religious music" and music for liturgical worship, repertories (in many situations) and congregational expectations will necessarily have to change.

This generation has also seen the emergence of a large number of church musicians who see as part of their vocation the composing of new music for worship. This has been a tremendous blessing for the Church, and the Church has been greatly enriched through their efforts. But it is also incumbent on those who are so talented to remind themselves of the dangers and pitfalls to which all of us who write music for the Church are susceptible. The lack of attention to the study of one's craft, the striving of the easy effect, the subtle notion that piety can somehow substitute for competence, or that cleverness and flair can replace mastery and skill—all these are very real temptations for young or old composers for the Church. Artistic morality presupposes skill at one's craft, but it also involves being worthy of one's heritage by both nurturing it and by extending it through the creation of music of commensurate emotional and intellectual rigor.

One more thing needs to be said, and that involves the crucial relationship between church musicians and the pastors. No one has said it better than A. R. Kretzmann, who some years ago reminded us all that doxology is the name of the game, and that "If we [pastors and church musicians] are to rise to the heights of a common doxology, we must rise together,"[6] because it is in the corporate worship of the assembly that we share a ministry of proclamation, praise, and nurture centered in the Gospel of Jesus Christ. Against the common notion that the work of the church musician is simply that of a "hired hand," Kretzmann speaks clearly and forthrightly:

The "whole" man is redeemed by Jesus Christ and the "whole" man responds to the message. The two media, preaching and music, are thus not only culturally and aesthetically involved, but they have a proclaiming and theological dimension which can hardly be estimated unless we have fallen prey to the popular but erroneous feeling that the "spoken" Word is *the* thing.[7]

Such an understanding, he reminds us, ought to draw pastors and church musicians together in dialog and understanding as nothing else can. It is the same Gospel that should sound out with equal clarity from both pulpit and choir loft, from both the chancel and the organ. There is no need to expand the distance that often is found between pulpit and choir loft into a great impossible gulf. Where this happens, Kretzmann advises us, search for the reason: "Who has forgotten the Gospel, and why has it happened? Can you explain moods and temperaments in the light of the cross? Has the congregation come to expect tensions born of pride? Why should there be pride when the only interest is the glory of God?"[8] The list of questions could go on.

One could speak no better words in conclusion than those of Austin Fleming, who has caught the spirit of the church musician as steward of the mysteries better than anyone. Speaking directly to the church musician, he reminds each of us that

- Yours is a share in the work of the Lord's Spirit who draws us together into one, who makes harmony out of discord, who sings in our hearts the lyric of all that is holy.
- Yours is the joy of sounding that first note which brings the assembly to its feet ready to praise God.
- Yours is none other than the Lord's song; you draw us into that canticle of divine praise sung throughout the ages in the halls of heaven.
- You help us respond to God's word, to acclaim the Gospel; to sing of our salvation in Christ.
- Yours is a ministry that gathers our many voices into one grand choir of praise.
- Come to your work from your personal prayer.

THE CHURCH MUSICIAN AS STEWARD OF THE MYSTERIES

- Let your rehearsals begin with prayer in common, let your practice be marked by unanimity in spirit and in ideals.
- Be gentle in correcting one another: the kingdom will not fall on a flatted note.
- Open the choir to those whom the Lord has blessed with musical gift; help the not so gifted to discern the talents that are theirs.
- Take care to study the Scriptures for the liturgy in which you will serve; know well the word that calls for our praise.
- Let the lyrics of your songs be strong, true, and rooted in the scriptures; those who sing the Lord's word sing the Lord's song.
- Make no room for the trite, the maudlin, the sentimental.
- Open your hearts and voices to new songs worthy of God's people at prayer.
- Let your repertoire change as all living things must, but not so much that the song of God's people is lost.
- Be ambitious for the higher gifts, but not beyond your gifts; respect the range of talent the Lord has given you and your community.
- Let your music be always the servant of the Lord, of God's people, of the divine service they offer.
- Let the service of our music always complement but never overshadow the people's prayer.
- Let your performance become a prayer, and your art a gift.
- Let technique become no idol, but simply a tool for honing the beauty of your gift. Remember that your ministry is ever an emptying out of yourself; when the solo is assigned to another, let that singer's offering become your prayer.
- When no one comments on the new motet, be thankful that your work led the people to God and not to you.
- Waste no time wondering, "Do you think they like it?" but ask at all times, "Did it help them and all of us to pray?"

- When your ministry leads you to music, it has led you astray.
- When your ministry leads you to the Lord, it has brought you home.
- When your brothers and sisters thank and praise you for your work, take delight in the song their prayer has become, and rejoice in the work the Lord has accomplished through you.
- Be faithful in the work you do, for through it the Lord saves his people.[9]

Notes

[1] Humphrey Appleby, *Yes, Prime Minister* (Sidney: Doubleday, 1988), entry for 10 January.

[2] Martin E. Marty, "Dead End for the Mainline?" *Newsweek* (Aug. 8, 1993): 48.

[3] Ewald M. Plass, *What Luther Says* (St. Louis: Concordia, 1959), 980.

[4] 1 Chron. 15:22.

[5] Martin Luther, *Luther's Works*, American edition, vol. 53. *Liturgy and Hymns*, ed. Ulrich S. Leupold (Philadelphia: Fortress, 1965), 333 (preface to the Babst hymnal [1545]).

[6] A.R. Kretzmann. "The Pastor and Church Musician: A Constant Doxology," *Church Music* 70. no. 2 (1970): 8-11.

[7] Ibid., 8.

[8] Ibid., 9.

[9] Austin Fleming, *Yours Is a Share: The Call of Liturgical Ministry* (Washington, D.C.: The Pastoral Press, 1985), 16-20.

Learning from the Past: What the Lutheran Tradition Can Teach Church Musicians of Today

To posit the thesis that church musicians and pastors can learn something from the past experience of the Church concerning its music and worship necessitates two things: first, the assumption that there is indeed something to be learned from the Church's history and practice; second, that we are willing to hear and learn what the past can teach us. In the present climate, neither of those two statements is self-evident.

Much of American culture today suggests that the past has nothing to teach us, that we live in a time when the past is irrelevant and it is only the present that matters. While we quote George Santayana that "Those who cannot learn from the past are doomed to repeat it," we act as if the lessons of the history have no bearing at all on what we are doing, that we live in a time which is unique, facing challenges and situations never faced before, and that, for all practical purposes, there is nothing that the past has to teach us.

It is no different in the Church. Even if those who claim an interest in the music and worship of the Church are aware of its history, there seems to be a basic disconnect between the past and the present. With much of the Church and virtually all of the culture focused almost exclusively on the present, the tacit understanding is that whatever the significance and glory of our musical and liturgical heritage may have

---

Presented at the Institute on Liturgy, Preaching, and Church Music at Carthage College, Kenosha, Wis., July 26–29, 2005.

been, while we honor it in the abstract, it is, for all practical purposes inapplicable, no longer germane to our present needs, and ultimately immaterial to our present situation as we seek to reach out with the good news of the Gospel. That this is in fact true is painfully obvious if one simply observes what happens on Sunday mornings in too many Lutheran churches these days. The musical and liturgical heritage of the Lutheran church and its practice in regular congregational worship is not only conspicuous by its absence in many congregations, anyone brash enough to mention that obvious fact is often met with disdain and outright hostility.

This presentation would suggest quite the opposite view: that both the understanding of the role of music in the Church and its practice, particularly as reflected in Lutheranism's formative years in the sixteenth and seventeenth centuries, has a great deal to teach us—*if* we are willing to listen, hear, and learn. In addition, an awareness of the richness of the Lutheran tradition can help us avoid a danger peculiar to our time: being shaped either by a fashionable relativism in which there are ultimately no standards at all, or by contemporary cultural taste prescribed as the only solution to the question of how the Church is to be relevant in today's world. A knowledge and understanding of our Lutheran musical/liturgical heritage and its possibility for revitalizing congregational worship can provide a much-needed perspective in the discussions of church music practice today—if we will only listen to what it has to teach us.

In attempting to discern what lessons might be learned from our Lutheran liturgical/musical heritage which could be helpful today, I would suggest a look at several common characteristics of a group of early Lutheran church musicians who helped shaped the course of Lutheran music in that formative period between Luther and Bach, from the publication of the first collection of choral music for use by Lutherans in 1524 to the death of Heinrich Schütz in 1672, the period between Martin Luther and Johann Sebastian Bach. We cannot examine all the important musicians of that period, but shall focus on common characteristics of seven musicians: Johann Walter, the first cantor of Lutheranism; Georg Rhau, the composer, *Thomaskirche* cantor, and, most importantly, printer to the Reformation; Hans Leo Hassler, the first among the German composers to travel to Italy to absorb the new musical style emanating from that center; Michael Praetorius, the great preserver of the chorale; Johann Hermann Schein, whose use of the chorale as the basic material in his use of the "new style" of his day served as a model for others; Samuel Scheidt, the great organist and organ teacher of Halle; and Heinrich Schütz, generally acknowledged as the greatest Lutheran composer before Johann Sebastian Bach.

What characteristics do these early Lutheran musicians have in common in the first century and a half of Lutheranism? What can we learn from them? As a group whose thought and practice largely shaped Lutheran music in the period from Luther to Bach, they can serve as examples and as teachers for what we can learn from the early Lutheran musical tradition.

Common Attributes of These Early Lutheran Musicians

One of the characteristics of these church musicians was that *all were highly trained in the art and craft of music*. Whatever their particular origin—Johann Walter was a farmer's son, Hans Leo Hassler came from a family of musicians, Michael Praetorius and Johann Hermann Schein were sons of pastors, Samuel Scheidt was the son of a barkeeper, and Heinrich Schütz an innkeeper's son—they were musicians who had received the best musical training the time could offer. Some were schooled in court chapels (Walter, Schein, and Schütz), some were pupils of the most illustrious musicians of the day (Hassler, Schütz, and Scheidt). As a young boy in Nuremberg, Hassler, for example, came under the influence of Leonard Lechner, teacher at the St. Lorenz school who himself had sung as a boy chorister under Orlando di Lasso at the Munich court chapel. Hassler later went to Venice to study with Andrea Gabrieli at St. Mark's cathedral, and it was there that he began a lifelong friendship with Andrea Gabrieli. Samuel Scheidt studied for two years with Jan Pieterzoon Sweelink, the great Dutch organist, in Amsterdam. Schütz, at the young age of only 14 years, became a choirboy in the court chapel at Cassel under the direction of Georg Otto who, as a boy, studied at the Torgau Latin School and had sung under the direction of Johann Walter, first cantor of the Lutheran Church. Whatever their various origins, every one of these musicians had received the best musical training the time could afford—as singers, organists, composers.

As composers, their mastery of the contrapuntal art and their skill in writing four-, five-, six-, and seven-part traditional counterpoint with what seems like effortless ease is astonishing. Johann Walter, the earliest of these musicians, wrote polyphony that would leave many present-day composers in the dust. Heinrich Schütz, chronologically the latest of these composers, and who had explored, more than most, almost every facet of the new musical styles of his day, was no less committed to the necessity of traditional training in composition. In the preface to his *Geistliche Chormusik* (1648) he had this to say:

> no musician trained in . . . counterpoint, can start on any other kind of composition and handle it correctly, unless he has first trained himself sufficiently in the style without basso continuo and has also mastered all the prerequisites for regular composition, such as: disposition of the modes; simple, mixed, and inverted fugues; double counterpoint; different styles for different kinds of music; part-writing; connection of themes, and so on. . . . No composition of even an experienced composer lacking such a background (even though it may appear as heavenly harmony to ears not properly trained in music) can stand up of be judged better than an empty shell.[1]

Each of the other musicians who helped shape the music of early Lutheranism received comparable training, beneficiaries of the best and most rigorous musical training the period afforded.

While training in the art and craft of music was crucially important, it was no less important that these early Lutheran musicians understood and were committed to the theological understandings of the Reformation. Luther's thinking in this area was foundational and his thoughts on music in the church were widely known. Prominent figures such as Philipp Melanchthon and Johann Bugenhagen contributed their thinking in prefaces to choral collections, extolling the important place of music in the worship and life of the church. Johann Walter developed an entire theology of music in his poem (*In Praise of the Noble Art of Music* [1538]) which treats at length the purpose of music from the Creation to his time.

These early Lutheran musicians lived and worked in an environment in which theology was not only important, but determinative in their understanding of their role as church musicians. To be a Lutheran musician at the time of the Reformation was not only to be an excellent and well-trained musician, but also to know and be committed to the theology of the Reformation, and to exhibit both in their vocation as church musicians. Luther once remarked that if your vocation is that of a shoemaker, you exercise that vocation by being the best shoemaker possible, not by making third-rate shoes and putting a cross on them. If one was a church musician, one exercised that vocation by being the best church musician possible.

Questions:

- How and where are church musicians being trained today?
- What kind of training—not only musical but training and study in understanding the Lutheran tradition and the place of music in worship—is available?
- What are the implications of the large number of volunteer church musicians serving Lutheran parishes today, many of whom have only the vaguest notion of how Lutheran understandings of worship and music should shape what they do week after week?
- What problems can arise when musicians serving in Lutheran congregations come with ideas of church music rooted in a theology at variance with Lutheran understandings?

Another characteristic of these early Lutheran musicians is that *all were musicians who found the historic liturgy and the worship of God's people to be the most natural and appropriate context for the greater part of their music.* It was the historic liturgy in which these musicians had been nurtured and which shaped their experience of worship. That historic liturgical heritage, it should be emphasized, was in no way rejected by Martin Luther. It was later affirmed in no uncertain terms: "It is not now nor ever has been our intention to abolish the liturgical service of God completely," Luther declared.² Nor was he shy about maintaining the traditional practices in the conduct of the service. Luther remarked, "Let the old practice continue. Let the mass be celebrated with consecrated vestments, with chants and all the usual ceremonies, in Latin."³ In his Latin and German Masses Luther continued the basic liturgical tradition of the medieval church, changing only that which he found contrary to his understanding of the Gospel. (Two places where his understanding conflicted with the tradition were the Canon of the Mass and the Offertory.) Otherwise, anyone who was familiar with the medieval Mass would find the reformed Mass of the Lutherans familiar. Luther understood the root meaning of the word *traditio*, from which we derive our word "tradition," as the act of "handing on" to each new generation—in this case—the treasure of the Church's liturgy and song. Luther went out of his way to criticize those who caused general upset, dissatisfaction, and offense with the great variety of new masses cropping up. "Every one," Luther remarked, "makes his own order of service."

> Some have the best intentions, but others have no more than an itch to produce something novel so that they might shine before men as leading lights, rather than being ordinary teachers—as is always the case with Christian liberty: very few use it for the glory of God and the good of the neighbor; most use it for their own advantage and pleasure.⁴

The import of all this for the church musician was that the music which served the medieval Mass could, for the most part, find a comfortable place in the newly reformed orders of the Lutherans.

This is reflected in the various collections published for use among Lutherans. These collections, chiefly those published by Georg Rhau, contained much music from the past, including pieces by Catholic composers in addition to newer composers writing specifically for Lutheran services. Both Catholic and Lutheran orders had similar musical needs. In fact there was little difference—with the exception of the use of the evangelical chorale—between the music used in Catholic and Lutheran worshipping communities in the sixteenth century. Polyphonic settings of the Ordinary and Proper Mass texts for the church year, the music for Vespers, Psalm settings with antiphons, responsories, hymns based on the old church melodies, motets on biblical texts— all these were common building blocks for musicians in both Catholic and Lutheran communities. One need only look at such collections as Walter's *Geistliche gesangk Buchleyn* (1524), his Passion settings (1525-30), psalm settings in the homophonic style (1540), and *Magnificat* settings of 1540 and 1557, both simple and polyphonic, to see this understanding in practice. Likewise, Rhau's publications for the Mass and for Vespers (1540, 1544), as well as his *Newe deudsche geistliche Gesenge . . . für die gemeinen Schulen*, drew on a wide variety of composers, old and new, Catholic and Lutheran.

In addition, Hassler's Mass settings, his settings of the chorale melodies in both simple and polyphonic style (1607, 1608), virtually the entire musical output of Praetorius, which revolved around the chorale, Schein's *Cantional* (1627/45), his *Opella Nova* (1618/26), Scheidt's *Tabulaturbuch, 100 geistliche Lieder und Psalmen*, and Schütz's *Becker Psalter* (1628) and Passion settings (1665/66), all show their reliance on the liturgy as the basic source for their inspiration and their composition of music for use in the worship of early Lutheranism.

A particular theological contribution of the Reformation, one reflected in the music of these early Lutheran musicians, was the understanding that the role of music in liturgical worship was both proclamatory and didactic. Luther had written that

> after all, the gift of language combined with the gift of song was only given to man, to let him know that *he should praise God with both words and music, namely by proclaiming* [the Word of God] *through music*[5] (emphasis mine).

Johann Walter emphasized this point in his poem "In Praise of the Noble Art of Music" where he states that the reason God supplied music was to "keep fresh in human memory" the story of God's unmerited free grace. In other words, music's purpose was to help us tell again and again the story of salvation.[6] Music and words together had a particular didactic purpose in the telling and retelling of the story of salvation. This didactic purpose is clear in many of Luther's own texts. His "catechism hymns" are a case in point.

Questions:

- What is the effect in congregational life when worship leaders summarily reject the liturgical and musical tradition of Lutheranism, opting instead for musical and worship practices rooted in traditions and practices at variance with Lutheran understandings?
- If the historic liturgy was the inspiration for the music of early Lutheranism, what is the inspiration for present-day composers? Do they find their inspiration in the liturgical needs of the liturgy, or simply from some desire to write "religious" music?
- Does the majority of the music in most church choral libraries serve the liturgy or some other need?
- Are our choral libraries well stocked with music for the psalmody, music for participation in the singing of hymnody, settings of the canticles, Passion settings, and so on? Or have Lutheran church musicians simply adopted, by default, the typical "Protestant" practice of the use of such materials as "Calls to Worship" (often parading under the misleading title of "Introits"), anthems, and the like?
- Does the ubiquitous anthem have a legitimate place in Lutheran liturgical worship?
- Does the musical repertoire of early Lutheranism have anything to teach us as an example and guide for our own understanding?

A third characteristic of the musicians of early Lutheranism is that *they were, with few exceptions, involved in the secular musical life of their day.* In the sixteenth and seventeenth centuries the role of cantor often extended beyond their work of preparing music for the weekly services. According to Herbert Nuechterlein, "The cantor, because of his vocation, found himself closely attached not only to the church but to the community as well."[7] Their duties often involved preparing music for a variety of civic events in the towns in which they served. Where they served as leader of the *Stadtkantorei* ("city cantorei") they were continuously in the public eye at weddings, funerals, and other important civic functions.

Where employed by a court, these church musicians were to provide music not only for its religious needs but for its secular occasions as well. Michael Praetorius's *Terpsichore*, Johann Hermann Schein's *Banchetto musicale*, and Samuel Scheidt's *Ludorum musicorum* were collections of dance movements for instruments for use at the court or whatever secular occasion might be appropriate.

Most of these early Lutheran musicians wrote a variety of kinds of secular music. Hassler's Italian *Madrigali*, Schein's *Venuskränzlein, Studentenschmaus, Diletti pastorali,* and his *Musica boscareccia* were collections of secular choral music, and even Heinrich Schütz wrote a collection of 19 Italian madrigals. Georg Rhau included secular choral pieces in his publications intended for the church's schools, notably three secular choral pieces in his *Symphoniae iucundae*, the preface of which, by Martin Luther himself, is the source for the most-often quoted passages showing Luther's support for music. In addition, Rhau's *Bicinia gallica, Latina, germanica* (1545) included both sacred and secular two-part songs designed largely for pedagogical purposes. The involvement of these musicians in the secular musical culture presupposes at least a modest knowledge of musical life outside the church.

The involvement of these musicians in the secular musical life of their communities is a direct reflection of Luther's view that all of music, sacred and secular, is God's good gift for the enjoyment and enrichment of God's people. Johann Walter, for example, could write that

> Then too, since sin acquired at birth
> > Would bring to Adam's seed on earth
> Much woe and—earth itself now spoiled—
> > Small joy in all for which they toiled
> As antidote against that blight
> > To keep man's life from wilting quite,
> And also to rejoice the heart,
> > God soon supplied sweet music's art.[8]

Luther could equally affirm the goodness of music apart from its use in worship. In his poem "A Preface for All Good Hymnals" (a short poem written as an introduction to Walter's longer poem) he says directly and clearly:

Of all the pleasures, joys, and mirth
    There is no finer on the earth
Than sound of woodwind or of string
    Or of the voice with which I sing.
No ill mood can be present where
    A group with singing fills the air.
For anger, hatred, envy, strife,
    Downheartedness, and cares of life
Flee from the sound of joyous song
    And take attendant ills along.
The great good news has set men free
    From fear that song a sin might be.[9]

While Luther acknowledged that God's good gift of music could be misused, the role of secular music to "rejoice the heart" was, in Luther's view, clearly part of the vocation of the musician.

Questions:

- To what extent are Lutheran church musicians involved in the broader, secular musical life of their communities?
- Do we attend concerts of our local symphony or attend any of the large variety of musical events available in most communities?
- How knowledgeable are most church musicians about what is going on in the world of serious secular music? Should they be? Does it matter?

A fourth characteristic of these early Lutheran church musicians was—with the exception of Johann Walter and Georg Rhau who were too early to be affected by the new developments, especially in their role as composers—that *they all wrestled with the challenges and opportunities presented by a new musical style.*

By the end of the sixteenth century, new breezes were blowing from Italy which would dramatically change the musical landscape, heralding a new period in church music, and music in general, which would last a century and a half. The latter years of the 1500s saw a group of innovative musicians, centered chiefly in Venice, pursuing a variety of innovative musical ideas which composer and theorists of the day would refer to as the *secunda prattica*[10] ("second style" or "new style") as opposed to the *prima prattica* ("first style" or "older style"). Elements of the "new style" were taken up, in various ways and in varying degrees, by the most important composers of the time in both their church music and their secular music.

These new developments gradually made their way from Italy to Germany through students who went to Italy to learn the "new style," as well as those who learned from the many new manuscripts which were increasingly available as a result of the new technology of printing. Most composers who adopted aspects of the "new style" continued to write also in the "old style." Hassler, in his sacred music, largely remained a practitioner of the "old style," yet his polychoral works reflect something of the "new style" associated with Venice. Michael Praetorius, on the other hand, clearly reflects his debt to the "new style" in his *Polyhymnia* (1612–19), his *Urania* (1613), a collection of polychoral settings, and especially in his use of *basso continuo* in his later large-scale works. Johann Hermann Schein's *Opella nova* (1618), a collection of settings of chorales for two, three, and four voices with continuo, was a landmark leap into the "new style." Using the chorale melodies as the basic material, Schein "distorted the chorale tunes, broke them up into fragments, vivified the rhythm, and infused them with extraneous chromaticism or *gorgia*."[11] Scheidt's *Newe geistliche Conzerten* (1631) followed in a similar pattern.

What is striking about these composers' reactions to these new musical developments is that they did not simply reject the old as outmoded and old-fashioned, replacing the old with the new, but rather sought to utilize some of the new techniques, assimilating elements of the new practices which they thought would be compatible with a Lutheran understanding of music and worship of the Church. Some composers, after experimenting with elements of the "new style," reverted back to the "old style" in their mature years: Heinrich Schütz is perhaps the best example.

These composers, while experimenting with elements of the "new style," generally retained a strong connection with their musical heritage, reflected in their continued use of the chorale as a basic musical element in much of their use of the "new style" as well as in their continued orientation toward liturgical church music.

Generally speaking, the incorporation of elements of the new baroque style into the music of the early Lutheran composers was gradual and incremental. This is true of the adoption of most of the new styles the Church has encountered throughout its history. Such a "cultural lag," waiting to see and test newer stylistic innovations as to their musical and liturgical appropriateness for worship, is seen by some today as a missed opportunity for immediate cultural relevance, a failure to be on the cutting edge in the use of new musical ideas, styles, and approaches. It is perhaps better seen as a tendency on the part of the Church not to adopt too quickly every passing cultural and musical fad.

One does not have to go back more than a few decades to see musical fads in both hymnody and church music which were quickly adopted by elements in the church as the answer to what was perceived as the need to be immediately relevant, only to see them soon fade from oblivion. What was viewed as the solution to a perceived lack of relevance was soon cast aside as out of fashion and passé.

While some of these fads have persisted in use, their irrelevance becomes more and more obvious, both in liturgy and music. This is nowhere seen so clearly as in the misleading use of the terminology of "traditional worship" and "contemporary worship." Such terminology overlooks the obvious: that what is called traditional worship in many Lutheran congregations usually bear little or no resemblance to the great tradition of the Church; and what is called contemporary worship is, from any musical vantage point, hardly contemporary at all, but a leftover from the now-dated styles of the 1960s or reflecting the invasion of Christian popular music described by Michael Linton as

> that brew of white gospel, rock n' roll, Scofield dispensationalism, Azusa Street enthusiasm, Vegas theatrics, Vineyard spirituality, sex, and cash so curdled that it would have made even the stomach of Flannery O'Connor churn.[12]

Questions:

- What can we learn from early Lutheranism as to how new musical styles are incorporated into the musical vocabulary of the Church?

- Why do you think many "contemporary church musicians" reject out of hand the musical tradition of the Church?
- What is the musical pedigree of "contemporary Christian music?" Its texts?
- Are there examples of serious church musicians attempting to incorporate new musical elements into their music?

A final characteristic worth considering is that *all of these early Lutheran musicians were influential, in one way or another, as teachers.* Some of their teaching consisted of formal instruction; other times it was of a more informal nature. Some of their pupils went on to become well-known musicians in their own right. Others' names would be largely unknown except by historians. Occasionally one or another pupil rose to particular prominence, but many pupils of these early musicians labored in relative obscurity. But these pupils went on to participate and lead music-making in courts, chapels, and congregations throughout the countries which had adopted the Reformation, taking with them the lessons they had learned and absorbed from their teachers.

In most cases the relation between teacher and pupil meant not only the direction of their musical skills and a concern for their professional advancement through recommendations to suitable positions, but a concern for their personal, material, and spiritual welfare as well. Thus many of these early Lutheran church musicians were mentors in the best sense of that term. Through their pupils and others who were influenced in a variety of ways by these shapers of the early Lutheran music tradition, the concern for the Church, its liturgy and music, the chorale, and the craft of musical composition was transmitted to a new generation of young musicians.

Perhaps most importantly, in their role as teachers, these early Lutheran musicians saw their role as, first of all, to preserve and carry on the received tradition. They were custodians of the heritage they had received from their teachers; their first, but certainly not their only, responsibility was to transmit the heritage they had received to the coming generation. It was to their pupils, then, that the task was given of carrying on the tradition, moving it forward, restating, reinterpreting, and transforming it for their own day.

Questions:
- What does the historic role of church musicians as teachers have to say to our responsibility as church musicians today and to our chief responsibility as nurturers and as carriers of the tradition?
- Do Lutheran church musicians see their role as, first of all, carriers and "handers-over" of the tradition?
- How do church musicians intentionally work to hand on Lutheran liturgical and church music practices and repertoires which have proved their worth over time in countless parishes?

Conclusion

In conclusion, let me make some general remarks about the situation today in the light of the role of these early Lutheran musicians.

The Lutheran church in the United States has yet to come to terms in a significant way, I believe, with *the Lutheran view that music in the liturgy is indeed a proclaimer of the Word*. Music is not just a mood setter or a tool to be used for a variety of other purposes, worthwhile as those purposes might be. Proclaiming the good news of the Gospel means saying and singing explicitly about what God has done for us. It means telling the story of salvation in a way appropriate to the particular Sunday or festival. It does not mean saying or singing any kind of "religious" words, repeating moral platitudes, or voicing amorphous religious statements. It means telling the story of salvation. To put that into practice will necessitate, among other things, a sea change in the repertoire of church choirs and congregations.

That *the liturgy of the church is the foundational context and discipline for church music* seems self-evident, yet today it is honored by its absence in too many Lutheran congregations. In many churches "the liturgy" is whatever order worship leaders have pasted together from a variety of "resources." The hymnal, the church year, the appointed lessons are optional "possibilities" from which pastors and other worship leaders may choose or not as they see fit. Where worship leaders reject the discipline of the liturgy and the Church's song it is not long, as James White has pointed out, before worship becomes centered less in Word and

Sacrament and more in preaching apart from the sacrament, where the sacraments are increasingly viewed from an Enlightenment perspective as largely symbolic, where freely chosen readings soon lead away from the full counsel of God toward the pet topics of particular preachers, where worship soon loses its distinct Trinitarian character and reflects, at best, a simple Unitarianism of the second person of the Trinity, and where worship is seen less and less as nurturing the Christian community and more and more as an evangelistic tool.[13] When that is the direction that congregations take—and many are being encouraged to do just that—what you have is generic American Protestantism, no matter what the sign of the front lawn says. What is lost is the richness and depth of a liturgical and musical heritage that both nurtures the Christian community and also reaches out to the world; what is left is a sectarianism that pretends to look out, but is ultimately centered in the self.

Such cavalier reshaping (or misshaping) of the liturgy from week to week brings with it serious unintended consequences: the gradual loss of communal memory, the loss of a basic repertoire of hymns in the congregation's memory bank, Bible stories becoming less and less familiar, prayers easily becoming vehicles for promoting social or political programs, and congregations finding themselves increasingly subject to the liturgical and musical whims of individual worship leaders. Such gradual movement from a regular use of the historic liturgy to the use of freely devised "orders" in which the hymnal is simply one resource among many from which one may choose or not, depending on worship leaders' perception of what a congregation might "need," is an affliction in which the purported cure is worse than the ailment it pretends to remedy.

The training of church musicians today presents its own set of challenges and responsibilities. For a significant part of our (LCMS) history we have had teacher/church musicians who supplied many of our congregations, all of whom had a significant theological education, most of whom had achieved at least a basic level of musical proficiency to lead music in the parish. Today the pattern is reversed. On the one hand, one often finds more skilled musicians who are, for the most part, theologically illiterate in the Lutheran tradition. In addition, a large number of volunteer church musicians have only basic musical skills and their theological understanding and discernment is largely nonexistent. Add to that the large number of pastors who see music as simply a means toward other ends and you have a recipe for disaster.

There is much good that can be cited. Church colleges and universities offer training at both the undergraduate and graduate levels in church music. The program for in-service training of church musicians through the Commission on Worship is a good start. This conference reflects an awareness of the need for continuing education. But congregations need to encourage their church musicians to receive ongoing education and training in honing their musical skills and theological understanding.

In addition to their musical skill and theological understanding, early Lutheran church musicians brought their musical and theological *judgment* as they sought to deepen and extend the faith in the congregations they served. But mature judgment is not the same as opinion. Everyone has an opinion but not all exercise good judgment directed toward a practice which will help congregations grow in faith and mature in understanding of music in the lives of Christian people.

Challenges presented by new styles. The church has addressed the matter of new musical styles in virtually every age of its existence. This is nothing new in our day. In every age the Church has looked at its musical culture, adopting or adapting elements into its worship where such might be desirable, at other times avoiding the elements of current styles. Pastors and church musicians need to examine carefully the theology and theological suppositions underlying much of the new material as well as the music itself. Here, seasoned musical and theological judgment needs to be exercised.

But perhaps the most significant forward step we could take today is the restoration of the idea that the church musician is, first and foremost, a "hander-on" of the tradition. Where pastors, church musicians, and congregations come to understand this, worship and its music has the opportunity to deepen and enrich congregational life in ways we can hardly imagine.

In recent years there has been an increasing clamor for church musicians and worship leaders to "think outside the box"—the box presumably representing what is perceived as the confining and constricting restraints advanced by those obsessed by the glories of a musical and liturgical heritage that are simply no longer relevant in today's world.

Spurred on by declining numbers in some congregations, such importuning is often promoted by those who have little or no knowledge or experience with what might actually be found *in* that box, who are captive to the present culture, who mistakenly find novelty and change to be the key to relevance, and who have too readily accepted the often soft conclusions of the social sciences as the unquestioned guide for setting the direction the Church should follow.

What has been forgotten is that the Church has a unique culture of its own, a new and larger vision of reality, a culture of worship and song born in baptism with the sign of the cross, a sign which nurtures and nourishes the Christian life until it is made over us one final time as we are laid into the grave. That culture has developed a unique musical and liturgical heritage, a dynamic and glorious body of song, ritual, and tradition that has in Fred Pratt Green's words "borne witness to the truth in every age," (*Lutheran Worship*, #449) a heritage we as Lutherans can rightfully call our own. What is needed today is a musical expression that is not wedded to the popular commercial culture but a musical expression which reflects a greater reality, a larger and more inclusive version of the church. For the ever-present danger is that when the church becomes captive to the culture it loses its voice, the Gospel itself is turned out, and we find ourselves on the road to producing results aligned with a particular, and unbiblical, view of success.

If the purpose of the Christian life is the praise of God and the proclamation of the Gospel—to God in thanks and praise for what he has done for us, to each other in the mutual building up of the people of God in the faith, and to the world in the proclamation of the Good News—then perhaps we might want to take a second look at what is in that box before dismissing it so cavalierly. Among the riches we will find there is a treasure of psalms, hymns, and spiritual songs that is as timely and relevant for our day as it has been for the countless generations of Christians whom it has nourished and for whom it has been a life-sustaining vehicle of praise and prayer.

That treasure, that past, to paraphrase William Faulkner, is never dead and buried—it isn't even past.[14] It is alive and well in many Lutheran parishes which have discovered, or are recovering, the richness and vitality of a treasure that is part of our unique heritage and tradition as

Lutherans. We just have to listen, and learn, think *inside* that box, and, in our vocation as church musicians and pastors, put those riches into practice in our parishes.

Notes

1. Quoted in Carl Schalk, *Music in Early Lutheranism: Shaping the Tradition (1524-1672)* (St. Louis: Concordia Academic Press, 2001), 171-72.
2. Martin Luther, "Order of Mass and Communion for the Church at Wittenberg [1523]," in *Luther's Works* (hereafter *LW*), American edition, vol. 53, *Liturgy and Hymns*, ed. Ulrich S. Leupold (Philadelphia: Fortress, 1965), 20.
3. *LW* 36:254 ("Receiving Both Kinds in the Sacrament" [1522]).
4. *LW* 53:61 ("Preface to the German Mass of 1526").
5. *LW* 53:323-24 ("Preface to Georg Rhau's *Symphoniae iucundae*").
6. *LW* 53:197. Ulrich Leupold's comment that "Luther's hymns were meant not to create a mood, but to convey a message. They were a confession of faith, not of personal feelings" has, in Lutheranism, been sometimes rejected with the suggestion that "hymns should be devotional rather than didactic or homiletical" ("Introduction to the Common Hymnal," *Service Book and Hymnal*, 1958).
7. Herbert Nuechterlein, "Cantor," in *Key Words in Church Music*, ed. Carl Schalk (St. Louis: Concordia, 2005), 12.
8. Johann Walter, "In Praise of the Noble Art of Music," tr. by F. S. Janzow, quoted in Carl Schalk, *Music in Early Lutheranism: Shaping the Tradition (1524-1672)* (St. Louis: Concordia Academic Press, 2001), 40.
9. Ibid., 195-96. Here Luther sets himself apart from Augustine who had qualms about being attracted by the beauty of music. Luther commented that "St. Augustine was afflicted by scruples of conscience whenever he discovered he had derived pleasure from music and had been made happy thereby; he was of the opinion that such joy is unrighteous and sinful. He [Augustine] was a fine and pious man; however, if he were living today, he would hold with us" (Martin Luther, *Sämmtliche Werke*, vol. 62, Erlangen edition, 111).
10. Some of these new musical ideas included a polychoral style which contrasted high, low, or similar choirs; a progressive use of instruments used in more idiomatic ways; experimentation with a variety of echo effects; the aurally sensuous use of broad masses of sound; and ultimately a freer use of dissonance; a growing concern for greater dramatic expression; and a move toward a more harmonically oriented musical texture.
11. Manfred Bukofzer, *Music in the Baroque Era* (New York: Norton, 1947), 85.
12. Michael Linton, "Rockin' with Jesus," *First Things* 100 (February 2000): 63-69.
13. James White, *Protestant Worship: Traditions in Transition* (Louisville: Westminster John Knox, 1989).
14. William Faulkner, *Requiem for a Nun* (New York: Random House, 1950).

A Primer for Lutheran Worship and Music

Introduction

This primer attempts to begin to answer the question "What is the Lutheran tradition in worship and music and how can it apply to Lutheran congregations in America?" For some the Lutheran tradition in worship and music consists of what they grew up with in their home parish. For others it is whatever happens to be found in their current hymnal or service book. For others it is simply whatever their pastor says is Lutheran. None of those answers may necessarily be true.

The task for those who serve as church musicians, pastors, and worship leaders is first to *discover* or, in some cases, *rediscover* or simply to be reminded of what that tradition is, and then to begin to *recover* that

---

This essay is based on a set of 12 theses with brief explanations, each thesis preceded by "We believe and affirm . . . ," developed by the Association of Lutheran Church Musicians (ALCM). The statement was the work of a committee of the ALCM, appointed by its president and representative of the Lutheran churches in its membership: the Evangelical Lutheran Church in America (ELCA), The Lutheran Church–Missouri Synod (LCMS), and the Wisconsin Evangelical Lutheran Synod (WELS). The committee consisted of Gregory Peterson, chair (ELCA), Carl Schalk (LCMS), Paul Weber (ELCA), Grace Wessel (WELS), Paul Westermeyer (ELCA), and Daniel Zager (LCMS). The statement especially sought to reflect areas of agreement among its members as to the role of music and worship in the Lutheran tradition. It was discussed and adopted without dissent on July 3, 2003, by the ALCM at its convention in San Diego, Calif.. The statement can be found on the ALCM website: alcm.org/about/worship_statement/.The statement as adopted by the ALCM consists of the theses titles in bold type together with the brief explanation in italics. The further explanation is that of the author.

This essay was also presented to the South Wisconsin District Pastoral Conference, April 10–12, 2007.

tradition for the life and worship of parishes where it is unknown or has been forgotten.

Countless congregations where this tradition is alive and well can attest to the vitality of the Lutheran tradition of worship and music. It is the hope that this "primer" might serve as a reminder, both to experienced church musicians as well as to those who have recently come to serve in Lutheran churches, of some basic insights into the role of worship and music as practiced in the Lutheran tradition. It might also serve as a basis for discussion by worship committees or other groups in the congregation.

Foreword: Worship and Music in the Lutheran Church

Lutherans believe and teach that worship in its essence is faith in God through Christ. The Apology of the Augsburg Confession, contrasting worship which flows from faith to that which is from the Law, states that "Faith is that worship which receives the benefits that God offers; the righteousness of the law is that worship which offers God our own merits."[1]

Lutherans believe with all Christians that worship is *Trinitarian*. The Athanasian Creed says simply: "This . . . is the catholic faith: that we worship one God in trinity and Trinity in unity." The proper object of worship is always the triune God—Father, Son, and Holy Spirit—God's proper name into which all Christians are baptized and whose name is invoked at the beginning of worship and whose blessing is given at its close. When one person of the Trinity is emphasized to the exclusion, omission, or minimizing of the others, the Christian faith in inevitably distorted.

Lutherans believe that Christian worship is *incarnational*, that it is expressed through words, actions, gestures, music, and the arts, that external ceremonies, while not in and of themselves worship, are nevertheless necessary for corporate worship. Martin Luther notes in his Large Catechism regarding the Third Commandment that "Places, times, persons, and the entire outward order of worship have therefore been instituted and appointed in order that God's Word may exert its power publicly."[2]

While acknowledging the necessity of outward order and ceremonies on the one hand, Lutherans also acknowledge, on the other, that "It is not necessary for the true unity of the Christian church that uniform ceremonies, instituted by human beings, be observed everywhere."[3] This should not be interpreted as a license to do whatever one might want, but rather to acknowledge that within the greater unity of the Lutheran tradition, variety is welcome when and where it contributes to a healthy worship practice in the local parish.

Such foundational concerns are part of the context which underlies the statements in this document. They cannot be properly understood without them. This statement and the commentary on each of the individual theses deal with understandings and practices that have long characterized Lutheran worship and its music throughout its history and which characterize Lutheran practice today where it continues to be faithful to its own history. These understandings and practices have grown out of the long tradition of the Church before the Reformation and as they have been modified and adapted by the church of the Lutheran Reformation. They have nourished countless Christians throughout the ages. They can continue to do so as they are understood, acted upon, and put into practice in congregations today.

1. Worship is the indispensable center of the church's life.

For Lutherans, the worship of the Christian community is the center of the church's life from which all other facets of its life and mission derive their strength, purpose, and direction.

Worship is faith's first response of the believing heart to the good news of the Gospel. Confronting the dying Christ, standing at the foot of the cross, the response of the centurion in an act of profound worship was to confess simply and directly: "Surely this was the Son of God." Moses' response, when confronted by the angel of the Lord in the burning bush, was simply to stand in awe and wonder and to do what the Lord said: "Take off the shoes from your feet for the place where you are standing is holy ground." Worship is faith's first response; it is the heart and center of our lives together as the Church. It is that glowing center from which flow all other aspects of the Church's life and ministry, not one program among many.

The Church is simultaneously a worshipping, nourishing, and witnessing community. But first and foremost, it is a worshipping community. For Lutherans, corporate worship is not simply a pleasant option, something to do on a Sunday morning; nor is it simply a strategy ultimately directed toward other ends. It is the fundamental, indispensable, and central work of the gathered community. There are many tasks the church has been called to *do*—mission, education, stewardship, evangelism, and many more—but what the church *is*, first and foremost, is a worshipping community.

Worship is both our duty and delight. On the one hand, it is the obligation which we as creatures owe our Creator. The reply to the invitation preceding the *Venite* in the Order of Matins in the Common Service had it right. Responding to the invitation "O come, let us worship the Lord," our reply was not "Because it is a pleasant thing to do on a Sunday morning," "Because we enjoy the music," "Because we like the pastor," or "Because we haven't seen our friends in quite a while." The response was simply "For He is our Maker." As created beings, worship is our obligation, our duty as created beings of the Creator. On the other hand, as redeemed children of God, it is also our delight. It is what we cannot help but do in response to God's goodness. Luther's comment was simple and direct: "He who believes this [Gospel] earnestly cannot be quiet about it. But he must gladly and willingly sing and speak about it so that others also may come and hear it."[4]

Worship, nurture, and witness are complementary aspects of a single action. Worship is that centripetal force in which we are drawn together to be nurtured and nourished by Word and Sacrament, only so that we may, in turn, be thrust back into the world where we bear witness to our faith in our everyday lives. Worship, nurture, and witness are never—or should never be—in competition.

The classical view of the mission of the Church can be described as threefold: the praise and worship of God, the nurturing of the Christian community, and the Church's witness to the world. They must be taken together as part of the whole cloth of the Christian's response to the

Gospel. When we place them in competition we are disjoining what is a single thread in the life of the Christian community. In recent years some churches have renamed their sanctuaries "worship centers" when the life of those communities is, in fact, centered somewhere else and where worship has become simply a means to other ends. When Lutheran worship is disconnected from its witness to the world, it separates what is in reality one larger action. When, for example, worship becomes simply a tool for evangelism, the church has misunderstood its more comprehensive role as a worshipping, nurturing, and witnessing community.

Part of Lutheranism's genius, in spite of many calls to do otherwise, is that it continues to see worship as the center of its life together. Where this is not the case, where congregations give other matters the pride of place in its life, church musicians, as part of their high and holy calling, can be a leaven to help to restore worship to the central position it should hold in the life of God's people.

2. Worship centers in God's gift of Word and Sacrament.

The norm for the weekly gathering of Lutherans at worship consists of the celebration of both Word and Sacrament. In addition, daily prayer and occasional services complement the Sunday gathering.

For Luther, the norm for worship in congregational life was the weekly Sunday celebration consisting of Word and Sacrament. The Augsburg Confession states simply: "Among us the Mass is celebrated every Lord's Day and on other festivals. . . . We also keep traditional liturgical forms such as the order of readings, prayers, vestments, and similar things."[5] And in the "Order of Mass and Communion for the Church at Wittenberg" (1523) Luther states that "It is not now nor ever has been our intention to abolish the liturgical service of God completely."[6] That was the pattern of the Christian church since its beginning and Luther was determined to preserve it. In addition to the regular weekly celebration of Holy Communion, Luther encouraged the daily use in congregations of Matins (Morning Prayer) and Vespers (Evening Prayer), enriching and complementing the Sunday celebration of Holy Communion with additional opportunities for worship, instruction, and nurture in the faith.

For Martin Luther, God's revelation of himself was and is to be found in Word and Sacrament. That is where God promises to meet his people. God's revelation is a "mediate" one, Luther believed, mediated through such earthly "means" such as water, Word, bread, and wine. Luther rejected the views of the Enthusiasts who believed that God came "immediately," that is, directly, without the use of any intervening means. Nor, for Luther and the reformers, was God's grace revealed to us in Jesus Christ to be validated either by our own powers of reason or by our feelings, but by trust in God's promises, promises available to us in the Word and Sacraments.

With the devastating effects of Pietism and Rationalism in the latter part of the seventeenth and into the eighteenth centuries this central practice was largely lost to Lutheranism. The celebration of Holy Communion became less frequent, often only four times a year, with some communing even less than that. Beginning with the Confessional Revival of the nineteenth century, Lutheranism began the slow and difficult process of recovering its earlier practice of a weekly celebration of Holy Communion. Many congregations today celebrate Holy Communion weekly. Where that has not yet occurred, church musicians have a unique opportunity to help congregations move toward that particular and salutary Lutheran practice.

3. Worship in Lutheran practice stands unashamedly in the liturgical tradition.

> *Rooted, reformed, and renewed in the history and experience of the Church, Lutherans– together with much of Christianity– share a concern for ordered worship. It is a Lutheran conviction that the needs of the people at prayer are most effectively met by forms and practices which draw on the collective experience of the whole Church. Lutheran worship is characterized neither by eccentricity nor faddishness, but values stability and continuity with the whole Church. Thus, historic patterns, the church year, appointed readings, and psalms, and a central core of hymnody have a prominent place in Lutheran worship.*

Lutherans in the sixteenth century were determined to "keep traditional liturgical forms" and Luther stated that it has never "been our intention to abolish the liturgical service of God." To stand in the liturgical tradition is to be concerned with "ordered" worship. Lutherans, together with most of the Church catholic, share a concern for "ordered" worship. But what is unique about the "orderedness" of Lutheran worship—together with other churches of the liturgical tradition—is not simply that it is ordered. All activity undertaken by any group of people is inevitably ordered if it is not to fall into chaos and disorder. What is unique about the "orderedness" of Lutheran worship is that it is rooted in the cumulative experience and the great tradition of the Church handed down from generation to generation, rather than primarily in the ingenuity, creativity, cleverness, or resourcefulness of individual worship leaders.

While some seek variety and excitement in a constantly changing "disorder" of worship, Lutherans, together with most of the Christian Church, seek continuity and stability in the shape of worship, the *ordo*, which has been handed down through the entire history of the Church and which has been received with grateful thanks as a wonderful gift of God.

To affirm the historical tradition does not mean that Lutheran worship is devoid of interest and variety. Indeed the rites of the Church, when used in their richness and fullness, provide both for variety and richness as well as continuity and stability in their shape, form, texts, ritual actions, and music. That we have not always taken advantage of the richness and variety inherent in those forms has sometimes given rise to the unjust criticism that these inherited forms are somehow stultifying, inhibiting, unattractive to modern congregations, and ultimately boring. Just the opposite is true. Where the church regularly uses the rites and forms handed down from the beginning and employs them with the richness and fullness that is part of their uniqueness, worship is enriching, satisfying, engaging, and nourishing

The liturgy of the church is, by its very nature, traditional, that is, rooted in the past experience of the Church at prayer throughout the centuries, yet not paralyzed by it. This does not mean that having paid lip service to the Church's past one can move into the future mindless of the Church's tradition. Where the Church has moved forward, cut off from the tradition, it has easily fallen prey to the theological and sociological fads, fancies, and trendiness of each new generation in the name of a relevance which has repeatedly failed to achieve its often highly touted goals.

Some would suggest that the liturgical tradition is but one among a variety of approaches to worship, that we are all locked into our particular perspectives and prejudices, and that we should certainly not impose them on others who may have different view. "The liturgical tradition may be fine for some, but it is, after all, what works for the individual that ultimately matters." Those who appeal for greater freedom in their approach to worship—"different strokes for different folks"—miss the irony of their attempt to impose on the Church their own subtle absolutes based on their own individualistic and relativistic views. Rather, the very nature of the Church presumes continuity from one age to the next. Rather than thinking of this as confining, continuity presents us with a

> freedom from the idolatry of fads, radically liberating because it locates new life in God rather than in human ingenuity no matter how momentarily intriguing or able, and highlights the finest of human crafting for the glory of God over very long periods of time so that we are not stuck in the mistakes and constraints of any one time or place, including our own.[7]

All this speaks to the fact that Lutheran worship is incarnational. Lutheran worship is not simply a matter of the spirit, if by this is meant disembodied thoughts or intellectual appropriation of ideas about religion. Lutheran worship, as is all of Christian worship, is incarnational in that God comes to us and reveals himself through means—water, Word, bread, wine, and, in a larger and somewhat different sense, through music, ritual action, and the arts. This means, for example, that worship's Trinitarian structure, the regular repetition of the content of the biblical narrative, the church year, the use of appointed reading from Scripture, appointed psalms, and a central core of hymnody, especially the Hymn of the Day, are of crucial importance and have a prominent and indispensable place in the liturgical worship of Lutherans.

For Lutheran church musicians and for all those entrusted with leadership in worship, this is the place where we must begin: with a continuing and prayerful immersion in an ever-greater understanding of the meaning and celebration of the church year, with study of the appointed lessons for a particular Sunday or festival, the psalms appointed for the day, and for the appropriate use of a central core of hymnody. Out of such study and contemplation emerge appropriate choices of music for worship.

All of this, of course, has significant practical implication. In many situations it may well mean the reordering of priorities on the part of pastors, musicians, and congregations alike, priorities which have been based on concepts or ideas inimical to a Lutheran understanding of the place of the liturgy and the role of music in worship. One works from the liturgy outward, not from predetermined viewpoints as to what can or should be done and then impose them on the liturgy. To do this may be a difficult task for many church musicians already accustomed to other patterns of thinking about music. But that is where Lutheran church musicians must begin.

4. Music in the liturgy is God's good gift to the Church to glorify him and to edify his people.

Music is given that the Creator might be praised and glorified, and that the Word of God's redemption in Jesus Christ might, through the power of the Holy Spirit, be proclaimed to the Church and the world. To those who would condemn sacred art of any kind, Lutherans respond with an understanding of music as God's creation and gift, next in importance to theology.

For Lutherans, music is God's good gift to be used for his praise, for the nourishment of the Christian community, and for the proclamation of the Gospel to the world. On the one hand, Luther could highly commend music, and all the arts, as he did in his preface to the Wittenberg hymnal of 1524: "I would like to see all the arts, especially music, used in the service of Him who gave and made them."[8] But simply because music is God's good gift does not mean that it cannot be used in ways detrimental to a Lutheran understanding of the use of music in worship.

Luther understood that such was a distinct possibility for in the same preface he could warn that youth needed "something to wean them away from love ballads and carnal songs and to teach them something of value in their place."[9]

Music's proper use and role in worship is as a vehicle for glorifying God and edifying his people. That means that Lutherans, at their best, are always open to music in the liturgy—whether simple or complex—that reflects the highest level of musical excellence and creativity. Luther carried the argument a step further when he noted that it was in the cultivation of music at the highest artistic levels of excellence that the perfect goodness and wisdom of God is revealed.

> When [musical] learning is added to all this and artistic music which corrects, develops, and refines the natural music, then at last it is possible to taste with wonder (yet not to comprehend) God's absolute and perfect wisdom in his wondrous work of music.[10]

Luther condemned anyone who would find no place in worship for sacred art of any kind, saying he must be a "clodhopper indeed," and "should be permitted to hear nothing but the braying of asses and the grunting of hogs."[11]

However, not all music that is excellent or even "religious" is necessarily useful or appropriate for corporate worship. Some would suggest that any music which is artistically excellent is suitable for the liturgy; others suggest that any music which is in some sense "religious," however vaguely, is equally useful for the liturgy regardless of its musical excellence or lack of it. Still others suggest that the appropriateness of music for worship is related somehow to the sincerity or intent of those who perform it. A Lutheran understanding affirms none of these viewpoints.

Music appropriate for Lutheran worship is music which has its roots deeply embedded in the liturgy and worship practice of the Church, which speaks the Gospel clearly, distinctly, and unambiguously, and which is appropriate to the Sunday or festival. Such music, whether simple or complex, always strives for the highest level of artistic achievement possible in particular circumstances, whether a simple congregational hymn or chorale or a more complex choral or instrumental work.

5. Music in the liturgy is the living voice of the Gospel bound to the Word, proclaiming the Gospel to the Church and the world.

For Lutherans, music and the Word are intimately connected. The Word, Lutherans affirm, is preached through music. Lutherans take care that texts sung in worship fulfill their purpose by speaking the Gospel clearly and unambiguously. God is praised when the Gospel is proclaimed, and when the Gospel is proclaimed God is rightly praised.

For Lutherans, music and the Word are intimately connected. Texts are crucially important, for if the Gospel is to be proclaimed then it must be the *Gospel*, the good news, which is indeed being proclaimed, not vague religious sentiment. The writers of the Old Testament psalms did not simply praise the majesty, goodness, and power of God; they identified God's goodness, power, and mercy by his actions (see, for example, Psalm 136). In the New Testament to speak the Gospel is to speak of God's saving action in Jesus Christ. To praise God is not to talk *about* the Gospel, but to *speak* and *sing* it, to tell the story of what God has done, particularly in the life and work of Jesus Christ centered in his death and resurrection.

It is in the liturgy and hymns, through both text and music, that the Biblical narrative is uniquely kept alive in the Christian community. Luther was clear in this regard:

> After all, the gift of language combined with the gift of song was only given to man to let him know that he should praise God with both words and music, namely, *by proclaiming* [the Word of God] through music and by providing sweet melodies with words[12] (emphasis mine).

It is in that sense that Lutherans understand that *God is rightly praised when the Gospel is proclaimed*, and conversely, that *when the Gospel is proclaimed, that is the way God is rightly praised.* Not all religious texts, even biblical texts, are equally useful or suited to liturgical worship. Nor is all music, even when set to a religious text, equally useful for liturgical worship. One characteristic of the church musician is a growing discernment for those texts and musical settings that are liturgically useful and that speak the Gospel clearly and unambiguously.

Music has an equally important role to play in the proclamation of the Gospel. Lutherans do not view music in a purely functional way, simply as a neutral vehicle for carrying words. For Lutherans, the substance of what is proclaimed is intimately linked with the way it is proclaimed — that is, the musical vehicle that carries the words. Views which arbitrarily separate words from music—the theological substance from the musical vehicle—are contrary, not only to a Lutheran view of the role of music in worship, but to common sense. The honesty and integrity of the Gospel message itself must be matched with an equal honesty, integrity, and craftsmanship of the musical vehicle which is united with those words.

It is in this way that we can best understand Luther's remark that "next to the Word of God, music deserves the highest praise."[13] Here music and the Word stand not in a hierarchical relationship, but in a reciprocal relationship, "next to," side by side, the Word providing the substance, the music giving life to the words in a way that by themselves they cannot do.

6. Music in the liturgy is an integral part of catechesis, assisting in the formation of Christians in the faith.

The Christian life is shaped and disciplined not only by teaching and instruction in the faith, but first and foremost through worship. Participation in the liturgy with its music and hymnody plays a crucial role in forming Christians, young and old.

The music of the liturgy together with the music of hymnody plays an important role in shaping and disciplining the Christian life. It cannot be overemphasized that the liturgy is a discipline—a discipline for all who participate: congregations, pastors, and musicians. The liturgy is a discipline that shapes us to God's ways, not something we use to shape God to our own needs, desires, and understanding. Discussions of liturgy designed to "meet people's needs" too easily ignore the distinction between needs and wants and the understanding that what many people may feel they "need" are simply things they think they "want." Liturgy helps to shape and form us to God's ways and to a new and ultimately more realistic view of reality.

The formation of Christians, young and old, is carried out in a significant way by the texts and music sung in the liturgy and by the hymnody of the Church. Such formation is accomplished, in part, by the intentional "handing over"[14] of the vocabulary of the faith as expressed in the words and music of the liturgy and the Church's hymnody. Therefore, it is incumbent upon leaders of worship to see that where texts not appointed in the liturgy are used in worship, it is the faith of the Church that is being taught, not human speculation or ideas.

Formation and catechesis, in this sense, is an ongoing task in which the entire congregation is always participating. It can never be left to chance; it must always be intentional. Where church musicians, pastors, or other worship leaders view the liturgy and the Church's song simply as opportunities to advance a variety of personal agendas, the liturgy, the Church's song, and catechesis inevitably suffer.

Part of the teaching function of the Church is to safeguard the faith of the Church, to see that what has been handed down to us by our fathers and mothers in the faith is handed over to our children and to each succeeding generation. Fred Pratt Green's words make just this point: "So has the Church, in liturgy and song, in faith and love, through centuries of wrong, borne witness to the truth in every tongue."[15] To hand over the vocabulary of faith in liturgy and song is one of the greatest gifts we can give to our children and one of our highest responsibilities.

It should be obvious that the liturgy of the Church and its hymnody are ways of teaching the faith. But we need to teach intentionally, teach at all age levels, and at all levels of maturity in the faith, using every opportunity we can find as church musicians to lead each generation to a new appreciation of the treasure of the Church's liturgy and song. If we neglect this responsibility we may well wake up some day to find our heritage of liturgy and hymnody has passed into oblivion and the Church's song has disappeared—and no one noticed.

7. Music in the liturgy reflects the truth of the Gospel and the beauty of holiness.

Music, apart from its association with texts, participates in the proclamation of the Word as it faithfully reflects in its own terms the honesty, integrity, truthfulness, beauty, and winsomeness of the Gospel. It is never simply functional or utilitarian. Music as

> *God's creation and gift requires a concern for craft and integrity of composition.*

Music, as a vehicle for the Gospel, even apart from words, must reflect in its concern for the craft, integrity, and artistry of its composition the honesty, integrity, and beauty of the Gospel itself. Whether the music is simple or complex, careful attention must be given to the craft of its creation.

Since music for worship—whether congregational or choral song, instrumental ensemble or solo voice—must always be viewed in the larger context of corporate worship, it is not enough that music is seen as simply a pious expression of an individual's faith. Just as the vocation of a shoemaker who is a Christian consists in making the best shoes possible, not second-rate shoes with little crosses on them, skill in the craft of music is necessary if it is to achieve the seriousness of purpose it is to serve. For the church to willingly accept the second-rate in its liturgical music of hymnody, even with the most pious intent, is to fail to hold its composers to the highest ideals of their vocation.

In the Old Testament, Chenaniah was chosen to "direct the music" in the temple "for he understood it" (1 Chron. 15:22), that is, he was skilled in it. While not addressing the matter of music directly, St. Paul notes that leadership in the church was dependent, at least in part, on the gifts—the skills and abilities—of those chosen to exercise leadership in the church ("And his gifts were that some should be apostles, some prophets, some evangelists, some pastors and teachers to equip the saints" [Eph. 4:11]). Just so, not all in the Church have equal knowledge and understanding of the gift and practice of music to exercise leadership in music in public worship.

The music of worship, whether old or new, should always be the firstfruits of our artistic efforts. Whether choral, instrumental, solo, or congregational, the music of worship should be the very best of that which we are capable. Skill and care in its creation and competence in its preparation and presentation necessarily accompany such a goal.

8. Congregational song is the pre-eminent music of the church.

> *Congregational song, re-established as a vital ingredient in corporate worship at the time of the Reformation, is a central*

> *feature of Lutheran worship. It is not enough that people are merely present at worship. Faith inevitably erupts in song. Wherever a Lutheran understanding of congregational song prevails, the chorale—among all the jewels in the treasury of the church's song—holds a place of particular worthiness and honor.*

The sixteenth-century Reformation established congregational singing as an important part of corporate worship. For Luther, faith inevitably erupted in song. But it was not enough that the congregation simply sing occasionally in worship, a pleasant psychological change of pace, a momentary diversion from the liturgy. Singing was to be a way of helping the congregation to *sing the liturgy* itself, thus enabling them to participate in the proclaiming of the Gospel.

To help the congregation sing the liturgy there developed in the early Reformation hymns (chorales) that were metrical paraphrases of parts of the liturgy (especially the *Kyrie, Gloria in excelsis,* Creed, *Sanctus,* and *Agnus Dei*)[16] as well as others which were psalm paraphrases. Early on there gradually evolved a set of hymns or chorales particularly connected to specific Sundays and festivals of the church year. These were the *de tempore* hymns (or Hymns of the Day) sung on the appointed Sunday or festival year after year. All these helped to shape both the congregation's understanding of the role of music in worship and, in more general terms, their piety.

The role of hymnody from a Lutheran perspective is to help us all sing the Gospel. We are not singing our song, our story, but the Church's song—that is, God's story of the good news in Jesus Christ. As Ulrich Leupold has noted, "Luther's hymns were meant not to create a mood, but to convey a message. They were a confession of faith, not of personal feelings."[17] Not every hymn is centered in telling that story. Much hymnody, often written for personal, devotional purposes, is centered more on the personal, individualistic thoughts of particular authors rather than on the song of faith of the community of the church.

There is much hymnody that is religious, devotional, even "spiritual," yet is not particularly appropriate for use in corporate worship. This calls for careful and thoughtful discretion on the part of those choosing hymns for worship. It is not enough that people "like" this or that hymn or that a hymn is an "old favorite." Neither is it enough that a hymn is, depending on one's perspective, either "old" or "new." The first criterion is: does it speak the Gospel clearly and unambiguously in the context of the Sunday or festival in which it is intended to be used?

It is because the Lutheran chorale—among all the rich treasures of the church's song—speaks the Gospel so clearly and unequivocally that it holds a place of particular importance in the Lutheran tradition. This is reflected particularly in the development of the Hymn of the Day, a hymn of significant textual and musical weight which relates to the appointed readings for the day, but with a breadth which can bear the larger weight of meaning the Church has assigned to a particular festival or day of the church year. In recent years, although the terminology of "Hymn of the Day" is widely accepted and has found a place in Lutheran hymnals, congregational practice in many places still reflects the persistence, mindset, and spirit of the old "sermon hymn."

Where the chorale is well known and used in congregations, it should continue to be carefully nurtured through regular and frequent use. Where it may be little or less known, it needs to be winsomely introduced so that where the chorale is not known congregations may learn to treasure it and welcome it into its core of hymnody.

9. The cantor is the leader of the congregation's song.

The term "cantor" is the historic designation for the vocation of the Lutheran church musician. The cantor normally serves as organist, director of choirs and instrumental groups, and teaches, encourages, and nurtures the musical talent of the congregation. The cantor's calling, however, extends beyond the preparation of music for the various services. The cantor takes an interest in the personal and spiritual lives of those with whom he or she works, and is often musically active in the larger community in which the congregation is situated.

The role of cantor in the Lutheran tradition is both a vocation and a calling. As leader of the Church's song in a particular place, the cantor stands in a long line of leaders in the people's song: Heman, Asaph, Ethan, Azariah, Chenaniah, and all the Levites mentioned in 1 Chron.

15. That line can be extended to Johann Walter, first cantor of the Lutheran church, and other Lutheran cantors such as Georg Rhau, Johann Hermann Schein, Samuel Scheidt, Heinrich Schütz, Johann Sebastian Bach, and in more recent times Hugo Distler, Paul Bouman, Paul Manz, Ronald Nelson, and a host of others. That is heady company.

The cantor is first a conservator, a guardian, a "hander on" of the tradition, as well as one who, as appropriate and possible, moves the tradition forward. The cantor is one who, on the one hand, resolutely holds fast to the old which is tried and true, and at the same time, on the other hand, offers a disciplined introduction of what is best among the new. Those are the two focal points of the cantor's calling: (1) to hand on the tradition, and (2) the disciplined instruction of the new. It is only when the balance between care for handing on the tradition to each new generation and the gradual introduction of the new is in proper balance that the cantor best serves the congregation.

While some parishes may view the cantor "as an affliction sent by God, so that those who have not suffered for their faith may not be denied the opportunity to do so," countless congregations can testify to the rich blessings which faithful church musicians have brought to the prayer life of the parish community as, through winsome and persistent example, they have led the Christian people to a fuller and richer understanding and practice of the faith through the Church's song.

10. Presiding and assisting ministers, choirs, organ, and other instruments enhance, enrich, and elevate the congregation's song.

In a Lutheran understanding of worship, the role of solo voices, choir, organ, and other instruments is to enhance the musical participation by the congregation. This is accomplished by supporting and enriching the singing of congregational hymns, bringing richness and variety to worship as portions of the liturgy are entrusted to those who have rehearsed on behalf of the congregation and presenting attendant music as appropriate and possible.

From a Lutheran perspective, the congregation is the chief musical instrument in corporate worship. That instrument, however, may be enhanced and enriched through the song of presiding and assisting ministers, choirs, organs, and other instruments.

Corporate worship in the Lutheran tradition has normally been sung. A sung liturgy adds a beauty and solemnity to worship, elevating worship beyond the personal and idiosyncratic to that of truly corporate worship. This is the case also for those who lead worship; presiding and assisting ministers have their particular role to play in singing the liturgy. Thus it is normal that when presiding and assisting ministers engage the congregation in dialogue—as in greetings, the exchanges at the beginning of the preface—it is appropriate that both sing their parts. Where there are choirs, their primary responsibility is to assist the congregation in its liturgical song. Where congregations do not participate fully in their sung portions of the liturgy, choirs should help teach them their role and ultimately, when it is well established, to spur on their singing, enriching it with descants, through singing alternating hymn stanzas, and the like.

An equally important role for the choir is to sing those parts of the liturgy assigned them in the liturgy. In our day, that means that choral participation should be focused first on the singing of the psalms, the Verse, the Hymn of the Day, and the Offertory. Where there is still rehearsal time, and where the choir has the ability, additional choral materials, attendant music—music which attends or serves the liturgy—such as motets, music for communion, anthems, liturgical settings of the Passion story for Holy Week, and so on, may be prepared.

In many congregations, focusing first on the liturgical contribution of the choir may mean a reordering of priorities, initially, on the part of the church musician, who must then lead the choirs and congregation (and often pastors as well) to a renewed understanding of their role. For many choirs and congregations who have come to view the choir's role as simply presenting an anthem each week, with little or no attention to the choir's primary role in worship, this can present a real challenge.

Likewise, soloists, organists, or other instrumentalists exist to serve the liturgy. Not all may view their role this way, seeing it rather as a vehicle to display their—sometimes considerable, sometimes not so considerable—technical ability. Many organists, some of them excellent concert performers, spend little or no time learning the unique art of accompanying the congregation—which is their primary function. Organists need to see their basic responsibility as effectively leading the congregation in the singing of the liturgy and hymns.

11. Simple congregational song and music of the highest artistic achievement join together in the praise of God and in the proclamation of the Word.

In contrast to Christian traditions which, on the one hand, emphasize only congregational singing, or, on the other hand, only sophisticated art music, the Lutheran tradition has from its beginning encouraged the reciprocal interaction of simple congregational song and art music of the most sophisticated kind. The result is an environment in which congregations, musicians, and composers all contribute to a vibrant worship life.

Early Lutheranism found itself between two distinct points of view. By the time of the Reformation, Roman Catholicism had a highly developed body of art music for the liturgy with little, if any, room for the participation of the people. Those who followed Calvin encouraged the congregational singing of the people, but allowed for little or no art music of any kind in corporate worship. Luther's genius was to admit to worship both the people's song and the most sophisticated art music of his day—Gregorian chant and Renaissance polyphony—and find a place for both in the worship of the Christian community.

What united these two seemingly disparate elements was the Lutheran chorale, the popular song of the people, which served as the basic musical material for much of the glorious art music for choirs, organs, and instruments which developed following the Lutheran Reformation. The flourishing tradition of Lutheran music between the time of Luther and culminating in the music of Johann Sebastian Bach—the period of Johann Walter, Johann Hermann Schein, Samuel Scheidt, Heinrich Schütz, Dietrich Buxtehude, and many more—was the happy result.

In the centuries following the Reformation, Lutheran music, at its best, continued to draw strength and inspiration from the texts and melodies of the chorale. In the twentieth and twenty-first centuries the chorale continues to be the basis for much of the music, both choral and organ, developed for worship in the Lutheran tradition.

12. Music in worship encompasses the repertoire of both the church universal and the congregation in particular.

The musical culture of the Church is both universal and parochial, reflecting the diversity of the Body of Christ and God's mission in and to the whole world. Congregations reflect the unity of the Church by using the music of Christians around the world and acknowledge their context by fostering the individual gifts of their members.

The hymnal, as an indicator of the repertoire of the church's song in any given period, is a remarkably catholic and comprehensive collection of the Church's song, widely representative of the various cultures in which the Church has taken root. Even the most conservative of Lutheran hymnals today contains hymns from a wide spectrum of countries and cultures: Greek, Latin, Scandinavian, Slovak, Welsh, French, Italian, Finnish, Dutch, African American, Hispanic, Caribbean, German, British, American, and Canadian. There are songs from the Old and New Testaments, the early church, together with texts and melodies from the medieval, Renaissance, and Reformation periods, along with significant hymns which the Church has taken to its heart from more recent times. Clearly, the traditional hymnal is the most cross-cultural book which the Church regularly uses. It is unfortunate that it is usually not recognized as such.

It is also unfortunate that as a result of faulty ecclesiastical presuppositions, a misreading of the Second Vatican Council and its concerns about inculturation, together with an increasingly consumer culture, some parts of the Church have been led to abandon its rich legacy of hymnody. In its place is often to be found material which blurs, at best, or distorts, at worst, the message of the Gospel and which reflects an almost abject surrender by the Church to the surrounding culture.

To sing the songs of the Church which nourished the faith and proclaimed the Gospel to the world from every period of the Church's history is to unite us with Christians who have gone before us—"all the company of heaven"—in ways that go beyond simply intellectually reminding ourselves that they once sang these songs. The same is true of hymns from the medieval church, the Reformation church, from all the periods since the Church began. To sing such songs is to remind us that we are part of a communion of saints that was here long before we were born, a community into which we were born by baptism, a community that does not begin and end with us.

But congregations also minister in the midst of particular cultural circumstances. If we are to minister to the variety of cultures in which the Church finds itself today, then, depending on the situation of particular parishes, Christian hymns and songs which proclaim the Gospel in other cultural idioms may well be in order.

But careful discernment and use is both appropriate and necessary. Many newer hymns come with theological biases inimical to a Lutheran understanding of the faith. Because a hymn or song has a religious content and is Norwegian or German (or Swedish, Finnish, or Icelandic), for example, does not necessarily mean it speaks the Gospel or is liturgically appropriate. The same must be said of hymns or songs that come from cultures newer to Lutheranism's experience such as African-American, Hispanic, Asian, or any other culture. Hymns and songs from cultures new to Lutheranism need to undergo the same careful process of examination as any other hymns which would aspire to take their place as part of the Church's song. In that process it is only an awareness of the history of Christian song, both its music and its theology, that helps prevent us from being blinded by the vagaries of contemporary cultural taste.

And just as English-speaking American Lutheran congregations, presumably rooted in the breadth of the Church's song, are being introduced to hymnody from cultures new to Lutheran experience, so too must cultures new to Lutheranism be exposed to the breadth and depth of the historic song of the Church of which they also are a part. Such congregations need to take care that their repertoire of hymns also reflects the breadth of the church's song. Where a congregation's hymn repertoire, by design or by default, utilizes largely only one kind of music—*whatever the musical idiom may be*—the music of worship easily becomes curved in on itself, a solipsistic reflection of a congregation's musical parochialism.

We need also to remind ourselves that it is not simply, or even basically, a matter of absorbing from the surrounding culture whatever the Church can utilize or adapt for the purposes of its life and mission in frantic pursuit of an always-nebulous diversity. The Church needs to remind itself that it has its own unique culture, a distinctive and incomparable culture shaped by Word and Sacrament, marked by an observance of time which stands in stark contrast to the surrounding culture, and animated by a unique song that has developed out of the particular needs of the Church's worship. In a very real sense the Church's worship and its song is always counter-cultural, standing against whatever the culture may be. At the same time the Church's worship and song is supra-cultural, standing in the midst of, and yet always beyond, all time and culture.

Afterword

The Lutheran church can claim a rich and varied heritage of worship and music that has nourished countless Christians throughout the centuries. It is a heritage which must be learned and treasured anew by each successive generation. This happens only as it is intentionally handed down from one generation to another and as each successive generation learns to treasure it anew, keeping it alive and vibrant in congregational worship. This does not happen by accident. Pastors, church musicians, and worship leaders need to be intentional in taking up the task of handing down the tradition from one generation to another. It will not happen in any other way.

Ours is a time when the rich Lutheran heritage of worship and music is, in many places, being challenged by a variety of well-meaning but misguided attempts to lead worship down different paths. Often this challenge comes from leaders who have never experienced the riches of their own tradition, or who view worship simply as a tool, a penultimate means to other ends. Church musicians need to rise to the challenge, to show the way not only to a *discovery* of our tradition as Lutherans, but to a *recovery* of it in the life, worship, and mission of every congregation.

"The greatest gift the Church can give our society," writes Robert Wilken, speaking of the Church's worship, "is a glimpse, however fleeting, of another city. But we can only do that if our worship is self-consciously, confidently, and unmistakably oriented to God. . . . Indeed if the visitor does not feel uncomfortable, out of place and out of step, something is terribly wrong."[18]

To give us all a glimpse of another city in our worship and its music will be no small task. But it is a task worthy of the calling of every church musician, an ongoing task that must be undertaken anew by each successive generation of church musicians. It is a task to which our heritage as Lutherans can continue to make a significant contribution.

The Anniversary of the Presentation of the Augsburg Confession
June 25, 2006

Notes

[1] Robert Kolb and Timothy J. Wengert. *The Book of Concord: The Confessions of the Evangelical Lutheran Church* (Minneapolis: Fortress, 2000), Ap IV, 49 (Apology of the Augsburg Confession).

[2] Ibid., LC, 94 (Large Catechism).

[3] Ibid., AC VII, 3-4 (Augsburg Confession)

[4] Martin Luther, *Luther's Works* (hereafter *LW*), American edition, vol. 53, *Liturgy and Hymns*, ed. Ulrich S. Leupold (Philadelphia: Fortress, 1965), 333.

[5] Kolb and Wengert, Ap XXIV, 1.

[6] *LW* 53:20.

[7] Paul Westermeyer, *Let the People Sing: Hymn Tunes in Perspective* (Chicago: GIA, 2005), 6.

[8] *LW* 53:316.

[9] Ibid.

[10] *LW* 53:324.

[11] Walter Buszin, *Luther on Music* (St. Paul: North Central, 1958), 6.

[12] *LW* 53:323-24.

[13] *LW* 53:323.

[14] The word "tradition," from the Latin *traditio*, means "the act of handing over."

[15] *Lutheran Service Book*, #796; *Evangelical Lutheran Worship*, #850, 851; *Christian Worship* #248.

[16] These were "Kyrie, God Father in Heaven Above," "All Glory Be to God on High," "We All Believe in One True God," "Isaiah, in a Vision Did of Old," and "O Christ, Thou Lamb of God."

[17] *LW* 53:197.

[18] Robert Wilken, "Angels and Archangels: The Worship of Heaven and Earth," *Antiphon: A Journal for Liturgical Renewal* 6, no. 1 (2002): 10-18.

III

The Lutheran Heritage of Hymnody

The Roots of American Lutheran Hymnody

Any discussion of the roots of American Lutheran hymnody must of necessity begin with developments in the sixteenth-century Reformation. Moreover a thorough discussion needs to take into account not only the textual and musical aspects of hymnody, but must also look at the larger theological context in which Lutheran hymnody appears, particularly its role in worship in the context of the Reformation. Such a discussion also needs to take into account the impact of the social and political forces operative as Lutheran hymnody worked its way through the intervening centuries from the Reformation to the present day.

Martin Luther's (1486–1546) unique insight into congregational song was not simply that the congregation should be involved in worship through the means of song. While that statement is mostly true, it must be joined together with Luther's insight, understanding, and conviction that the purpose of the congregation's involvement was not just to sing, but to sing the good news of salvation, and to sing it in words that could be understood by the congregation, and with musical vehicles that could be readily employed by the people. Hymnody was not only a means whereby the congregation expressed what it believed, but a vehicle by which they sang the good news of the Gospel to God (pleading it before him and thanking him for it), to each other (in mutual consolation and the building up of each other in the faith), and to the world (in proclamation and praise.) Where both of these aspects of Luther's

---

This essay was first published in *Hymns in the Life of the Church*, ed. Daniel Zager (Ft. Wayne, Ind.: Concordia Theological Seminary Press, 2004), 101–15, journal for the Fourth Annual Conference of The Good Shepherd Institute (Pastoral Theology and Sacred Music for the Church), November 2–4, 2003). Used by permission.

understanding are not present, we have only a truncated view of Luther's use of hymnody.

We need to be reminded of Ulrich Leupold's words in his introduction to the hymns in volume 53 of the American edition of *Luther's Works* that "Luther's hymns were not meant to create a mood, but to convey a message. They were a confession of faith, not of personal feelings."[1] Such a comment speaks directly to the matter of the content of Reformation hymnody. In the years following the Reformation such a view would come into conflict with other views which tended to reshape the understanding of the role of hymnody in Lutheran worship, not always for the better. Many of the problems the church faces in connection with hymnody today are the direct result of a misunderstanding or lack of understanding of the basic Reformation perspective.

Various musical sources were employed by Luther and his colleagues to enable congregational song to accomplish that goal. Those sources of Reformation hymnody, a hymnody which came to be known collectively as the Lutheran chorale, are well known and only need to be mentioned here. They include (1) the *repertoire of Gregorian chant*, which, after all, had been the musical language of the Church for a millennium and a half, a treasury which was adopted and adapted for greater ease in congregational singing. (One chant, for example, the *Veni Redemptor gentium*, became the germ from which developed several Lutheran chorales: "Nun komm der Heiden Heiland," "Verleih uns Frieden gnädiglich," and "Erhalt uns, Herr, bei deinem Wort."); (2) *Leisen*, pre-Reformation German folk songs characterized by the use of some form of "Kyrie eleison" ("Nun bitten wir den heiligen Geist," would be an example); (3) *Cantiones*, pre-Reformation Latin or Latin/vernacular spiritual songs which, while religious, were not necessarily associated with the liturgy. ("In dulci jubilo" would be an example.); (4) *Contrafacta*, songs that came about by providing a sacred text to an already existing popular secular melody. (Luther's "Vom Himmel hoch da komm ich her" adapted from "Aus fremden Landen komm ich her" would be an example.); and (5) *Newly composed songs*, a category for which Luther himself set an example with his various newly written texts from "Ein neues Lied wir heben an" to "Sie ist mir lieb, die werte Magd."

Characteristic of the texts of early Lutheran hymnody was their intimate connection to the liturgy. Some were paraphrases of portions of the liturgy such as the five hymn paraphrases of the parts of the Ordinary of the Mass ("Kyrie, Gott Vater," "Allein Gott in der Höh," "Wir glauben all an einen Gott," "Isaiah, dem Propheten das geschah," and "Christe, du Lamm Gottes"). Others were paraphrases of Scripture which found a place in other liturgies, such as "Mit Fried und Freud ich fahr dahin" or "Vater unser im Himmelreich." Some were paraphrases of psalms, such as "Aus tiefer Not schrei ich zu Dir" or "Ein feste Burg ist unser Gott." Many were translations of Lutheran office hymns, sequences, and antiphons. Many were hymns for the seasons of the church year. Where pre-Reformation texts were employed, they were often corrected and improved, "verbessert" in Luther's words, bringing them in line with Luther's understanding of the Gospel.

Parenthetically, while ready to freely change the words of songs he found contrary to the Gospel, Luther could complain with the best of them about those who would change his words. In "A New Preface by Martin Luther" to the Weiss hymnal of 1528, Luther complained about the situation in which there seemed to be

> no end to this haphazard and arbitrary revision which goes on from day to day and that even our first hymns are more and more mutilated with each reprinting. . . . I beg and admonish all who love the pure Word no more to "improve" or enlarge our booklet without our knowledge.[2]

Luther, it seems, was certainly concerned about maintaining the integrity of his own texts.

The characteristic liturgical orientation of texts in early Lutheran hymnody was also reflected in the hymnals of the period. While the earliest small collections were often *ad hoc* collections created by compiling a number of broadsides, by the middle of the sixteenth century Lutheran hymns were being clearly organized by the liturgical demands of worship, chiefly the church year and the sacraments. The *Geistliche Lieder* (1545), for example—the so-called Babst hymnal—contained 129 hymns in two sections. The first section, containing 89 hymns, was largely given over to hymns for the church year and the sacraments together with the Litany, various chants, and similar material; the second section, containing 40 hymns, was designated as containing "psalms and spiritual songs written by other faithful Christians" ("Psalmen und Geistliche lieder welche von fromen Christen gemacht"). The clear division in this hymnal of hymns for liturgical use from other songs which were helpful and useful for devotional purposes but not necessarily for use in public worship is important to note. This hymnal, described as "the finest hymnal of the Reformation period"[3] and as "the most significant hymnal of the sixteenth century,"[4] set the standard for future Lutheran hymnals of the time.

It was this developing hymnic tradition together with a gradually developing basic repertoire of chorales that was soon exported to those countries where Lutheranism took root. This basic core of hymnody, translated into the vernacular of the particular countries where Lutheranism established itself, soon became the common property of Lutherans everywhere. Thus many of what were originally—through an accident of history and geography—German chorales became the common property of Lutherans in Norway, Sweden, Denmark, several of the Eastern European countries, and wherever Lutheranism took root. The German chorale thus became the Lutheran chorale, a true cross-cultural vehicle for the spreading of the Gospel.

These basic understandings of Lutheran hymnody soon came under pressure from a variety of social, theological, and political forces which would result in changes in Lutheran hymnody as it made its way to North America in the seventeenth, eighteenth, and nineteenth centuries.

Early Lutheran Hymnody in North America[5]

The earliest evidence of Lutheran hymnody in North America is associated with the ill-fated expedition of the Danish explorer Jens Munck who set sail from Denmark in 1619 with two ships and 66 men in hopes of finding a northern route to East India, the so-called "Northwest Passage."[6] To set this in context, in 1619 the Thirty Years' War had just begun, Michael Praetorius (1571-1621) was still living, and Heinrich Schütz (1585-1672) was just 34 years old. Munck's expedition entered Hudson's Bay and arrived at its western shore near the Churchill River and established a settlement called "Nova Dania" (New Denmark) a year before the Mayflower set sail from England bringing the earliest English settlers to the New World. Munck's expedition included a pastor, Rasmus Jensen, who conducted services. Munck noted in his "Dagbog" (journal) that in 1619 on "the holy Christmas day we celebrated jointly in a Christian manner; we had preaching and the Lord's Supper."[7] Presumably hymns were sung. They would likely have been taken from Hans Thomisson's *Den danske Psalmebog* (1569), the first hymnal specifically prepared for Lutheran services in Denmark, which contained a number of translations from the earlier German collections together with their melodies. This Danish settlement was short-lived. Most of the settlers died within the first year and only two sailors and Munck himself managed to return home safely in September of 1620.

If the members of this expedition sang hymns, as they undoubtedly did, we can say that this hardy band of Danes were the first to sing Lutheran hymns in North America. The sounds of their hymns, however, were as short-lived as their settlement.

Two other groups of Lutherans came to America in the early seventeenth century. These were the Dutch sent by the Dutch West Indies Company, which numbered Lutherans among the settlers. In the early 1600s strong Lutheran congregations existed in such Dutch cities as Amsterdam, Rotterdam, and Leyden. In 1623 just such a group reached America, settling at Ft. Orange near the city of Albany. Two years later a similar group settled on Manhattan Island founding New Amsterdam. Lutherans, however, found the practice of their faith somewhat difficult since the Dutch officials were Calvinist (or Reformed). When Lutherans began holding services they were often fined and threatened with heavier fines if they repeated the offense. It was not until the English conquered New Amsterdam in 1664, renaming it New York, that Lutherans found greater religious freedom there. In 1669 the Lutherans in Holland sent Jacob Fabritius to serve as pastor to the Lutherans there. He restored traditional Lutheran hymnody and liturgy as it was practiced among the Lutherans in Holland. And in 1703, in what was probably the first regular ordination in the New World, Andrew Rudman ordained Justus Falkner in "Old Swedes Church" in Philadelphia in a full Latin service with choir.

The second group consisted of Swedish Lutherans who came up the Delaware River in 1638 and established a settlement near present-day Wilmington, Del., soon to be followed by another group in 1640 who served the colonists at Fort Christina. Describing the worship of these colonists, Amandus Johnson points out that

> the Swedish order of service was followed in the colony . . . in 1644 . . . 'the services with its ceremonies are conducted as in Old Sweden' and in the 'good old Swedish language.' The order of services at 'High Mass' as given in the Psalm-book of 1614 which was used here. . . (1640–97).[8]

The service of the Psalm-book of 1614 included the singing of Decius's "All Glory Be to God on High," another hymn between the Epistle and Gospel, Luther's setting of the Creed ("Wir glauben all an einen Gott"), a hymn before the sermon, the congregational singing of the *Agnus Dei* ("O Lamm Gottes unschuldig"), and a final hymn.

Among the contributions of the early Swedes were their upholding of the liturgical tradition of their homeland at a time when most American groups were confining their hymnic participation to metrical psalms and, according to Edward Wolf, their "extensive use of hymnbooks, their intonations of such liturgical texts as the collects, and their early introduction of organ support for the services."[9]

These early seventeenth-century Lutheran settlements were soon eclipsed, however, by the rising tide of German immigration in the first half of the eighteenth century. And it is to that development that we now turn.

The German Immigration and Early American Lutheran Hymnody

The great tide of Lutheran immigration into colonial America came not from Sweden but from the German immigration in the first half of the eighteenth century. Germans from the Palatinate moved up the Hudson River in the first decade of the century and established both Lutheran and Reformed congregations as far north as the Mohawk River. But while the number of German immigrants generally continued to grow, the most astounding growth occurred in Pennsylvania where by

1750 the Lutheran population had grown to 60,000, a number which continued to increase throughout the latter half of the century.

The hymnody which the immigrants brought with them largely reflected the post-Reformation-era developments in Germany in which the strong, confessional, objective hymns of the early years of the Reformation were gradually displaced by the hymns of Pietism which reflected an emphasis on the more personal, introspective, and devotional rather than on the proclamatory or didactic emphases of the early Reformation. It is not difficult to trace this development when one compares texts by Luther and his contemporaries through Paul Gerhardt to the excesses of the hymnody of later Pietism.

Pietism, it should be said, had any number of salutary effects on Lutheranism, among them the development of orphanages, hospitals, printing presses, an emphasis on mission work, together with other social activities. The hymnody of Pietism, however, while a welcome addition to the more dogmatic and proclamatory hymnody of the early Reformation, in time displaced the earlier hymnody, leaving a body of hymnody largely concerned with overly personalistic, introverted texts which emphasized human feelings, eventually largely apart from any substantive Gospel proclamation.

This change from a churchly, confessional hymnody (*Bekenntnislieder*) to hymns of a more personal and devotional character (*Erbauungslieder*) is nowhere more clearly evident than in the first Lutheran hymnal compiled and produced for the growing Lutheran population in America—the *Erbauliche Liedersammlung* of 1786, largely the product of the "Father of American Lutheranism," Henry Melchior Muhlenberg (1711–87).[10] Muhlenberg saw the production of one book for American Lutherans as a way of alleviating the confusion in worship caused by the variety of hymnals which the immigrants had brought with them from their homelands. (Upon his arrival in America Muhlenberg found hymnbooks from Marburg, Cöthen, Württemberg, and Wernigerode, among others, in use.) One book could also be a way, Muhlenberg thought, of bringing a sense of unity to Lutherans who were scattered about the new land. In the preface to the 1786 hymnbook Muhlenberg wrote concerning this sense of unity:

if only there were one hymnbook for all American [Lutheran] congregations which would contain the best of the old and new spiritual songs, how much more convenient and harmonious it would be.[11]

Muhlenberg's hymnbook, a text-only book containing 706 hymns, was to follow in its composition and arrangement several rules set out by resolution of the Pennsylvania Ministerium, two of which are of particular interest for our purposes. They were (1) "As far as possible to follow the arrangement of the Halle Hymn Book," and (2) "Not to omit any of the old standard hymns, especially those of Luther and Paul Gerhard[t]." The "Halle Hymn Book" referred to was the *Geistreiches Gesangbuch* of 1704 published in Halle and edited by Johann Anastasii Freylinghausen and the *Neues Geistreiches Gesangbuch* of 1714, also printed in Halle, both of which were subsequently bound together and published in 1741 and contained 1,581 hymns with 597 melodies. The "Halle Hymn Book" itself included melody with figured bass for many of the hymns. Muhlenberg himself had been given a copy of this book on the day of his ordination by the wife of August Hermann Francke (1663-1727) who along with Philip Spener (1653-1705) was considered one of the chief leaders in the Pietist movement. Francke had established a center for Pietism at the University of Halle, and it was Francke's son, Gotthilf August Francke (1696-1769), who had persuaded Muhlenberg to accept the call of the "United Lutheran Congregations" in Pennsylvania in September of 1741.

While retaining a significant number of the hymns of the early Lutheran *Kernlieder* of the Reformation ("Aus tiefer Not," "Christ lag in Todesbanden," "Christ unser Herr zum Jordan kamm," "Durch Adam's Fall," "Ein feste Burg," "Wir glauben all an einen Gott," and "Komm, heiliger Geist" to name a few), Muhlenberg's *Erbauliche Liedersammlung* also included an even larger selection from the newer hymns of Pietism.

Musically, the hymns were sung to the isometric, or equal-note, forms of the melodies which had developed in the time since the early Reformation. Instead of the vigorous melodic forms of the Reformation, Pietism favored the isometric forms of the tunes in the belief that they evoked a more solemn and devotional attitude in both the singer and the hearer. In other words, the more slowly and "devotionally" the hymns were sung, the more religious and heartfelt was the experience. This form of the melodies was also employed in the *Choralbuch für die Erbauliche Liedersammlung* which appeared over a quarter-century later in 1813 and which contained harmonizations in four parts of the isometric forms of the melodies for Muhlenberg's hymnbook. This *Choralbuch* was for the organist, the congregation using only the text-only book. Where an organ was not available, the congregations sang unaccompanied, often following the "lining out" procedure common in early America.

Muhlenberg's *Erbauliche Liedersammlung* (1786) was the vehicle which carried to America the legacy of the hymnody of German Pietism, a legacy in which a substantial number of the early Reformation core hymns continued to be included but which also included an even larger number of the more recent Pietist hymns. It was a legacy which was soon to erode under the influences of rationalism, unionism, and revivalism, three movements which were to have a significant impact on the development of Lutheran hymnody in America in the nineteenth century.

Also, as the early Lutherans in American began to reach out to their neighbors in the language of their newly adopted country, they found that the old melodies were not always familiar to those at home in another language. In his *Journals* Muhlenberg notes that "I soon discovered that the English people did not know our tunes, so I selected familiar English melodies which fitted some of our Lutheran hymns."[12] The "familiar English melodies" were undoubtedly the tunes associated with the singing of the psalms together with the melodies associated with the metrical psalms and hymnody of Isaac Watts (1674-1748) and the hymnody of John (1703-91) and Charles Wesley (1707-88) which were the common fare of much of Protestant America at the time. Harry Eskew and Hugh T. McElrath, both from the Baptist tradition, point to Watt's hymnody as Calvinistic in theology, and characterize the Wesleyan hymns as largely Arminian in their theology.[13] One sees, even at this early stage, the beginning of the domination of American Lutheran hymnody by English hymnody, some of it of a largely Calvinistic, Arminian bent.

It was also at about the beginning of the nineteenth century that the transition to the English language began among these early German immigrants. In the course of this transition serious questions would be raised as to whether good translations of the German hymns were even possible, if possible whether they were desirable, and whether the literary quality of the result was worth the effort. All these questions and how they were answered were to impact the development of Lutheran hymnody in the nineteenth century and would continue to trouble Lutherans to the present day.

Rationalism, Unionism, and Revivalism in Lutheran Hymnody

Rationalism, unionism, and revivalism were each, in their own way, attempts at accommodation with the culture. Rationalism, which sought in human reason the answer to religious questions, ultimately replaced a Pietism which sought religious assurance in human feelings. Unionism was fostered in part by a spirit of religious indifference (brought on in part by rationalism), but also because it frequently appeared to be the most prudent course of action in the common cause of the evangelization of America. Revivalism, promoted by the evangelical religion of the frontier, brought its own set of problems.

The epitome of rationalism in American Lutheran hymnody was *A Collection of Hymns, and a Liturgy, for the use of the Evangelical Lutheran Churches*, printed in 1814 and largely the work of Frederick Quitman, then President of the New York Ministerium. It was a collection which completely rejected the heritage of the Lutheran chorale, turning instead to English sources which were freely altered to conform to the rationalistic tendencies of the time. Quitman's "improvements" took two turns: first, it was necessary to bring hymnody into line with the theology of the time, a theology largely characterized "by its high Arminian view of human potentiality, its ethical moralisms, its sweetly reasonable descriptions of a benevolent deity, its criticism of dogma, especially the Trinity";[14] second, it tended to emphasize the literary infelicity of many of the older texts (meaning, largely, the chorale), especially those translated from other languages. Texts were freely altered, stanzas summarily omitted, and it used an organization in which Quitman substituted for the church year an arrangement which organizes the hymnbook by a dogmatic scheme common to most Reformed hymnbooks of the time. Quitman's hymnal was probably the lowest point in the history of American Lutheran hymnody.

Unionism, on the other hand, was fostered by a natural attraction of Lutherans and Reformed. Both groups had come from Germany; they had a common ethnic origin which was often as important as their various religious convictions. In addition, as the year 1817—the occasion of the 300th anniversary of the Reformation—approached, it was inevitable that there would be any number of conversations about joint activities. And since many Lutheran and Reformed churches often shared a church building, so-called "Union Churches," it was not long before a call would be heard for a single hymnal which could serve both congregations. The result was the publication in 1817 of *Das Gemeinschaftliche Gesangbuch*, explicitly for "use in the worship of Lutheran and Reformed Congregations in North America." It contained only one hymn of Luther ("Aus tiefer Noth"), and was characterized by Luther Reed by "the omission of the classic hymns of the church and the insertion of weak and frivolous hymns."[15] Such unionism was condemned by the Saxon immigrants some years later as exemplified by a poem printed in the 1860s in *Der Lutheraner* as an example of how such "union dizziness" had taken hold in the Ohio Synod. The final lines of that poem read as follows:

> Lasz jeden bleiben, was er ist; Sei jeder nur ein wahrer Christ!
> Wo alle steh'n vor Gottes Thron, Da ist die rechte Union.
> Wo alle Halleluja schrei'n Stimmpt Zwingli auch mit Luther ein.[16]

Das Gemeinschaftliche Gesangbuch and a later *Neues Gemeinschaftliche Gesangbuch* (1850) continued to be published and their use continued to be an issue into the latter part of the nineteenth century. "Union churches" can still be seen today in the Pennsylvania countryside.

But it was the hymnals of the General Synod, formally organized in 1820, that most clearly reflected the impact of the "new measures" of frontier evangelism during the early and middle years of the nineteenth century. Specifically, it was the General Synod's *Hymns, Selected and Original, for Public and Private Worship* of 1828 together with later editions of 1841, 1850, and 1852 which clearly demonstrated a sympathetic approval of the rising tide of revivalism. The fact that Quitman's earlier rationalistic book was now to be replaced with a book "thoroughly impregnated with Calvinistic and Arminian material of highly subjective character and with a dogmatic scheme which practically ignored the church year,"[17] did not prevent its becoming the most widely used Lutheran hymnal up to its time. The enlarged and revised editions in 1850 and 1852 contained over 1,000 hymns.

Of particular interest in *Hymns, Selected and Original* are the sections of the hymnbook devoted to "Revivals" and "Temperance." The section of temperance hymns included such texts as "Round the temp'rance standard rally, All the friends of human kind," and

> We praise Thee, Lord, if but one soul
> While the past year prolong'd its flight,
> Turn's shudd'ring from the pois'nous bowl,
> To health and liberty and light.

In addition, it is surprising to find a hymn on "The Millennium" in a Lutheran book, but that is what one finds at no. 916 in the revised edition.

Hymns, Selected and Original belonged to the period of "American Lutheranism," a movement in the mid-nineteenth century championed by Samuel Simon Schmucker (1799–1873), which sought to adapt Lutheranism to the American scene and make it more palatable in America. Both the movement and the hymnbook reflect the influence of the Second Great Awakening which attempted to embody the full scope of the new evangelical theology and experience, the worship style, "new measures," and the hymns and songs of the revivalism which were sweeping the country. At the head of the list of signers of the preface was S. S. Schmucker. The ultimate rejection of his Definite Platform, a document which promoted Schmucker's "American Lutheranism," was a victory for the more conservative Lutheran voices that were gradually being heard. The effects of the hymnbook for which Schmucker was chiefly responsible, however, lingered on.

Each f these three hymnbooks—Quitman's *A Collection of Hymns and a Liturgy* and *Das Gemeinschaftliche Gesangbuch*, and Schmucker's *Hymns, Selected and Original*—enjoyed widespread use in their various contexts. It was not until their influence began to gradually recede before the developing interest in the Confessional Revival and its impact on Lutheran hymnody that one began to see a gradual change in the hymnic climate of American Lutheranism.

Movement toward a More Confessional Hymnody

The hymnals and hymnody of early American Lutheranism were rooted in the Pietistic hymnals of the eighteenth century. It was this hymnody and its music that formed the basic musical diet of early American Lutheranism. But by the time rationalism, unionism, and the influence of the frontier revival were wreaking havoc on Lutheran hymnody, voices began to be raised urging a return to a more confessional approach to worship and hymnody. The Confessional Movement, as it came to be called, originated in Germany in the first half of the nineteenth century and, as it impacted hymnody, it advocated two things: (1) a return to the unaltered texts of the Reformation hymns which had been drastically altered in a variety of ways in the ensuing centuries; and (2) a return to the use of the original forms of the melodies which had been flattened out into even-note melodies, especially during the period of Pietism. These two approaches were advocated not only in the name of some sort of theological repristination, but also because it was felt that they could be an important practical factor in reviving congregational singing and restoring to it the vigor it had once enjoyed.

The voices which attempted to return American Lutheranism more closely to its Reformation heritage came from two distinct and quite different places. The first was a group of voices from among those Lutherans who were the spiritual descendants of Henry Melchior Muhlenberg, such as Charles Porterfield Krauth (1823-83), Joseph A. Seiss (1823-1904), Beale M. Schmucker (1827-88), and Frederick Mayer Bird (1838-1908), a noted hymnologist of the time. Several of these men played an important role in the formation of the General Council in 1867, created in reaction to what was perceived as the liberalism of the General Synod. This resulted in the creation of the *Church Book* of 1868, arguably the best Lutheran hymnal to its time, and, some 20 years later, the adoption of the *Common Service* in 1888 by the General Council, the General Synod, and the General Synod of the South. Both publications were landmarks in the history of American Lutheran hymnody and liturgy.

The *Church Book* was able to draw on the fruits of the Oxford Movement in England, particularly the translations into English of many of the Latin and Greek hymns from the early and medieval times, as well as some translations of German texts by Catherine Winkworth. Nevertheless, the *Church Book* contained only a few of the Reformation chorales in contrast to the General Council's *Kirchenbuch* (1877) which included a large number. Interestingly, the *Church Book with Music*, issued in 1872, was the only Lutheran hymnal to have a woman as music editor, Harriet Reynolds Krauth (1845-1925).[18]

The movement toward a more confessional hymnody was aided also by two Lutheran immigrant groups which came to America in 1839. These were a group of Prussian Lutherans under the leadership of J. A. A. Grabau who emigrated in 1839 and settled in and near Buffalo, N.Y., and later near Milwaukee, Wis. A second group was a group of Lutherans from Saxony under the leadership of Martin Stephan and then C. F. W. Walther who settled in Perry County, Mo., and later in St. Louis. Both groups came committed to restoring to use the body of Reformation-era hymnody, a fact clearly evident in the hymnals it published, Grabau's *Evangelisch-Lutherisches Kirchengesangbuch* of 1842, and Walther's *Kirchengesangbuch* of 1847. These two books together with the General Council's *Kirchenbuch* of 1877 sought to reclaim for use the *Kernlieder* of the Reformation period. Grabau's book, in particular, was a repristination with a vengeance of the Babst hymnal (*Gesangbuch*) of 1545 not only in its selection of hymns but in its organization and its use of Latin hymns as well as German hymns. *Choralbooks* for the organist were ultimately prepared for Walther's hymnbook as well as for the General Council's *Kirchenbuch*, providing organists with four-part settings of the chorales in their original rhythmic melodic forms.[19]

In a sense the immigrant groups had the easier task since the hymnody they sought to restore was in the language of their people. Those who had long been in America had to introduce not only tunes that were often unknown to their people, but texts which existed in what were often crude and inelegant translations from the German. In one way or another, the matter of translation became a matter of contention for all Lutherans when the transition to the English language was in full flower by the end of the nineteenth and the early twentieth century.

The Movement toward Consolidation

By the early twentieth century a movement toward consolidation and merger among many of the Lutheran groups with a similar ethnic origin or theological orientation had begun. This movement was sometimes occasioned by the preparation of a common hymnbook to serve groups which had a common ethnic identity. At other times a common book was the result of talks moving toward consolidation. It was not always clear which provided the initial motivation.

The first Lutheran hymnbook resulting from such a movement toward consolidation was the *Lutheran Hymnary* (1913) which brought together a number of Norwegian groups. Other books around which various Lutheran groups came together or books which resulted from working toward merger include the *Common Service Book and Hymnal* (1917) which brought together the General Council, the General Synod, and the United Synod of the South; the *American Lutheran Hymnal* (1930) which brought together the Iowa, Ohio, and Buffalo synods; *The Lutheran Hymnal* (1941), a product of the bodies making up the Synodical Conference; and the *Service Book and Hymnal* (1958) which brought together eight Lutheran church bodies which participated in its preparation. Most of these hymnbooks involved bringing together groups of similar ethnic origins or compatible theological viewpoints. More recently, *Lutheran Book of Worship* (1978) which brought together in its preparation the American Lutheran Church, the Lutheran Church in America, the Evangelical Lutheran Church in Canada, and The Lutheran Church—Missouri Synod (which subsequently withdrew from the project at the very end of the process) represented an attempt to bring together Lutheran groups with the most widely disparate pieties yet attempted in America.

If the first concern of those determined to recapture a more confessional hymnody was a return to the unaltered texts and melodies of the Reformation period, a subsequent concern was that of translating those hymns into English in order that the Lutheran heritage of hymnody might be passed on to future generations. The possibility of successful translation from another language into English was a subject of much discussion, especially by those who were concerned with literary quality as a chief characteristic to be considered in hymnody in English. There is little doubt that the early attempts at translating this heritage often left much to be desired. The *Lutheran Hymnary* (1912), the *Evangelical Lutheran Hymn-Book* (1913), and *The Lutheran Hymnal* (1941) are clear evidence that the attempt was made, even though the translations from the Norwegian and German that they contained were criticized by some as inelegant or simply rhymed dogma. Nevertheless the attempt was made, and we are the beneficiaries of the efforts of our forebears.

As English increasingly became the accepted language of worship and hymnody among Lutherans in America, other concerns arose. The foreword to *Worship Supplement* (1969) indicates that "concerns for social structures, colleges, armed forces, missions, the inner city, and radically or culturally conscious groups have raised a need for updating liturgical and hymnodic materials both as to language and form."[20] Likewise *Lutheran Book of Worship* (1978) raised awareness of the need for more and new hymns for baptism and Holy Communion, clearly reflected in the number and choice of hymns for those rites which appear in the book and which, to a large extent, have carried over into *Lutheran Worship* (1982).

Matters of language in hymnody continue to be a concern among all Lutherans. Concerns over the use of archaic words and forms of language, the use of gender-neutral language, and the matter of God language continue to excite both critics and defenders of whatever is the current practice. Satisfactory answers to those concerns are not easily arrived at.

In addition, the momentum in the 1960s and '70s toward Muhlenberg's dream of "one hymnbook for all American [Lutheran] congregations"[21] was shattered when the so-called Blue Ribbon Committee of The Lutheran Church—Missouri Synod, appointed to review *Lutheran Book of Worship*, recommended that "the Synod consider using a revised edition of *Lutheran Book of Worship*."[22] It subsequently appeared as *Lutheran Worship* in 1982. The irony is that in their hymnic content *Lutheran Book of Worship* and *Lutheran Worship* are closer than any of their predecessor books had been.

By the beginning of the twenty-first century the situation is more confused. American Lutheranism, which had been working toward a single book which could be used by all, today has four official hymnals: *Lutheran Book of Worship* (ELCA, 1978), *Lutheran Worship* (LCMS, 1982), *Christian Worship: A Lutheran Hymnal* (WELS, 1993), and *The Evangelical Lutheran Hymnary* (ELS, 1996).

In addition, a host of both official and unofficial supplements—among them *With One Voice* (1995) and *Hymnal Supplement '98* (1998)—containing both new and less-traditional hymnic material, praise songs, choruses, and a variety of so-called "world music" together with other experimental material are available. They have become part of the general hymnic scene among all Lutherans in America.

What of tomorrow? Let me end with a true story. About a year ago, my wife and I took a trip on the Yangtze River in central China from Chongquing to Yichang to see the Three Gorges Dam being built. When finished, we were told, the dam would be the largest in the world, as high as a sixty-story building and as wide as five Hoover Dams. It was immense. One could not help but being impressed. More than a million people are being dispossessed. And as we speak, over the objection of many Chinese who have raised serious concerns about the environmental and human effects of the project, water is rising to a height of 200 feet above the banks of the river flooding countless towns, inundating untold numbers of cultural treasures, and submerging priceless archeological sites, the very cultural heritage of China, which have existed for centuries along the banks of the Yangtze.

Is this a parable for our time as we work to retain and pass on to our children and grandchildren a magnificent musical and theological hymnic heritage? Are we allowing our glorious heritage of hymnody to be drowned beneath a flood of theologically and musically questionable third- and fourth-rate material? What are the consequences for our children and grandchildren if we fail to pass on that heritage to future generations?

In large part, the answers to those questions are in our hands.

Notes

1. Martin Luther, *Luther's Works*, American edition, vol. 53, *Liturgy and Hymns*, ed. Ulrich S. Leupold (Philadelphia: Fortress, 1965), 197.
2. Ibid., 317–18.
3. Ibid., 194.
4. Johann Daniel von der Heydt, *Geschichte der Evangelischen Kirchenmusik in Deutschland*. 2nd ed. (Berlin: Trowitzsch, 1932), 54.
5. For a more detailed treatment of the larger subject of the development of early Lutheran hymnody in America, see Carl Schalk, *God's Song in a New Land: Lutheran Hymnals in America* (St. Louis: Concordia, 1995), and its companion, *Source Documents in American Lutheran Hymnody* (St. Louis: Concordia, 1996).
6. See William J. Finck, *Lutheran Landmarks and Pioneers in America* (Philadelphia: General Council Publication House, 1917), 15–21, and James P. Delgado, *Across the Top of the World: The Quest for the Northwest Passage* (New York: Checkmark Books, 1999), 24–25.
7. Quoted in Finck, 19.
8. Amandus Johnson, *The Swedish Settlements on the Delaware, 1635–1644*, cited in *Church Music and Musical Life in Pennsylvania in the Eighteenth Century*, vol. 1 (New York: AMS Press, 1972), 187–88.
9. Edward Christopher Wolf, "Lutheran Church Music in America during the Eighteenth and Early Nineteenth Centuries" (Ph.D. diss., University of Illinois Urbana-Champaign, 1960), 34.
10. A meeting of the Pennsylvania Ministerium in 1782 appointed a committee consisting of Revs. Muhlenberg Sr., John Christopher Kunze, J. H. C. Helmuth, and Muhlenberg Jr. to prepare a new hymnal. While the committee was to prepare the book it would be difficult to escape the conclusion that the senior Muhlenberg was the driving force behind it. He was also later asked to write the preface.
11. From the preface to Henry Melchior Muhlenberg, *Erbauliche Liedersammlung* (1786).
12. Henry Melchior Muhlenberg, *Journals*, vol. 1 (Philadelphia: Muhlenberg), 300.
13. Harry Eskew and Hugh T. McElrath, *Sing with Understanding: An Introduction to Christian Hymnology* (Nashville: Broadman, 1980), 120–25.
14. Martin E. Marty, *The Infidel: Freethought and American Religion* (Cleveland: Meridian, 1961), 4.
15. Luther Reed, *The Lutheran Liturgy* (Philadelphia: Fortress, 1947), 171.
16. *Der Lutheraner* vol. 17 (July 31, 1861), 1906–7
17. Reed, 177.
18. Harriet Reynolds Krauth (1845–1925) was the daughter of Charles Porterfield Krauth. She later married Adolph Spaeth and had five children, one of whom was Samuel Spaeth, the noted American writer on music.

[19] A variety of choralebooks served Walther's *Kirchengesangbuch* of 1849, the chief ones being the second edition of Friedrich Layriz' *Kern des deutschen Kirchengesangs* (1849), the *Evangelisch-Lutherisches Choralbuch für Kirche und Haus* (1863), Heinrich Hoelter's *Choralbuch* (1886), and Karl Brauer's *Mehrstimmiges Choralbuch* (1888), all of the latter based on Layriz' work. The *Choralbuch mit Liturgie und Chorgesängen zum Kirchenbuch der Allgemeinen Kirchenversammlung* (1879), prepared by John Endlich, served the General Council's *Kirchenbuch*.

[20] *Worship Supplement* (St Louis: Concordia, 1969), 9.

[21] From the preface to Muhlenberg's *Erbauliche Liedersammlung*.

[22] Robert Sauer, "Lutheran Worship (1982): The Special Hymnal Review Committee," in *Lutheran Worship: History and Practice*, ed. Fred L. Precht (St. Louis, Concordia, 1993), 199.

Paul Gerhardt: Some Thoughts on His Hymnody

Introduction

Paul Gerhardt should need no introduction in Lutheran circles. His hymns have ranked with those of Martin Luther in popularity, although their character, in many respects, is quite different. His hymns are amply represented in the most recent Lutheran hymnals in America: Of his 134 hymns, *The Lutheran Hymnal* includes 21; *Lutheran Book of Worship*, 11; *Lutheran Worship*, 17; *Christian Worship: A Lutheran Hymnal*, 18; *Lutheran Service Book*, 17; and *Evangelical Lutheran Worship*, 9. German hymn books contain a significantly larger number.

Gerhardt is being celebrated this year as we commemorate the 400th anniversary of his birth in 1607. At the hymn festival this afternoon we sang ten of Gerhardt's most frequently sung hymns in a variety of glorious settings. He is also being widely celebrated in print, as witness the fine article about Gerhardt in the current issue of *Lutheran Witness* by Dr. Uwe Siemon-Netto of this seminary's faculty.[1]

His Life

The facts of Paul Gerhardt's life and career are quite clear and straightforward. Born on March 12, 1607, the son of the mayor of the little town of Gräfenhainichen, located between Halle and Wittenberg, Gerhardt's father died while Paul was a young man. At the age of 21 he began studies at the University of Wittenberg. The Thirty Years' War undoubtedly disrupted his studies since he was still at Wittenberg until

---

Banquet speech delivered at the Paul Gerhardt Festival, Concordia Seminary, St. Louis, Mo., March 18, 2007.

1642 when he went to Berlin where he became a house tutor in the home of Andreas Barthold, a prominent attorney. It was here in Berlin that his poetic talent began to flourish. At some point he became acquainted with Johann Crüger, organist at the *Nicolaikirche* ("Nicolai Church") in Berlin, who published 15 of Gerhardt's texts in the second edition of what was to become the most important hymn collection of the seventeenth century, the *Praxis Pietatis melica* ("The Practice of Piety in Music") in 1647. These 15 texts by Gerhardt were set to tunes by Crüger. By the fifth edition of the *Praxis Pietatis melica* the number of Gerhardt's hymns had increased to eighty-one. In 1657 Gerhardt accepted a call to be the third assistant pastor at the *Nicolaikirche* where he and Crüger, who had been cantor at the church since 1622, would become colleagues for a little over a decade. The fruit of their unique collaboration, one of a number of such historic partnerships between Lutheran pastor/poets and musicians, was to blossom and would prove to be a great blessing to the Church's song in the years that followed.

Gerhardt's life was beset with a variety of personal and professional tragedies. In 1637 Swedish soldiers set fire to his home town where his father had been mayor. The Gerhardt's family home, possessions, and their church were destroyed. Later in his life he lost his wife and four of his five children to disease and then there was the matter of his personal health. Because of political and ecclesiastical conflict between Lutherans and Calvinists, Gerhardt, who gained a reputation as a popular preacher of the time, certainly in Berlin, ultimately lost his position as pastor at the *Nicolaikirche*. In 1669 Gerhardt was called to be archdeacon at Lübben where he remained for seven years until his death in 1676.

In the town of Lübben today, there stands the sanctuary where this great poet last served and is now buried, now named the Paul Gerhardt Kirche as a reminder of the life and work of this great poet of Lutheranism. It is the ultimate irony that this church is now a Union church. And in Berlin, the *Nicolaikirche* is now essentially a museum. But a plaque on the outside of the church commemorates the fact that it was there that Paul Gerhardt and Johann Crüger, the cantor with whom he served, once worked in those tempestuous years of the seventeenth century.

His Hymnody

Concerning Gerhardt's hymnody itself, I would mention four factors which were the heart of the context in which Gerhardt's hymns were shaped.

First, there is the gradual abandonment in the seventeenth century of the Meistersinger tradition in which the poet and the composer of the melody were the same person. The hymnody in the early years of the Reformation reflected this Meistersinger tradition. Luther wrote both words and tunes, at least in a number of cases, as did Johann Walter, his musical friend and advisor, and others of the time. The seventeenth century saw the gradual dissolution of this practice in favor of a new paradigm in which the poetic task and the musical task were separated and poet and musician were two separate people.

The favored musical form of the Meistersinger tradition was the so-called bar form, a tripartite AAB form. Philip Nicolai is often cited as the last great example of a hymn writer in the Meistersinger tradition. Nicolai wrote both the texts and the tunes for two of the great Lutheran chorales: "Wie schön leuchtet der Morgenstern" and "Wachet auf, ruft uns die Stimme," both in bar form. The new pattern involved two separate persons, one writing the texts, the other the tune. With few exceptions, this is the general pattern which has prevailed ever since.

But the abandonment of the Meistersinger tradition was not a precipitous one. Several texts by Gerhardt set to music by Crüger clearly demonstrate that the bar form continued in use, for a time at least, as a viable musical form, even while it was undergoing subtle alterations and permutations. "Auf, auf, mein Herz, mit Freuden" ("Awake, My Heart, with Gladness"), "Wie soll' ich dich empfangen" ("O Lord, How Shall I Meet Thee"), and "Zeuch ein zu meinem Toren" ("O Enter, Lord, Thy Temple") would be three such examples. All three of these examples were sung to tunes by Crüger. Other text writers of the time also continued to some extent to use this form.

A second factor was the matter of the stylistic changes in the German language which occurred at this time. The chief influence in this regard was Martin Opitz (1597-1639). His *Buch der Deutschen Poeterey* (1624) reflects the new approach to language. Opitz also organized a literary group of poets to promote the new views. Among its members was Johann Rist, a highly respected writer of the day, made poet laureate by Emperor Ferdinand II in 1644. Rist wrote a number of hymns which are still included in Lutheran hymnals.

Opitz advocated a greater concern for metrical regularity and purity of language. Metrical regularity was viewed as reflecting a more sophisticated manner in contrast to the more irregular, rugged, and, to the presumably more refined and sophisticated tastes of the seventeenth century, cruder rhythms of the preceding century. While such views were based on a misunderstanding of the earlier Meistersinger patterns of poetry, nevertheless, the rhythmic groupings of two's and three's which characterized the earlier Reformation melodies, which were largely unbarred, and whose origins were ultimately to be found in Gregorian chant, gradually gave way to the more regular duple and triple meters, whether or not they were barred as such in the music.

The impact of this development was to give the German hymnody of the time, and Gerhardt's hymn texts among them, a smoother and more polished character, both rhythmically and poetically, joined together with a theological content which was warmer, more closely tied to the life situations of the people, yet always, at least in Gerhardt's texts, clearly Christocentric. None of these developments, of course, occurred overnight, but the emerging hymnody of the time increasingly reflected these new characteristics. Gerhardt's texts and Crüger's tunes reflected these new directions, both in the nature and character of the hymn texts as well as in the musical style of the tunes.

Third, Gerhardt, as well as the people he ministered to, were not strangers to the devastation of the Thirty Years' War (1618-48) which ravaged most of Europe. This experience could not but have influenced his contribution to Lutheran hymnody. Johannes Riedel expressed the impact of the Thirty Years' War on the populace in general: "Confronted with the horrible killing and pillaging of the Thirty Years' War, the individual sought enlightenment, self-understanding, comfort, and consolation in a personal and subjective approach to God."[2] It was inevitable that the hymnody of the time would seek to relate more closely to the life situations in which the people found themselves, a fact reflected in so many so-called "cross and comfort" hymns or *Trost und Trotz* ("consolation and defiance") hymns which were so much a part of the hymnody of this period. Gerhardt's texts illustrate the transition to a more subjective tone. James Mearns has counted 16 of Gerhardt's texts that begin with the word "I." Yet it is not so much the individual soul that is laying bare its moods, as it is the representative of the Church speaking the thoughts and feelings shared with fellow members.

Fourth, it is important to note, as a number of scholars have pointed out, that many of the hymn texts written during this and succeeding times and which centered more and more on the needs of the individual were written for personal or private devotional use. They were not primarily or initially intended for corporate worship. Many pastors of the period wrote devotional verse, some of which was published in small collections and used in the home for personal devotional reading or family devotions. Some of these hymns inevitably found their way into use in corporate worship. This distinction between hymns conceived for use in corporate worship and those intended primarily for use in personal, family, or private devotions has largely been lost to the modern churchgoer.

That Paul Gerhardt's hymns continue to enjoy a genuine popularity in Lutheran parishes throughout the world is a tribute to their richness, their depth of substance, and their ability to connect with the human condition. They are personal without becoming individualistic. They touch the reality of the human condition when confronted with the despair and hopelessness which that condition inevitably brings, yet always point to the hope that is to be found in Jesus Christ. Gerhardt's hymns are always centered in Christ without succumbing to the danger of becoming Christo-monistic, a problem that increasingly beset many of the hymns of later Pietism.

Conclusion

Gerhardt's texts are both pastoral and theologically informed. They are accessible to all, yet saturated with the saving news of the Gospel. And at the same time they reveal the careful art of the craftsman who shapes words and phrases in ways to elicit the outcome he desires. Gerhardt's texts, unlike much of what passes for contemporary hymnody today, are not third-rate efforts of an inferior poet, covered over by an outward patina of piety. They are miniature masterpieces which invite our serious reflection and meditation.

Some in our time parrot the idea that hymns must be easy to sing at the first try and be readily understandable at a first reading, that a passion for textual and musical perfection is a kind of undemocratic snobbery, or excuse the use of inferior hymns as temporary stepping stones to something better. They had best be prepared for the sharp words of one whose teaching graced this seminary over a quarter-century ago.

Martin Franzmann spoke of the contemporary fascination with the *Ersatz* that has always been a characteristic of a sick Church, a Church "grown so languid that it cannot bear to live in the tensions of the last days." Against those who would argue that after all, "a man can make music on a tin whistle to the glory of God, and God will be pleased to hear it," he remarked, "True, true, true—if God has given [us] nothing more than a tin whistle; but God has given us infinitely so much more . . . then the tin whistle is no longer humility but a perverse kind of pride." As to the argument that "Yes, certain hymns are inferior, but they can be used as stepping stones to something better," he remarks that by indulging in such a condescension we may find the frequent use of the inferior ultimately becomes a habit too powerful for us to overcome.[3]

With our song we proclaim the good news of the Gospel of Jesus Christ and guide each other to the heart and center of our faith. In the hymns of Paul Gerhardt we have been given precious gifts which do exactly that. It is fitting that we celebrate this good gift today with both singing and reflection. It is both our privilege and our sacred responsibility that we have been given Gerhardt's hymns so that these great songs of the Church will continue to be sung, not only by us on our pilgrim way, but by our children and our children's children as well.

I cannot conclude without quoting a favorite Gerhardt text of mine which fell out of more recent Lutheran hymnals, but is restored for our use in *Lutheran Service Book*. It is a song for Christmas which has all the tender appeal which is so much a part of Gerhardt's popularity, yet which speaks the Good News clearly and unambiguously. It reads as follows in its English translation:

O Jesus Christ, Thy manger is my paradise
 at which my soul reclineth.
For there, O Lord, doth lie the Word made flesh for us;
 herein Thy grace forth shineth.

Thou Christian heart, whoe'er thou art, be of good cheer
 and let no sorrow move thee!
For God's own Child, in mercy mild, joins thee to Him;
 how greatly God must love thee!

The world may hold her wealth and gold; but thou, my heart,
 keep Christ as thy true treasure.
To Him hold fast until at last a crown be thine
 and honor in full measure.

(Lutheran Service Book #372)

Paul Gerhardt and his hymns are worth caring about because they have so much to teach us about the faith and how to sing it. And if we attend to them, they might even teach us something about how to sing that faith in our own time.

Notes

[1] Uwe Siemon-Netto, "Lutheranism's Sweetest Voice," *Lutheran Witness* (March 1, 2007).

[2] Johannes Riedel, *The Lutheran Church: Its Basic Traditions* (Minneapolis: Augsburg, 1967).

[3] Martin Franzmann, *Ha! Ha! among the Trumpets* (St. Louis: Concordia, 1966), 96.

Friedrich Layriz: A Forgotten Influence on Congregational Singing in American Lutheranism

Friedrich Layriz (Layritz) (January 30, 1808–March 18, 1859)—a German pastor, theologian, and hymnologist, a figure of great importance in the reform of Lutheran liturgy and church music in the first half of the nineteenth century—is a name largely forgotten or unknown to most American Lutheran church musicians. His name and especially his contribution to the use of the rhythmic chorale among many American Lutheran immigrants in the nineteenth century and the resulting contribution to congregational singing in the Lutheran churches in American deserves to be remembered.

Born in Nemmersdorf, Franconia. on January 30, 1808, the young Layriz studied theology, philosophy, and philology at the universities of Leipzig (where he received a Ph.D. in 1829) and Erlangen (where he joined the theological faculty in 1833). In 1837 he became pastor at Merkendorf, in 1842 at St. Georgen near Bayreuth, and in 1846 at Unterschwaningen.

His hymnological and liturgical contributions to church music were part of the larger "Confessional Revival" which developed in Germany in the early nineteenth century. This revival would also exert a significant influence on the Lutheran emigrants who left Germany during the 1800s to settle in America. The confessional revival, conveniently dated

---

First published in *CrossAccent: Journal of the Association of Lutheran Church Musicians* 13, no. 3 (2005): 29–36. Used by permission

beginning about 1817 with Klaus Harms' new "Theses" published for the tercentenary of Luther's posting of the 95 Theses on the church door at Wittenberg, was in part a reaction against the ravages which Pietism and the Enlightenment had inflicted on the Church, its worship, and its hymnody. It was also part of a more general reawakened interest in the nineteenth century in German history, German literature, and the Reformation in particular at that time.

Part of the impact of the confessional revival as it related to worship and hymnody was the impetus to recover the unaltered and unadulterated texts of the early Lutheran Reformation together with the original rhythmic forms of their melodies which had, in the intervening centuries, been flattened out into largely even-note melodies. While part of the impetus for the revival of the original texts and melodies of the early Reformation chorales was historical and theological, an equally important motivation for their use was the desire to revitalize congregational singing which, by the early nineteenth century, had fallen into an abysmal state. One report from Germany in 1847 spoke of congregational singing as proceeding in "a creeping, dragging fashion. . . . The hymns of Luther have had their wings clipped and have put on the straitjacket of 4/4 time."[1] The return to the rhythmic chorale and to the more orthodox hymnody of the early Reformation would, it was hoped, reinvigorate and energize congregational singing.

This revival nourished and was nourished by a number of significant, monumental studies in hymnody during the nineteenth century including Carl von Winterfeld's *Der evangelische Kirchengesang und sein Verhältniss zur Kunst des Tonsatzes* (3 vol., 1842-47), Philipp Wackernagel's *Bibliographie zur Geschichte des deutschen Kirchenliedes in 16. Jahrhundert* (1855) and *Das deutsche Kirchenlied von der ältesten Zeit bis zum Anfang des 17. Jahrhundert* (5 vol., 1864-77), Ludwig Schoeberlein's *Schatz des liturgischen Chor- und Gemeindegesangs* (1868), and Johannes Zahn's *Die Melodien der deutschen evangelischen Kirchenlieder* (6 vol., 1888-93). Layriz's contribution to that research was to play an important role in that revival, both in Germany and, through the influence of the German immigrants who came to America in the 1800s, among the Lutherans in North America.

Layriz's interest in the reform of church song is first seen in the publication of his *Offener Sendbrief an die protestantische Geistlichkeit Bayerns . . . in Betreff der Gesangbuchs-Reform* (1843)[2] and his *Kern des deutschen Kirchenlieds von Luther bis auf Gellert* (1844), both part of his protest against the *Bayrische Gesangbuch* of 1811. His interest in a revival of the old Lutheran liturgy is seen in his *Die Liturgie eines vollstimmigen Hauptgottesdienstes nach lutherischen Typus nebst Ratschlägen zu deren Wiederherstellung* (1849).

However, Layriz's greatest and most lasting contribution was his *Kern des deutschen Kirchengesangs zum gebrauch Evangelisch-Lutherischer Gemeinden und Familien* (hereafter *Kern*). This latter publication, referred to by W. G. Polack as Layriz's "Choralbuch,"[3] published over a period of eleven years from 1844 to 1855 in four volumes (1844, 1849, 1853, 1855), was a work which would have a profound effect, not only in Bavaria and more generally in Germany of his day, but also—through the German immigrants who would come to America during his lifetime and plant Lutheranism especially in the Midwestern states of the United States—on Lutheranism generally in America. The heart and center of Layriz's *Kern*[4] is the return to the original rhythmic forms of the chorales.

The first three volumes,[5] which constitute Layriz's "Choralbuch," consisted of 613 four-part settings of chorales in note-for-note homophonic style. Layriz indicates that he sought out the earliest forms of the melodies from collections of the sixteenth and later centuries.[6] He lists the hymn books or collections from which he has taken each setting but, unfortunately, he does not always indicate the source or the composer of each specific harmonization. Nevertheless, the origins of some, occasionally with slight alterations, are quite evident. The setting of "Es ist ein Ros entsprungen,"[7] for example, is clearly that usually ascribed to Michael Praetorius, however with a slight simplification at the end of the third phrase. The setting of "Gelobt sei Gott"[8] is that of Melchior Vulpius (see ex. 1).

What is clear is that the four-part settings of the chorales which appear in Layriz's *Kern* follow the cantional-style settings from the late sixteenth and seventeenth centuries: melody in the upper part, each part proceeding in a largely homorhythmic fashion, all of the voices for the most part singing the same syllables at the same time. The settings of

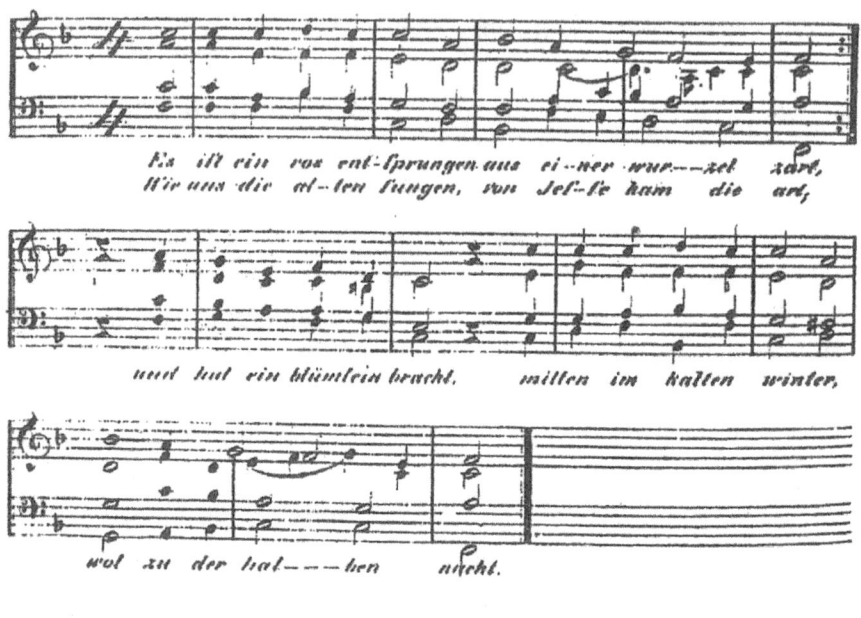

Ex. 1: "Es ist ein Ros entsprungen" and "Gelobt sei Gott" from Layriz's *Kern des deutschen Kirchengesangs.*

"Ein feste Burg ist unser Gott," although some freer than most, is another example (see ex. 2).

The inclusion in the title of the phrase *zum Gebrauch Evangelish-Lutherischer Gemeinden und Familien* ("for congregations and families") suggests its intended use: for congregational worship as well as for devotions within the home and family circle. In addition to their use as keyboard accompaniments, cantional-like settings would obviously facilitate use of the chorales in church as four-part choir settings, as well as use in the home where families could sing in parts, or simply in unison, as they were able.

The fourth volume consisted of 120 liturgical settings for choir or congregation including settings for the Communion service; eight com-

Ex. 2: "Ein feste Burg ist unser Gott" from Layriz's *Kern des deutschen Kirchengesangs*.

mon introits in four parts, according to the eight Gregorian tones; festive melodies for the *Benedictus* and *Magnificat* for Sundays and festivals set to the eight Gregorian tones; chants for the versicles and collects; chants for Matins and Vespers, including psalm tones for ordinary days; two settings of the *Te Deum* (one for two mixed choirs, one for male choir and mixed choir); additional canticles; and Good Friday Vespers. In publishing the *Kern*, Layriz was, according to Hans Joachim Moser, a "chief predecessor of 'Schöberlein and Riegel.'"[9]

In the foreword to the 1853 edition Layriz notes that he was aware of a growing interest in the rhythmic form of the chorale, not only within Germany but also beyond its geographical boundaries.

> The knowledge and intense interest in the rhythmic congregational song as the original way of singing in our Protestant [Lutheran] church has, for the past decade, spread throughout Germany and across to England and North America. And many, who at the beginning were opponents, became, upon closer examination, zealous advocates.[10]

That this was so will soon become apparent as we look to the use of Layriz's *Kern* among the German Lutheran immigrants in America.

But Layriz also saw clearly the need for education and for teaching the rhythmic chorales among the people if this musical reform was to succeed. To that end, in 1839, the same year in which a group of Saxons under the leadership of Martin Stephan emigrated from Germany to America in protest against the Prussian Union of 1817 and would ultimately found The Lutheran Church–Missouri Synod, Layriz published a small collection of 117 chorale melodies in their original rhythmic form set for two-part singing in order to help introduce the "new" rhythmic forms of the chorales. Titled *CXVII Geistliche Melodien meist aus dem 16. und 17. Jahr[hundert] in ihren ursprünglichen Rhythmen*, this slender volume, according to Zahn, "paved the way for the reform of church song in Bavaria."[11] It was followed in 1848 by a second volume in similar format titled *Geistliche Melodien meist aus dem 16. und 17. Jahr[hundert] in ihren ursprünglichen Tönen und Rhythmen, zum Gebrauche für Schule und Haus . . . Erstes Hundert*[14] (see ex. 3) and, a few years later in 1850, by a third similar collection of a second hundred melodies entitled *Geistliche Melodien . . . Zweites Hundert*.

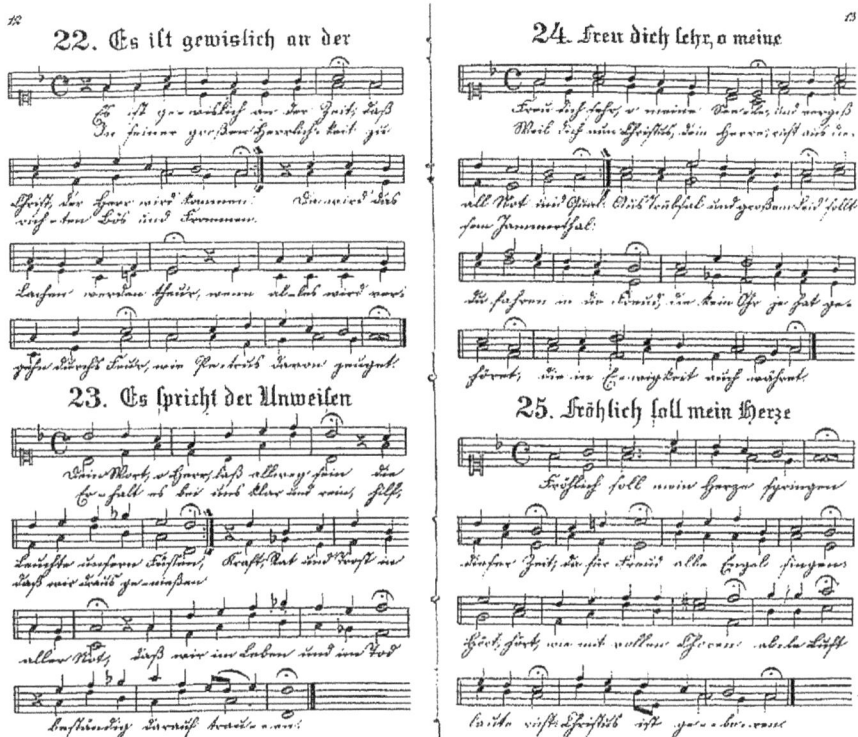

Ex. 3: Two-part settings from Layriz's *Geistliche Melodien* . . . *Erstes Hundert* (1848).

It was clear from the title of these slender collections that they were intended for use "in school and home" and would thus foster the learning and dissemination of the newly recovered rhythmic forms of the chorale melodies. These booklets were brought to America by some of the immigrant groups who had used them in Germany.[12]

Layriz's *Kern* in America

What books did congregations use to accompany congregational singing in the New World? Many of the Lutheran churches of the Pennsylvania Ministerium or who were otherwise the heirs of Henry Melchior Muhlenberg used the *Choralbuch für die Erbauliche Liedersammlung* of 1813 which contained 265 settings of chorales with melody and figured bass; however, the German immigrants who came to America beginning in the late 1830s turned to Layriz's *Kern*.

An early American example of a collection which relied on the work of Layriz was the *Cantica Sacra* published in 1854 by J. J. Fast, an Evangelical Lutheran minister in Canton, Ohio. It was printed in oblong tune-book format in open score and contained 137 four-part settings from Layriz's *Kern*, more than half the collection. Of particular interest is that it used shape-notes and the melody was placed in the tenor part. In addition, this collection included one choral piece by Layriz together with nine chants from the *Liturgie lutherischer Gemeindegottesdienste* of Friedrich Hommel (1813-92). The *Cantica Sacra* was apparently used in congregations of the Ohio Synod and was also promoted to a degree in the Missouri Synod, being sold through Otto Ernst in St. Louis. Its format suggests that it was used for part singing rather than for accompanying the congregation at the organ.

For many of the German immigrants, the second edition of Layriz's *Kern* served as their basic "Choralbuch." By the 1860s, however, this edition was apparently no longer available to the immigrants and the time had come for a new "Choralbuch." Mr. L. Volkening, a private publisher in St. Louis, Mo., announced in October of 1861 that

> because the second edition of Layriz's Choralbuch has been out of print for some time, and because the third and fourth editions have altered many chorales, and have made significant changes by the addition of strange and unfamiliar melodies, and since the high price of the new supply has made purchase more difficult, the undersigned, urged by many interested persons, has decided to arrange for a printing of only those chorale melodies which are found in our hymnal.[13]

By 1863 the new book was ready and appeared as the *Evangelisch-Lutherisches Choralbuch für Kirche und Haus*, a collection of the "most useful chorales of the Lutheran Church selected and printed without change from the *Kern des deutschen Kirchengesangs* of Dr. Layriz." This collection appeared in a number of later printings (1871, 1874, 1879, and 1883) and was commended to the Church by no less than C. F. W. Walther who remarked that it "has performed a service for our church which cannot be overestimated in that in our churches the old practice of singing in a slow and dragging fashion is being increasingly discontinued and the fresh rhythmic singing is being adopted in its place."[14]

The popularity of the rhythmic chorale was such that at least two similar collections, to my knowledge, with only the unison melodies in rhythmic form, were collected and published in America in the 1880s.[15] Their use was clearly pedagogical; both credited Layriz as their source.

In 1877 the General Council published its *Kirchenbuch für Evangelische-Lutherische Gemeinden* and in 1879 the accompanying *Choralbuch mit Liturgie und Chorgesängen zum Kirchenbuch der Allgemeinen Kirchenversammlung*. The sources for the chorale settings include Layriz, Tucher, Zahn, and others. John Endlich, the editor, could speak of the "glorious rhythmic chorale" and hoped that it would soon find a home also in the English Lutheran congregations.[16] In his preface, Endlich notes that it "would have been in order also to indicate 'settings by Praetorious' or 'Schein' and the date of the setting,"[17] but unfortunately he did not do so.

Two Lutheran chorale books which appeared in the 1880s and which relied heavily upon Layriz were the *Choralbuch* of 1886 (additional printings in 1895 and 1902), compiled chiefly by Heinrich F. Hoelter, and the *Mehrstimmiges Choralbuch* of 1888 (additional printings in 1897, 1900, 1903, 1906), edited by Karl Brauer. Hoelter (1846-1916) attended the teachers college in Fort Wayne, Ind., and served congregations in Washington, D.C., Pittsburgh, and St. Louis. Brauer (1831-1907) was a teacher in congregations in Philadelphia, St. Louis, Cleveland, and Baltimore, and from 1866 to 1897 he served at the Addison Teachers Seminary, the predecessor to Concordia Teachers College (now University), River Forest, Ill., where he was the first full-time music professor in The Lutheran Church—Missouri Synod. The prefaces of both these choral books attest to the importance of the second edition of Layriz's *Kern*, indicating that these books had become the treasured heritage of the congregations of the synod.

In addition, a volume similar to those of Hoelter and Brauer titled *Choralbuch zum Gebrauch für Evangelisch-Lutherische Christen in Kirche, Schule und Haus nach Layriz' Kern des deutschen Kirchensegangs*, compiled by Fr. Lutz,[18] director of the Wartburg Teachers Seminary in Waverly, Iowa, and published by the Wartburg Press in Chicago in 1902, is an indication that Layriz's influence extended beyond the boundaries of The Lutheran Church—Missouri Synod and into the Iowa Synod.

By the close of the nineteenth century, however, the Lutheran churches in America which had been founded by the immigrants of the 1830s and 1840s increasingly turned to the English language in their worship and hymnody. Crucial in this development was the publication of the Common Service in 1888 and its subsequent adoption, with some alterations, by most of the immigrant groups as they turned more and more toward the English language. In 1906 there appeared *The Common Service with Music*, published under the authority of the then English Missouri Synod, which contained two musical settings of the *Kyrie* giving Layriz as their source. The first *Kyrie* appeared in the "Morning Service, or Communion," the second in the "Evening Service, or Vespers." In addition, the "Morning Service, or Communion" contained two congregational offertories, one of which is attributed to Layriz. This slight volume was the basis, with some alterations, for the music in the *Evangelical Lutheran Hymn-Book* (1912) and ultimately *The Lutheran Hymnal* (1941), the first two English-language hymnals for the LCMS and, in the case of *The Lutheran Hymnal*, the other synods belonging to the Synodical Conference. The two *Kyries* from Layriz, without attribution, made their way into both these books where they continued to be sung throughout the twentieth century.

Layriz wrote a number of hymn tunes of which only one remained in use throughout most of the twentieth century: *Eins ist Not*, which first appeared in his *Geistliche Melodien . . . Zweites Hundert* (1850), but which he later discarded and returned to a tune by Freylinghausen in his *Kern*.[19] *Eins ist Not* has found its way into one or another Lutheran hymn book down to the present time. It was included in the *Evangelical Lutheran Hymn-Book* (1912), #83; *The Lutheran Hymnal* (1941), #366; and, most recently, *Christian Worship: A Lutheran Hymnal* (1993), #290. Both tunes, typical of a number of tunes from that period, change from duple to triple meter halfway through their respective melodies.

Layriz's greatest and most lasting contribution, however, was his persistence in promoting the restoration of the rhythmic form of the chorale melodies for use in Lutheran congregations. To that end his *Kern* became an important source in the promulgation of the simple cantional-like settings for the various Lutheran organ chorale books published for use in

America in the nineteenth century. That many of these settings persisted in use among Lutherans well into the twentieth century is reflected in the accompanying chart comparing the organ accompaniments of the tune *Erhalt uns Herr* in a number of Lutheran chorale books and hymnals with Layriz' original setting in his *Kern* (see ex. 4). This chart could easily be replicated with any number of chorale settings. In addition, his melody books were an important and necessary tool for teaching the new rhythmic forms of the chorales where they had fallen out of use.

Friedrich Layriz is a name that we should remember, as one of a number of important nineteenth-century Lutherans concerned for the worship life of the Church, and for his significant contribution to the restoration of an invigorated congregational singing through the reintroduction of the rhythmic chorale to congregations both in Germany and America. In many ways, though he is little known or rarely acknowledged, Friedrich Layriz's contribution persists wherever the rhythmic chorale flourishes and continues to invigorate, energize, and strengthen congregational singing today.

Ex. 4: Harmonization of "Erhalt uns Herr" from Layriz's *Kern des deutschen Kirchengesangs* compared with those of later American Lutheran chorale books and hymnals.

Notes

1. *Evang. Kirchenzeitung*, no. 84, (1847). Quoted in Johann Daniel von der Heydt, *Geschichte der Evangelischen Kirchenmusik in Deutschland* (Berlin: Trowitzsch, 1926), 195.
2. This publication prompted a response from E. S. F. Sittig in his *Offene Antwort auf den offenen Sendbrief des Herrn Dr. Fr. Layriz* (Nuremberg, 1844).
3. *The Handbook to the Lutheran Hymnal*, comp. W. G. Polack (St. Louis: Concordia, 1942), 535.
4. The German word *Kern* in the title *Kern des deutschen Kirchengesangs* means "kernel," the heart, center, or core. So the short title of Layriz's compilation might be translated as "The Core (or Heart or Center) of German Church Song." The term *Kernlieder*, then, came to refer to that central core of hymnody which reflected in its texts and melodies the central theological concerns of the Lutheran Reformation. That core, consisting largely of hymns from the Lutheran hymn writers of the first century and a half of the Reformation, was, nevertheless, a somewhat fluid list, some hymns falling out of use and others gradually coming into use over time. In Layriz's compilation, *Kernleider* refers to that basic, normative core of hymnody which is, or which Layriz thought ought to be, central to a Lutheran congregation's repertoire.
5. Although referred to as "volumes," the first three books, containing the hymns, are actually different editions of the same basic collection. Thus volumes two and three are enlarged editions of the first book, repeating the content of the prior publication along with new material.
6. In Layriz's listing of sources he mentions collections by Walter, Vopelius, Praetorious, Schein, Crüger, Vulpius, and others.
7. Friedrich Layriz, *Kern des deutschen Kirchengesangs*, vol. 2, #186.
8. Ibid., #195.
9. Hans Joachim Moser, *Die Evangelische Kirchenmusik in Deutschland* (Berlin: Merseburger, 1954), 239. Friedrich Riegel was a collaborator with Ludwig Schoeberlein in Schoeberlein's *Schatz des liturgischen Chor- und Gemeindegesanges* published in 1868.
10. Preface to Friedrich Layriz, *Kern des deutschen Kirchengesangs*, 1853 ed., vii. This and all subsequent translations from the German are by this author.
11. Johannes Zahn, *Die Melodien der deutschen evangelischen Kirchenlieder* (1893, reprinted Hildesheim: Verlagsbuchhandlung, 1963), vol. 6, 434.
12. I have in my personal library a copy of each of these two latter volumes (1848, 1850) bound together, the inside cover inscribed "J. H. A. Pinkepank, 1853, Frankenmut." It had obviously been used by the Lutheran immigrants who settled in the Saginaw valley of Michigan, particularly the city of Frankenmuth.
13. "Das Layriz'sche Choralbuch betreffend," *Der Lutheraner* XVIII (Oct. 30, 1861), 48. "Our hymnal" was the *Kirchengesangbuch für Evangelisch-Lutherische Gemeinden ungeänderter Augsburgischer Confession* of 1847.

[14] *Der Lutheraner* XXXV (Dec. 15, 1879), 192.

[15] Friedrich Layriz, *225 Melodien deutscher Kirchengesänge meist aus dem 16. und 17. Jahrhundert in ihren ursprünglichen Rhythmen und Tönen . . . Zum Gebrauch christl. Gemeinden deutscher Zunge in Nordamerika*, rev. ed. (St. Louis: 1884), and *335 Deutscher Kirchengesänge, meist auys dem 16. und 17. Jahrhundert.* rev. and enlarged ed. (St. Louis: 1887).

[16] Carl Schalk, *Source Documents in American Lutheran Hymnody* (St. Louis: Concordia, 1996), 77.

[17] Ibid., 76-77.

[18] Lutz was director of the Teachers Seminary from 1894 to 1905. For additional information of Friedrich Lutz see Ronald Matthias, *Still on the Move: Wartburg College, 1852-2002* (Cedar Rapids, Iowa: WDG Communications, 2002).

[19] Freylinghausen's tune for "Eins ist Not" may be found in *The Lutheran Hymnary* (1913), #227, and in *The Evangelical Lutheran Hymnary* (1995), #182.

IV.
The Role of the Composer

The Dilemma of Contemporary Composers of Church Music

The church composers of today stand between the old and the new; like the two-faced Janus they stand looking both backward and forward. Just this is the source of a composer's dilemma. Yet it can also be the source for a new vitality and freshness which, if composers seize upon it, can make an increasingly vital contribution to the Church's song.

Church composers in the second half of the twentieth century find themselves on the horns of a very real dilemma. In a sense it is the dilemma of composers of every age; in another sense it is unique to our day. As they stand midway between the old and the new, composers find their work inevitably drawing sustenance and inspiration from the past. The past's influence may be so encompassing that composers seek only to imitate what has gone before; it may also serve as the point of departure for a musical rebellion. But the past is decisive for composers' lives and works. Without it they would have no roots from which to draw nourishment and inspiration, nor anything against which to rebel.

But while composers stand with one face to the past, their other face points invariably to the future. If composers cannot live and work uninfluenced by the past, neither can they do so in regard to the present and the future. Composers cannot avoid being affected by the developing art of their own time and are, even when least aware of it, drawn along by their art as it moves into the future. The only alternative is a consciously cultivated musical archaism which has little to contribute to any fruitful discussion of the composers' dilemma.

In every age the dilemma of church composers is focused in the healthy conflict between the old and the new as it is manifested in the

---

First published in *Response* 7, no. 2 (1985): 69–78.

historical and cultural development of the musical environment in which they work. But the uniqueness of the dilemma which church composers face can be found in the actions and attitudes of both the Church and composers. Both Church and composers are responsible for the curious dilemma which composers for the Church face; resolving the dilemma, therefore, will take a reorientation on the part of both Church and composers.

The Church is responsible for composers' dilemma because it has chosen, almost without exception, to face only backward, looking almost exclusively to the past and, in general, avoiding any meaningful peek at the present or into the future which would challenge in any significant way its primary attachment to the past. For the Church, the forward look has always been the backward look. From Augustine to the *Motu Proprio* of Pius X it is the past which shines forth as that which must be imitated and emulated, and the new, if admitted at all, must be in conscious continuance of that past tradition.

Composers have contributed to their own dilemma because of their general inclination to throw off the past, to discard it rather completely, and to look with almost exclusive concern to the present and future development of their art and craft. Forgetting that both present and future come into perspective only in the light of the past, composers too often fall into the trap of attempting to free themselves completely from what they have considered the confining influences of the old. Arduously courting the new, they neglect to see that they are cutting themselves off from the very roots which can give nourishment, sustenance, and relevance to their endeavor.

The error of the Church's attachment to its musical past—a logical, understandable, and even theologically necessary one—has been to give that attachment an institutional and cultural cast not at all inherent in its theological concern. Misinterpreting its necessary attachment to the past by confining its efforts to the preservation of specific musical or liturgical evolvements, the Church has tended to forget that all creation, both old and new, has been redeemed and is worthy to be offered up in praise and celebration of the Church's Lord. If, in its attachment to the past, the Church has tended to say that the old—because it is old—is good, composers have tended to suggest that the new—because it is new—is better. Either viewpoint involves a distortion; for music can never be viewed simply and sharply from the perspective of either past or future, old or new. Church music is rather that two-faced Janus, drawing nourishment and sustenance from the past as it recreates its art and craft for its own present and moves with it into the future. The choice is never old or new, past or future. It is always old and new together, reshaped, reworked, recreated in the forms and harmonies of each new age as each generation offers its own song of praise in celebration of its Lord.

To summarize, the dilemma of composers for the Church has not sprung upon them full-blown. It has been caused, in part, by the Church's concern for its tradition and the preservation of its ritual against the inroads of what it has considered a pagan or secular music culture, and by composers themselves who have sometimes sought to advance their art and craft at the expense of the past.

The Historical Development of the Dilemma

Four factors help to bring into sharper focus the dilemma facing composers of church music in twentieth-century America.

The environment in which composers work has dramatically shifted in character from one characterized by isolation to one characterized by association.

Composers once nurtured their craft in comparative isolation. Their acquaintance with music beyond that of their immediate predecessors and a few of their contemporaries was negligible if not nonexistent. They learned their craft from a teacher or teachers and were content, by and large, to work within the context of the style to which they had thus been exposed. Living and working most of their lives in one or two towns, they learned their craft and did their work.

Today the opposite is true. Church composers no longer work in isolation. They work under the bombardment of a wide variety of musical styles from music's entire history which, both consciously and unconsciously, place composers at their mercy. Composers' whole lives are lived against a giant backdrop of disparate musical influences—some good, some bad—made up of equal parts of the classical concert hour, the musical commercial, Gregorian chant, J. S. Bach, William Byrd, Benny Goodman, Leonard Bernstein, the Beatles, Alban Berg, and the Mormon Tabernacle Choir.

Working in association with a host of influences, composers sense that they are in danger of losing their own creative identity, that, stylistically at least, they are no longer their own person. Convinced that their contributions as composers lie, first of all, in being stylistically unlike anyone else, composers turn to the new, the different, the experimental for the distinctiveness they seek. Overwhelmed by a situation which throws them into an intimate association with a vast musical heritage, sensitive composers are in danger of complete frustration and ultimately may give up the attempts to sing their "new song."

Secondly, American church composers have no overarching tradition against which to set their work.

In contrast to England, where a rather identifiable "style" of church music has developed, or Germany, where the heritage of the sixteenth, seventeenth, and eighteenth centuries provides a substantial and continued source of inspiration for even the most radical and modern experiments in liturgical music, America offers only a mosaic of disparate elements lacking any kind of coherent plan or structure. Viewed as bane or blessing, the kaleidoscopic character of American church music is largely peculiar to the American situation. Puritan psalmody, songs of the revivals, chorales from Germany—these influences and many more were brought to the New World and have continued to be widely influential—but influential among a growing pluralism of musical styles.

Faced with a musical tradition growing ever wider and broader, composers have an increasingly difficult time charting their own course for their "new song" for the Church. For what church composers of today see is a multifaceted group of styles from which they are free to pick and choose and against which they must fashion some direction for their own personal work. Free to pick and choose from a smorgasbord of church music styles, church composers of today have tended toward an eclectic and frequently purposeless course lacking direction, focus, and ultimately contributing little to either the Church or their art.

THE DILEMMA OF THE CONTEMPORARY COMPOSER

Faced with a mosaic-like church music culture, church composers have usually taken one of three courses: (1) they have borrowed an established musical tradition, (2) they have attempted to create one, or (3) they have chosen to continue the eclectic and mosaic-like "best of the past" situation which has caused their dilemma in the first place. Having no American church music tradition within which to work, most church composers have followed the most readily available course and borrowed one, a fact which can be seen in the endless number of church music compositions which are literal imitations of various historical styles. Other composers have followed the course of eclecticism, writing in any of a number of different styles and contributing to the further extension of the mosaic-like pattern of American church music. Some have sought to create a new style of church music unlike anything else. Whatever else the lack of a unified and overarching tradition in American church music may mean, it has contributed to the dilemma of practicing composers.

A third factor which contributes to the dilemma of church composers is that, in the eyes of many, they are no longer really necessary.

One of the traditional responsibilities of the church musician was the responsibility to provide a regular supply of music for the ritual life of the church. When Johann Pachelbel's contract with the church council in Erfurt said that he was to "be especially diligent in preparing thematic preludial music," it meant that he was to write it. In the seventeenth and eighteenth centuries the demand for church music was filled by the parish musician whose regular duty was to provide newly composed music for the weekly services. An organ prelude was required; he wrote it. A choral motet or cantata was needed for the next Sunday; the parish musician wrote it.

In the twentieth century, with its phenomenal growth in publications, church music is readily available in a way undreamed of 50 years ago. The demand for practical performing editions of the results of nineteenth and twentieth century musicological research in church music became a lucrative field, and church music publishing houses rose to meet the challenge. Centuries of Christian music—chants, motets, anthems, cantatas, instrumental literature from the entire heritage of Christian song—are available to all. If church composers of today manage to write at all, it is with the knowledge that they are superfluous, that they are really no longer necessary, and that their work will be but a ripple in the tidal wave of musical materials from all centuries which has inundated the church music scene.

Should composers succeed in convincing themselves that they are really necessary (convincing others is another matter), they are faced with the problem of publication. For unless their music is published and available, it has little opportunity to make any kind of contribution whatever to the art of church music. To be "successful" in publishing, composers' music must be wanted. To be wanted means that they must conform, in all important factors, to the prevailing patterns of supply and demand which already exist in the church music market. Encouraged to produce in accord with the established trends—or if they are especially clever in anticipating the trends—they remain, at best, within the confines of a market which does not know where it is going beyond the mosaic pattern it has set for itself. "Publish or perish!" is the fact of life for all church composers who feel that they have a contribution to make. In the usual course of events, however, publication can only be achieved by adding to the oversupply of characterless, but often neatly contrived, compositions already in existence.

Composers for the Church are no longer needed because the mechanics and economics of music publishing have made them, by and large, the least economic and the most expensive way of providing the steady stream of music the church program demands.

A fourth factor which has added to composers' dilemma is that training in church music has become increasingly a training for performance to the neglect of the craft of the composer.

This fact follows all too naturally from the third: if composers are, for all practical purposes, unneeded and unwanted, why train people in the art of musical composition for the Church? Any cursory examination of the courses of studies of those institutions whose purpose it is to train musicians for service in the Church quickly demonstrates that there are few opportunities within the church musician's formal training to learn the craft of composition. Academic courses which are available are usually offered only infrequently, and, when offered, they are blessed with a pitifully small enrollment. These facts simply underscore the observation that the ability to use the tools of the musical craft of composition—whether to harmonize a simple chorale or to compose a polyphonic motet—is found low down, if at all, in the list of priorities which characterize the ideal practicing musician whose ability can be more readily demonstrated at the console or by directing a choir. Choral directors or organists may compose, but usually only to demonstrate the proficiency of their choir or their dexterity at the keyboard. It remains as fact that apprentice composers find it virtually impossible to learn their craft within the Church, for the Church has tended to view musical composition as an essentially luxury item, a nonfunctional factor in a highly functionally oriented culture.

In adopting such an attitude, the Church has failed to realize that in neglecting to provide for competent training in musical composition as an accepted part of the equipment of the church musician, it is neglecting a function which it desperately needs. As it attempts to redeem all of creation and turn it once again to the praise and glory of its Lord, as it seeks for the "new song," it fails to provide the disciplined training from which that new song will ultimately arise.

The Developed Dilemma

This developed dilemma which threatens to engulf composers of church music comes at a particularly inappropriate time because it is at this particular juncture in contemporary history that the arts, and church music in particular, are increasingly being viewed as one of the few remaining "points of contact" with what appears to be an increasingly hostile and secularized "post-Christian" culture. As evidence of the fact that the Church has not given up the world—that it has something to say to people of our time, and that one way to speak is through involvement in the conversation between theology and the arts—the Church needs to demonstrate that the new, as well as the old, has a place in the musical culture of the Church.

This is the unique task of church composers: to speak meaningfully and forcefully in accents which ring unmistakably with the sounds, rhythms, and harmonies of our day. To accomplish this church composers will have to lead the way in showing that not only the old, but the new, as well, must be reclaimed, rewon, redeemed for the praise and glory of God. This is, first of all, formed into sounds and rhythms, melodies and harmonies, counterpoints and cadences. For the Church to fail to provide the stimulation and environment in which such a task can be conceived, or, more important, for composers themselves to fail to undertake it, will be for both to let slip past the unique challenge and momentous opportunity which is theirs.

The dilemma which faces composers is not entirely of their own making. Its roots are found in the attitudes of both the Church and composers. The heart of the dilemma may be stated simply:

Realizing more clearly than ever before the theological necessity of composers' tasks and the need for the highest level of both artistry and craftsmanship, in their relationship with each other both the Church and composers, paradoxically, expect too much and, at the same time, too little.

The Church Expects Too Little

Rather than expecting too much of composers, the Church's primary error is that it expects too little. It expects too little theologically. The Church's expectations are low because it often ignores the fact that Christian composers are gifts of the Spirit to the Church and that the "new song" which they bring is a useful and needed gift of God to the Church as it praises its Creator and edifies its members.

Expecting too little, the Church sees no need for composers to sharpen either their theological insights or the technique of their craft. The Church does not expect them to be composers, in the fullest sense of that term, or to take their work seriously. Expecting little, the results are usually commensurate with its expectations.

The Church Expects Too Much

At the same time that the Church expects too little, it, paradoxically, expects too much. Should the Church grant the propriety of the role of composers, their roles are frequently misconceived by seeing them against the background of nineteenth-century thought which viewed composers' work as a result of romantic inspiration. Composers were those who, in an experience of special illumination and under the guidance of some higher being, took pen to paper and created a masterpiece.

The Church of today continues to view composers' roles largely in this nineteenth-century manner. We treasure the stories of "inspiration" which surround many popular church favorites. Handel's "Messiah" or the hymn "Silent Night" take on particular significance because of the circumstances which surround their writing. We say that they were "inspired." A hymn is treasured because it was written in a fit of grief for a lost loved one or because the story surrounding its writing strikes a harmonious note on the harp strings of our sentiment. Craftsmanship in composers' works is largely forgotten. The genuineness of grief, the heartwarming character of the story surrounding a composition—everything takes precedence over the inherent artistic worth of the music itself. The Church hardly knows how to cope with musical artists quietly tending to the good of the work, creating music to the best of their ability with no reliance on homey stories or personal eccentricities. Expecting a twentieth-century model of a nineteenth-century view, the Church expects not only too much, but the wrong thing.

Expecting too much, the Church restricts composers' views of their work by assuming that music in the life of the Church is essentially a nonutilitarian item, a factor on the periphery of its life and worship, which is convenient to have available, but which can be dispensed with if necessary. It is the ecclesiastical equivalent of that music which accompanies our shopping or which serves as a constant background companion in the home. In asking composers to constrict their vision of their role in the life and worship of the Church to that of a manipulator of emotions, a producer of background noises for more important functions or ritual, the Church is asking too much.

The Church is not alone, however, in expecting too much and too little. The situation can readily be reversed because, as an examination of the attitude of many composers will quickly reveal, they are equally guilty in expecting of the church both too much and too little.

Composers Expect Too Much

Composers expect too much when they expect the Church to forget that it is within the context of the Church—the people of God, the *laos*—that they do their work. Within that context it is people who are to be reached, edified, and lifted up in their praise and adoration of

God. Church composers' responsibilities are threefold: to God, to their craft, and to their people. It is the third of these three responsibilities that composers are most likely to forget. Composers who place exclusive attention upon their craft, regardless of its implication for their people, have, in effect, short circuited their art.

Composers expect too much of the Church when they indulge in the speculation that their music is, after all, being written for future generations. Composers live and work in their own time, and their responsibility is to the people they are to serve. This need in no way detracts from their responsibility to develop their art and craft to the highest level of their ability, working with new forms, new sounds, new harmonies, melodies, and rhythms. It does mean that in their personal understanding and vision all of their work is carried out in the full realization that it is people who are to be served along with their Lord and their craft. If composers expect the Church to welcome them solely on the grounds of their art, they expect too much.

Composers expect too much if they expect the Church to adapt to their own preconceived notions of their particular role. "Contemporary music!" composers may shout. "Traditional!" the Church shouts back. And in such self-serving chauvinism both are equally wrong. For the issue in church music is not, first of all, contemporary or traditional, subjective or objective, Gospel song or chorale, or any of the other neat dichotomies which have been erected and around whose banners much energy and effort have been expended. The central issue of church music is the praise and honor of the Creator through attention to the highest integrity of the craft of music in order that the people of God might praise and in turn be edified. For composers to expect the Church to restrict its view of church music solely to that of artists and their craft, important and necessary as that element is, is to expect too much.

Composers Expect Too Little

Perhaps the greatest liability on the part of composers is that, in relation to the Church, they expect too little. Composers expect too little when they do not expect the Church to be the Church. To underscore the basic theological stance from which their work is to be done and to provide the necessary motivations for their work, composers must expect that the Church is exactly what it claims to be: the people of God gathered together in Word and Sacrament, accepting the varied gifts of the Spirit for the building up and edifying of the saints. Imperfect though the local manifestation of the Church which they serve may be, contentious and cantankerous though its members may seem, the Church is nevertheless God's people in that place. And unless church composers expect the people they serve to be what they know they are, these composers demean their work and the gifts which they have been given.

Expecting too little, composers often fail to see the necessity for honest, searching, self-criticism of their craftsmanship. Knowing that most will neither detect nor care about the integrity of their technique, they are content with a craftsmanship which is less than the best of their ability to produce. The awkward harmonization, the poorly worked-out counterpoint, the nebulous formal structure are let pass. Who will know the difference? What difference does it actually make? Content with slipshod work, composers fail to provide the honest craftsmanship which a proper stewardship of their gift of the Spirit demands.

Expecting too little of the Church, composers too easily acquiesce to the nineteenth-century image of composers. They attempt to play the role though they are particularly ill-suited to it, knowing all the while that it is nonsense. To the congregation, which continues to play the game, the contrast between the level of craftsmanship of the music nurtured within the Church under the influences of such a romanticized view of composers and that growing without is all too apparent. Refusing to accept a musical stone as bread, the Church rejects the craftless product of the Church's musical poverty; yet all the while it continues to nurture the image of composers as vehicles of a nebulous "inspiration" in which the knowledge of their craft is an unnecessary luxury. Too easily accepting the Church's distorted image of composers and unwilling or unable to attempt to change it, composers—in an area of primary concern to their role in the life and work of the church—expect too little.

The Way Out of the Dilemma

While, in a sense, composers are both prophets and priests, looking both backward and forward from the point in time which they happen to occupy, it is in pointing forward to the "new song" that the unique opportunity and challenge which is composers' resides. For the "new song" is not merely contemporary sounds, modern techniques of composition, or the avant-garde movement of any particular generation; it is rather each generation's recreation of the song of salvation for its own day. It is the making incarnate in rhythms and melodies the eternal song of salvation in a way which will have vitality and significant meaning for the people of its time.

The "new song" is a challenging song, challenging not only in its musical structures and sounds but in the theological accents which it strikes for the particular need of a particular time.

The "new song" is a conservative song in the root sense of the word, seeking not to conserve a superficial resemblance to the music of times past, but to conserve the underlying spirit which gave the Church of earlier times the need to sing its particular "new song."

The "new song" is a prophetic song because it seeks to call the Church to repentance and reformation.

Above all, *the Church's "new song" is an incarnated song.* It is the Song made rhythm, the Song made melody, the Song made harmony and counterpoint. Subject to all the frailties and weaknesses of our human conditions, it is the only song which composers of music for the Church can sing. Though they sing it with all the truthfulness, honesty, and integrity which they, as Christians and artists, can master, they sing it with the knowledge that it is only an imperfect imitation of that song sung at the creation of the world when all the morning stars sang together and all the children of God shouted for joy, and of that final perfect song of which the author of the Revelation of St. John speaks:

> And every creature which is in heaven, and on the earth, and under the earth, and such as are in the sea, and all that are in them, heard I saying, Blessing, and honour, and glory, and power, be unto him that sitteth upon the throne, and unto the Lamb for ever and ever. (Rev. 5:13, KJV)

Some Thoughts on the Writing of Hymn Tunes

Recent years have seen a tremendous increase in interest in the writing of hymn tunes, no doubt largely generated by what has been referred to as the "hymn explosion" of recent decades. This "hymn explosion," while largely an explosion of hymn *texts* written by an ever-increasing number of hymn *text* writers, has also resulted in a growing interest on the part of church musicians in setting these texts to newly written *tunes*. Few periods in the history of the Church—the period of Pietism in the late seventeenth and early eighteenth centuries, and the period of the rise of the gospel song in the late nineteenth century come to mind—can match the last half of the twentieth century for the sheer quantity of new hymn texts and tunes written by an increasing number of aspiring hymn text and hymn tune writers.

Several forces have contributed to bringing this situation about. First has been the large number of new hymns and hymnals published in the past 50years. Virtually every religious denomination together with publishing houses serving nondenominational groups have been involved in preparing new hymnals or revising older ones. Second, the practice of most hymnal committees and editors of "improving" the language of each successive hymnal, underscored by more recent concerns for gender and God-language issues has made available a whole set of new texts which are readily at hand and available for new tunes. Third, an increased awareness on the part of those responsible for putting together hymnals or hymnal revisions that each new hymnal should contain a significant representation of the work of contemporary hymn composers

---

First published in *CrossAccent: Journal of the Association of Lutheran Church Musicians* 4, no. 3 (1996). Used by permission.

has served to make hymn tune creation a matter of more than passing interest to many. Fourth, the readily available technology which can prepare and disseminate hymns for use by local congregations or other groups has provided a way for new hymns to be made available quickly to a wide variety of potential users. Finally, that hymn writing—both text and tune—has become of significant interest to an increasing number of music publishers, particularly in the acquiring of copyrights to texts and tunes, attests to the financial implications of this "hymn explosion," a situation with many parallels to the period of the rise of the gospel song in the latter nineteenth century when interest in the matter of acquiring copyrights first became an important consideration. Into this pool, then, many aspiring hymn writers—writers of both text and tunes— have cast their lines, some with good possibilities of catching a prize, others with little more chance than their personal piety would suggest.

For a variety of serendipitous reasons, my interest and involvement in writing hymn tunes has evolved so that at the present time I have written some eight hymn tunes which have been graciously and generously received. A good number of these have appeared in many of the currently available denominational hymnals and supplements. In general, my hymns have been written at the request of or commissioned by an individual, local congregation or denominational church body for some particular occasion. Thus the very first hymn tune (*Zion*) which I wrote —almost 40 years ago in 1958—was written for a marvelous translation by Martin Franzmann ("Rise Again, Ye Lion-Hearted Saints of Early Christendom") which had appeared in *The Lutheran Hymnal* (1941) but which had been little used in congregations. It was requested by and first sung at Zion Lutheran Church, Wausau, Wis., where I was serving at the time. My most recent hymn tune (*Ft. Wayne*) was written for a text by Stephen P. Starke—"Preach the Word!"—commissioned for the 150th anniversary of Concordia Theological Seminary, Ft. Wayne, Ind.

It always comes as a surprise and I view with amazement the fact that any number of my hymn tunes are sung as widely as they are. In such a context it is understandable that some should ask "What is your secret?" or "How does one go about writing a hymn tune that is satisfying musically and spiritually?" The simple, but superficial, answer is, "I don't know." A more cynical response is the suggestion that "there are three basic rules for writing a good hymn tune; the problem is that no one knows what they are." A better and more serious answer is a bit more complicated.

Many people are convinced that there must be a simple formula, a recipe, a set of "rules" which, when followed, will result in a "good" hymn tune. That is why, I believe, many people are attracted to hymn-writing workshops—"Just teach me the rules or recipe!" Many are convinced that behind all the rhetoric and the talk there are a few simple secrets to writing a good tune (or text) and we just need to search them out. True, recipes abound, but they are usually either too general to be of much help, or they presume that there is one particular musical style which embodies what congregational hymn style is all about. Such recipes are simply a reflection of that particular musical style.

But obviously more can and needs to be said. Is there something to say to fledgling hymn tune writers—or to those who have passed the fledgling stage—which can be of help in understanding the matter of writing hymn tunes for congregational worship?

Let us assume that one has at hand a text worth setting, a text which reflects the understandings and faith of the Church, which possesses intrinsic poetic worth, and which, for whatever reasons, calls for a new tune. Are there particular understandings and skills which can be helpful to bring to the matter of writing new hymn tunes and settings? Several areas of concern related to composing a new hymn tune for such a text may be worth exploring. None involves concocting a recipe. They include and are related to (1) the uniqueness of congregational song, (2) the problem of the ivory tower syndrome, and (3) the conflict between craft and piety.

The Uniqueness of Congregational Hymn Singing

First, by congregational singing I mean Christian song which is *congregational* in essence and which is, from a Lutheran perspective, rooted in a liturgical understanding of congregational worship. It is a song sung by largely untrained singers who do not ordinarily rehearse, but who long to sing their faith in songs that are theologically rich, challenging, and musically satisfying.

Such understandings help shape the congregational song we create. If, for example, the primary goal in the creation of a new hymn tune is simply "artistic self-expression," the results are likely to be something other than liturgically grounded congregational song. If the goal is to assist the congregation—through our song—to a more liturgically rooted worship, this will certainly affect the choice of texts; but it equally affects how we shape musically those tunes which we hope will give life to those texts. If our basic musical commitment is grounded simply in the goal of "personal self-expression," it will ultimately prove a commitment untrue to the goal of true congregational song.

A crucial factor in shaping a new melody for congregational singing—as well as determining its success or failure—is an understanding of the *uniqueness* of congregational singing. One frequently hears about the "limitations" of writing for congregational singing, limitations which presumably restrict the full and free exercise of the composer's musical imagination, instincts, and personal self-expression. To be sure, there are parameters within which congregational singing can best occur, within which one works if a new hymn tune is to be learned, assimilated, and sung with success by a congregation. Such matters as pitch, range of melody, the degree of rhythmic or harmonic complexity possible; all these are important factors which need to be considered in the writing of a hymn tune. But of paramount importance is the understanding that congregational song possesses a distinct uniqueness which sets it apart from all other musical writing.

A congregation is a unique singing group with strengths and weaknesses all its own. Some things it does well, musically, and other things it may do less well. The composer needs to remember— and congregations and pastors need to be reminded—that a hymn tune intended for congregational singing should never be a simplistic, undistinguished melody whose only purpose is functional. Nor is congregational singing, from my perspective, best approached or understood as either art song or as choral music. A congregation is neither a soloist nor a choir in disguise, a soloist or choir which, unfortunately, happens to sing rather poorly much of the time. An awareness of the unique parameters of congregational singing and an understanding of what congregational singing is *not*, together with a sensitivity to what is really and realistically possible with such a group will certainly improve one's chances at success than if those parameters and understandings are cavalierly ignored.

It needs to be pointed out that there are many fine tunes in the Church's repertoire of song written within historically accepted parameters which, according to the perception of some, are unexciting at first hearing, yet for which there is a welcome and needed place. Such tunes as *Jam Lucis* or *Hamburg*, for example, both of which have very restricted melodic ranges and are extremely simple rhythmically, are important, beautiful, spiritually rewarding, and necessary parts of the Church's song. However, few contemporary composers seem attracted to work within the more modest confines of such rhythmic or melodic "limitations." Here is a wonderful field for exploration by contemporary composers. There are many more examples of tunes, perhaps too many more, which emulate the more expansive, grand, and—dare we say it— triumphal sounds of such tunes as *Crucifer* or *Sine Nomine*. Perhaps we can remind ourselves that every new hymn tune need not be a "blockbuster."

However, having stressed the matter of a realistic appraisal of parameters in congregational singing, another fact needs to be mentioned. Many a strong hymn tune tends to stretch the boundaries of rhythm, melody, harmony, or form beyond which most congregations may think it is possible or even allowable to go. Certainly such tunes as *Kingly Love* (with its text by Martin Franzmann) or *Now* (with its text by Jaroslav J. Vajda) are set to texts which, formally at least, are radically unlike anything mostly congregations would mistake for a "hymn." Yet it is the unusual formal structures of these hymn texts which have been the catalyst for the creation of these tunes which are recognized widely as being tunes quite unlike anything congregations have sung before.

A successful hymn tune will demonstrate just how far the musical or formal boundaries can be stretched before they break. By extending those boundaries beyond what many congregations would regard as possible, a new hymn tune can help congregations realize the thrill of singing beyond what they may think of as their limits, but not beyond what they can actually do. The result can be the establishment of a new and broader musical horizon within which new voice can be given to the unique song of the Church which is congregational hymnody.

The Ivory Tower Syndrome

Probably the best way that a fledgling hymn tune writer can grow in a sense of where musical boundaries are located, and when and how those boundaries can be stretched, is to be part of a regular hymn-singing community which has at the core of its hymn repertoire a broad selection of the best of the treasury of the Church's song. Ideally this means participating regularly in a community that sings well, that draws its hymnody from the best of the Church's hymnody, past and present, and is led by an organist who knows how best to bring out the unique genius of congregational song.

Ongoing and regular contact with good congregational singing as a member of such a singing community will help develop an intuitive sense of what is possible, what is practicable, how far the boundaries can be stretched, what might best be avoided, and what hinders effective congregational singing. Moreover, it is extremely helpful for any aspiring hymn tune writer to carefully analyze the great hymn tunes of the Church. Analysis of such elements as form, cadence, word emphasis, melodic high points, and settings which undergird or detract from the melody not only help one understand what, from a purely musical viewpoint, makes these melodies "good," what makes them "work," but also sets a pattern for the rigorous self-analysis of one's own creation.

Isolation from a regular hymn-singing community is always dangerous for it tends to allow the composer's musical idiosyncrasies to remain unchallenged by reality. In such a context, musical mannerisms or affections are allowed free hand, unchecked by regular contact with a singing community which can bring a degree of realism to the endeavor.

The picture of a composer isolated in her ivory tower composing songs for congregations when that composer has no personal, immediate, and ongoing experience with congregational singing is, for me at least, a problematic one. If congregational song is, at least in part, the gift of the Christian community to itself, then it would seem that those who fashion the Church's song should not only be a regular part of the Church's worship, its mission, and witness, but also have —as part of their mission and witness—an ongoing and continuous relationship with the singing of the Church's song. That can hardly take place when the composer relegates himself to any modern-day equivalent of the ivory tower.

The Hymn Tune Writer and the Plumber

If one aspires to write a hymn tune intended for congregational use, it certainly ought to be a melody which reflects the highest level of competence—both in its creation and in its performance—of which the community is capable. This, let me hasten to say, has nothing to do with complexity; some of the most beautiful, noble, and exalted hymns are among the simplest musically. It has everything to do, however, with musical honesty, integrity, and craftsmanship. Moreover, the creation of a hymn tune cannot be seen simply, or even primarily, as a vehicle for its creator's "self-expression" apart from the congregation which will hopefully make this new song its own. It is rather a vehicle by which the congregation is nourished and through which its response of proclamation and praise can effectively occur. In all of this the *craft* of composition, *the attention paid to the thing being made*, needs to be uppermost in the mind of its creator.

The concept of the hymn tune—and certainly of all church music—as craft is one which is dutifully affirmed in theory and too often ignored in practice. In theory, craftsmanship in the work is held up and affirmed as not only highly desirable, but as a primary concern of the composer of the Church's song. Reviews of hymn tunes and church music often remark that a work is "well crafted" or "not well crafted." In practice what is too often substituted for craft is a piety which assumes that if one's intentions are good a work of art cannot be far behind. Piety, however sincere or well meant, or just the desire to write a hymn tune is simply not enough. Of primary importance is a solid grounding in the craft of musical composition. One may acquire that grounding in a number of ways, but it cannot be sidestepped.

The do-it-yourself plumber who succeeds in flooding the kitchen floor is usually long on good intentions, but short on competence—short in a knowledge of the craft of plumbing and how to apply it in a particular situation. One knows, for example, when a chair is well crafted: when it is appealing to the eye, when it does not collapse upon sitting in it, when one can sit in it for longer periods of time without becoming uncomfortable. In a similar fashion one can begin to recognize a well-crafted hymn tune: when it is appealing to the ear, when it does not fall apart musically when singing it, when one can sing it repeatedly without one becoming tired of it. Each of these characteristics has to do with elements of craft; none has to do primarily with intention.

One could ask rhetorically whether, upon being informed of the need for a heart operation, one would choose a pious Christian who had little or no knowledge of surgery or a non-Christian who knew his craft. The answer is obvious. One does not call a pious Christian with no knowledge of plumbing to fix the toilet. Many would-be hymn tune writers lack not only a similar competence in the craft of music, but some flaunt their lack of craft, implying that the piety of their intent will make up the difference. Simple reflection suggests that the greater one's technical competence in the craft of music—while certainly not guaranteeing a "good" hymn tune or setting—the greater the chance that one will at least be minimally successful in fashioning a melody and setting which can be both useful, practical, and, hopefully, spiritually rewarding.

Tunes to Grow Into

So many new tunes seem to lack substance and that indefinable something that make great tunes especially memorable. They are not tunes one wishes to grow into; they are tunes to grow out of. Trite rhythms, colorless melodic patterns, lackluster harmonic progressions—all these are hardly elements which will stimulate, ennoble, and excite congregations to greater singing. Likewise, hymn tunes which pander to the latest musical fads, which seek the lowest common musical denominator, or which self-consciously attempt to be "attractive" to particular age groups will hardly help congregations to grow—musically or spiritually. Good tunes are those which wear well with time and repeated use. These are the tunes to grow into.

Good hymn tunes, new or old, are seldom, if ever, written by musical dilettantes, however praiseworthy their intentions. But for those who are constantly sharpening the tools of their musical craft, who recognize the congregation as the unique singing group it is and the parameters within

SOME THOUGHTS ON THE WRITING OF HYMN TUNES

which such a group most effectively works, and who share the ongoing experience of hymn-singing with a vital music-making community, the experience of writing a new hymn tune can be an exciting and fulfilling experience.

And just maybe, once in a great while, that experience may result in a hymn tune which endures beyond the immediate present, that may enrich the song of the Church for years—or even generations—to come. That judgment, however, is finally beyond the immediate experience of any hymn tune composer. In the introduction to the first collection of my hymn tunes published some years ago, I remarked that my hymn tunes are "at heart a series of signposts along the way, markers made by one individual who has been privileged to be a small part of that happy task of providing songs for a pilgrim people along the way." To be involved in the creation of new tunes for new texts which place into the mouths of the faithful words of both proclamation and praise is to become involved in the craft of musical composition in a unique and wonderful way.

Perhaps the greatest gift that a composer of church music can give is a new tune for singing which—together with its text—enlivens, ennobles, and enriches the congregation's singing and nourishes and deepens its faith. But every composer of hymn tunes—and I believe that I can speak for everyone who has ever written one—can also testify that to hear a congregation sing one's hymn tunes with musical sensitivity, spiritual understanding, and with insight and appreciation is not only an experience thrilling and moving beyond description. It is ultimately the greatest gift that any hymn writer can possibly receive.

The Church and the Composer

The history of the Christian worshipping community is the history of a singing and music-making community. We can hardly imagine it otherwise.

> Wherever and whenever God's people have gathered to hear his Word and celebrate the sacraments they have sung songs, songs of death and rebirth, songs of sin and salvation, songs of repentance, renewal, and new life. The joining of music with Christian worship was hardly the result of historical or cultural accident. It was rather the deliberate result of the Church's concern for the faith joined together with an understanding of the power of music to move our minds and hearts. In theory the wedding of music and words may appear to be a wedding of convenience; in practice it is the unavoidable result of the new life in Christ. In theory it may be possible to imagine Christian worship devoid of song; in practice the Christian community fills its gatherings with psalms, hymns, and spiritual songs.[1]

And it is the composer who, throughout the centuries of the Church's existence, has provided that song where words and music combine to become a vehicle for the praise of God and the proclamation of the Gospel.[2] Throughout history the church and its composers have been inextricably linked. Whether anonymous or known, those who have brought into being, created, and shaped that song have given the Church a gift beyond compare.

The relationship between the Church and the composer has always been a reciprocal one. It is the composer who has given musical shape and form to the Church's response of proclamation, praise, and prayer,

---

First published in *CrossAccent: Journal of the Association of Lutheran Church Musicians* 8, no. 1 (2000): 3–8. Reprinted by permission.

to the good news of the Gospel. Whether that response is congregational song, or choral or instrumental music, it is the composer who imagines it, creates it, brings it to life, frames, shapes, and molds it. Any particular part of the treasury of the Church's song, while the creation of an individual, is not simply the song of the person who brings it into being. It becomes, when the Church accepts and sings it, the song of the whole Church. Such songs transcend the song of the individual and become part of the Church's treasury of song. Martin Luther, in his "Treatise on the Last Words of David," written toward the close of his life in 1543, expressed just that sentiment.

> St. Ambrose composed many hymns of the Church. They are called church hymns because the Church accepted them and sings them just as though the Church had written them and as though they were the Church's songs. Therefore it is not customary to say, "Thus sings Ambrose, Gregory, Prudentius, Sedulius," but "Thus sings the Christian Church." For these are now the songs of the Church, which Ambrose, Sedulius, etc., sing with the Church and the Church with them. When they die, the Church survives them and keeps on singing their songs.[3]

While it is the composer who shapes and forms that song, it is the Church which provides the context and the circumstances in which that song is sung. That context, of course, is the liturgy of the Church. When the composer ignores, forgets, or is oblivious to the context—and its musical, sociological, anthropological parameters—problems are sure to arise. Such forgetfulness or obliviousness may be musical, theological, or both. For the composer to write music oblivious to the abilities of the groups which are to perform it is to court musical disaster. For the composer to write music oblivious to the theological and liturgical context in which that music will serve is to court theological and liturgical disaster. Examples of both kinds of "forgetfulness" abound and are inflicted upon countless congregations week after week. When the Church forgets the imperatives of its own theology and liturgy, it is likely to fall into the trap of encouraging music which forsakes theology in favor of sociology, and which forsakes liturgy for group dynamics.

THE CHURCH AND THE COMPOSER

When composers lose their bearings in the music they present for use in the Church, the Church rightly and properly calls them to task. When the Church, or particular congregations, lose their theological or liturgical bearings, it is incumbent upon composers and all church musicians, to call the Church to task and point it to the riches of its theology and the liturgy. This reciprocal relationship between the Church and its composers is always somewhat tenuous since it is based on mutual respect, trust, and a shared understanding of the role of music in the life and worship of the Church. That such a shared understanding does not exist in many places is part of the problem the Church and many of its composers and congregations face today.

If composers are to make the contribution to the life of the Church which their vocation demands, and if the Church is to encourage and nourish those in its midst who shape and form the Church's song, several topics, among others, suggest themselves for further attention. They are (1) the return to a clearer understanding of the role of music in the Church as proclamation and praise, (2) the reestablishment of objective musical standards and the renewal of the understanding of the role of the composer as craftsman, and (3) the establishment of an environment of stability and continuity in which the composer may best work and flourish. Some of these areas are the particular province of the composer, others of the Church. Since both exist in a reciprocal relationship, both should be intimately involved in addressing each of these concerns.

Proclaiming the Gospel

The mission of the Church is to speak the Gospel—to God in praise, thanksgiving, and adoration, to itself as witness to the faith it holds, and to the world as the message of salvation.[4] The role of music—and the composer—in the life, worship, and mission of the Church, at least when speaking of music for the public worship of the Church, is to proclaim that same Gospel with all the skill, craftsmanship, and art which is possible. Music for worship is not a device for emotional manipulation, nor is it a tool for inducing a variety of psychological states presumably conducive to worship. Luther was clear:

> thus it was not without reason that the fathers and prophets wanted nothing else to be associated as closely with the

Word of God as music. . . . After all, the gift of language combined with the gift of song was only given to man to let him know that *he should praise God with both words and music, namely by proclaiming [the Word of God] through music* and by providing sweet melodies with words[5] (emphasis mine).

To proclaim the Gospel was, for Luther, to speak and sing about what Christ has done. "I have no one to sing and chant about but Christ," Luther says, "in whom alone I have everything. Him alone I proclaim, in Him alone I glory, for He has become my salvation, that is, my victory."[6] When Christians gather for worship, the song is the same: to sing and praise God for the victory won in the life, death, and resurrection of Christ. In the gathering of the Christian community, we sing that song: to God in praise, thanksgiving, and prayer; to each other as witness to the faith we hold; and to the world as message and proclamation. *God is praised when the Gospel is proclaimed; and the proclamation of the Gospel is the way Christians rightly praise God.* There is no artificial division between songs that "proclaim" and songs that "praise." For unless "praise songs" proclaim the good news of the Gospel they are not, in the Christian sense, praise songs at all.

To help the Church proclaim that Gospel is the privilege and responsibility of the composer for the Church. To proclaim the Gospel means to tell the story of salvation—or at least that significant part of the story which the particular time, season, festival, or commemoration might suggest. Moreover, to tell the story does not mean to tell *about* the story, but to tell it, the story of how God has accomplished our salvation.

Just as in family gatherings where we tell and retell the stories that make and bind us together as family, so in the weekly gathering of the Christian community we tell and tell again, week after week, the story of what binds us together as Christians. It is a story we tell in liturgy and song. That story is the story of what God has done for us—the good news of the Gospel. In Katherine Hankey's all-too-familiar "old favorite" we sing about how we "love to tell the story." Unfortunately, this "Gospel song" never gets around to telling it. Ronald Klug's text "Rise, Shine, You People!" on the other hand, encourages us to "Tell how the Father sent his Son to save us. / Tell of the Son, who life and freedom gave us.

/ Tell how the Spirit calls from ev'ry nation His new creation." (*Lutheran Service Book*, #825) Hankey's monotheism of the second person stands in stark contrast to the Trinitarian shape of Klug's proclamation. When the good news of the Gospel—which is a witness to something—is reduced to fuzzy love or transformed into anything that is "justifying" or "healing," "liberating" or "self-affirming," it has become something other than the good news of the *Gospel*.

The Gospel, Jenson reminds us, "is always some form of the claim, 'Jesus, the one who . . . , is risen from the dead,' with the ellipse filled by whatever narrative identification is needed in a [particular] context."[7] Luther said the same thing when he remarked in his commentary on 1 Cor, 15:

> and now St. Paul appropriately concludes with a song which he sings: "Thanks and praise be to God, who gave us such a victory!" We can join in that song and in that way always celebrate Easter, praising and extolling God for a victory that was not won or achieved in battle by us . . . but was presented and given to us by the mercy of God. . . . *But we must . . . sing of this victory in Christ*.[8] (emphasis mine)

All this, of course, says a great deal about the texts of the songs which composers choose to set when writing music for worship. Texts simply expressing some vague religious sentiment will hardly suffice. Nor will texts be adequate simply because they have been taken from the Bible. The exponential explosion of new texts in our day can be both bane and blessing. When they clearly and unambiguously sing of this Easter history in Christ they do what Luther enjoins us. When they consist of nebulous religious platitudes, they would best be set aside.

A Return to Objective Musical Standards

A second concern revolves around the idea of a return to more objective standards in the musical and liturgical life of the Church. It is, of course, the very idea of objective standards that is contested in the popular culture and is at issue where such thinking has infected the current discussion concerning the Church's song. Much thinking about culture these days, also within the Church, seeks to cast doubt on all absolutes, discards any assumptions inconvenient to the cause it is promoting, and scorns any notion of esteem for accomplishment or reverence for heritage. The result of such deconstruction is simply that everything is relative. No idea, work of art, culture, or piece of music is better than any other. It is all "a matter of taste." All depends on how I, as an individual, perceive ideas, art, culture, or music. Outside my own self and my own perceptions there are no objective standards.

Such a me-centered, "anything goes" attitude in the Church, which shrinks from ever saying simply and clearly that A is better than B, is omnipresent in the Church's thinking about worship and music. This kind of equivocation is brilliantly caricatured in an answer to the question: how many mainline church leaders does it take to change a light bulb? The answer?

> We choose not to make a statement either in favor of or against the need for a light bulb. However, if in your own journey you have found that a light bulb works for you, that is fine. You are invited to write a poem or compose a modern dance about your personal relationship with your light bulb (or light source or non-dark resource), and present it next month at our annual light bulb Sunday service, in which we will explore a number of light bulb traditions, including incandescent, fluorescent, three-way, long life, and tinted— all of which are equally valid paths to luminescence.[9]

In contrast to the notion that all are "equally valid paths to luminescence," it is the very concept that some ideas are better than others, some works of art more universal than others, and that some music is better suited to the life and mission of the Church that is at issue. The point in this deconstructive atmosphere is not to measure one's work and performance by any kind of absolute standard, but simply to feel good about taking part.

From such a vantage point the goal of music in the Church is simply to entertain—to be sure, to entertain religiously, but entertain nevertheless. It seems not to occur to many that to entertain is plainly a shallower goal than to be inspired, uplifted, or drawn to the Gospel; moreover, it is a self-absorbed and inward-looking pursuit, centered on the personal and, usually, passive side of life, rather than on the world. Entertainment promises to make you feel better, to help you forget your troubles, to liberate your from having to think at all. Even when it touches deep feelings it does so simply to reassure. In the midst of all of this it seems that no one can bring themselves to say what virtually everyone really knows—that the emperor has no clothes.

The unexamined notion is that everyone (including composers) is pretty much the same, that self-fulfillment is more important than objective achievement, that the "man in the pew" is always right. All this simply reinforces a populism which, coupled with a generally blissful indifference, leads to the common methodology of surveying an "audience," then groveling to its ever-changing whims. The results of such populist, egalitarian attitudes have, in large measure, led us to the situation in which the Church finds itself.

Such attitudes lead rather directly to the decline of any notion of the composer for the Church as one who learns a craft, dedicating his or her skill, knowledge, and ability to the praise of God through the highest use of their talent in musical composition.

The Composer as Craftsman

The composer's role involves a sensitivity to and knowledge of several related concerns: a sensitivity to the context of the liturgy in which his song is to find its home, a sensitivity of the realistic musical parameters within which the composer works, and, perhaps most important for our purposes here, an understanding of the work of the composer as craftsman.

The primary definition of craftsman in the *American Heritage Dictionary of the English Language* is "a skilled worker who practices a craft by occupation." A craftsman is an artisan, a skilled laborer, one who brings to the task at hand the skill and wisdom of one who has learned the technique of his trade or art. To learn a craft often involves many years of apprenticeship, practicing the skills necessary to become a master. This was certainly true of the Lutheran composers of the sixteenth and seventeenth centuries, all musicians highly trained in their art, most often pupils of illustrious teachers and composers of their day, and musicians who saw that the most proper exercise of their piety as composers was possible only by employing the highest degree of craftsmanship, technique, and skill of which they were capable.

Today, however, the music heard in too many churches reflects—even to the casual listener—a lack of craftsmanship, not simply in performance, but in its very composition. Much church music being written today seems to be written by those not only lacking basic musical skills, but who pride themselves on their lack of training as affording a more direct path to greater sincerity and self-expression than those concerned with the "technicalities" of their art. To put it another way, the nobility of their goal often obviates—in their minds, at least any compelling need for skill and expertise in their craft. When such material is published by presumably reputable publishers, it only tends to reinforce their prejudice against the need for skill, training, and competence in the craft they presume to practice. Here we have piety gone awry. Piety, however sincere and well meant, is not enough. Of primary importance is a solid grounding in the craft of musical composition. The do-it-yourself plumber who succeeds only in flooding the kitchen floor is usually long on good intentions but short on competence.

How does one judge a piece of music to be well crafted? How does one judge a chair to be well crafted, well made? If a chair falls to pieces the first time one sits in it, it is probably not very well made. On the other hand, if one can sit in it comfortably for long periods of time without tiring, it is serving the purpose for which it was intended. In judging a piece of music one can ask: does it fit the purpose for which it was intended? Does it bear repeated use without becoming boring or trite? Does it observe appropriate patterns of melodic, harmonic, rhythmic, and formal construction? Is the text effectively reflected in the music? Such questions can provide a starting point for frank and honest criticism and evaluation. But they must serve, first of all, as the basis for candid, honest, unreserved self-criticism by the composer.

This lack of self-criticism and careful, honest, and frank evaluation by composers themselves and by publishers (who sometimes have other criteria by which to judge what they will or will not publish) is all too evident in the flood of material which gushes forth year after year from a variety of presses. Too much of this music is shoddily written, often based on texts which, from a literary and theological point of view, leave much to be desired, clearly pander to popular tastes, and will soon be out of print once the initial enthusiasm—if there is any—has worn off. Good church music is seldom, if ever, written by musical dilettantes, however praiseworthy their intentions. But for those who are constantly sharpening the tools of their musical craft, who are always seeking greater skill and understanding of the art of musical composition, the rewards can be great indeed.

Where standards of craftsmanship are disdained, it is no wonder that the easy effect, the saccharine harmony, the obligatory and predictable rhythmic syncopation, and the arpeggiated bass line have become the new standards of acceptance. Erik Routley once remarked that

> there is . . . no miserable hymn or demoralising hymn tune, no mawkish anthem or organ voluntary, no spiritually depressing piece of church furniture, but somebody has thought it beautiful.[10]

What results in the ugly, Routley reminds us, is often pretentiousness, where behind the façade there is little or no substance. Such pretentiousness may manifest itself in a combination of cheap materials, large and impressive size, combined with a touch of bombast. It may also manifest itself in a piety which disdains craft and technique.

An Environment of Stability and Continuity

In nourishing and supporting the vocation of the composer, the Church needs to recognize the advantage to the composer of a relatively stable and settled environment in which to work. While American culture has been anything but stable and settled over the past half-century or so, with the publication in the late '70s and early '80s of *Lutheran Book of Worship*, *Lutheran Worship*, and, more recently in the early '90s, of *Christian Worship*, a more settled state of affairs has prevailed. That situation—at least as far as the official books within Lutheranism is concerned— has provided a stable liturgy, a set of generally established and accepted pericopes upon which composers could draw, and a situation in which composers could generally know what musical possibilities exist in the liturgy and could address them.

This relatively stable situation, however, was and continues to be disrupted by several developments. First has been the almost-constant process of change in the texts of the lectionary, of the appointed lessons, new Bible translations, and new concerns for language. More changes are undoubtedly on the way. Second is the predilection of many pastors to write or "create" their own liturgies week after week, a process usually consisting of pasting together snippets—with little knowledge or understanding of the liturgy—from a variety of "worship resources" which reflect little sympathy toward the historic practice of the Church. Third has been the urge on the part of a number of composers to produce new musical settings of the liturgy, many with texts at variance with official books of the Church and often questionable theology. Such developments are all too common in congregations today.

The constant changes in the texts of the pericopes and other portions of the liturgy have tended to make earlier musical settings of those texts out-of-date at best, and out-of-line at worst, and suggest that new settings of these texts will enjoy only a brief life span until the next revision occurs. This is hardly an incentive for the composer. The weekly invention of new "liturgies" clearly works against the development of communal memory in the worship life of the congregation. The seemingly endless flow of new musical settings of the liturgy, whether using official texts or not, reinforces the practice of dividing the congregation into groups determined by musical tastes, an apparently infinite number of musical fiefdoms, little pop-culture cubbyholes where each worshipper gets his or her own kind of fare. Neither of these scenarios contribute to the stability and continuity which composers find conducive to satisfying and productive work. Yet such developments are a publisher's dream—providing an endless stream of constantly changing liturgical and music material to congregations always seeking the latest developments.

The conflicting views reflected here are not likely to be resolved easily. But the Church should be aware that such instability and impermanence—where circumstances of vital importance to the composer's task are in a constant state of flux—does not bode well for the work of the composer seeking to advance a healthy musical and liturgical life in the Church and to contribute to the well-being and vitality of the worship life of the congregation. If such a situation continues, serious composers, I am afraid, will simply walk away, abandoning the field either to a battery of pious, eager, well-meaning dilettantes, or to more mercenary-minded composers all too ready to write whatever sells, leaving the Church in an even more perilous situation than that in which it now finds itself. That such is already happening should be quite clear, even to those with minimal powers of observation.

One of the current shibboleths of our time trumpets the need for change. There is much in the worship and music life of the church that needs change. For most congregations, what the term "traditional worship" usually describes is, at best, only a pale reflection of the fullness and richness of the Church's tradition. At its worst, it reflects that tradition's distortion, perversion, or abandonment. On the other hand, what often passes for music in so-called "contemporary worship" services is, by any reasonable standard, hardly contemporary at all, but rather the appropriation of some of the shallowest music of the contemporary culture usually coupled with highly questionable texts. The result is shoddy theology coupled with dubious musical material and workmanship served up as our firstfruits in the proclamation of the Gospel. Many have not been fooled at all; most will not be fooled for long.

What congregations need, and many long for, is neither a return to so-called "traditional" worship, nor a leap into the shallow waters of the so-called "contemporary." What is needed is a rediscovery of the depth, richness, authenticity, and relevance of the Church's treasury of worship and song—and the continued contributions to that treasury today by composers who know their craft, who know and love the liturgy, and who seek to draw worshippers into an ever-deepening experience of "wonder, love, and praise." That would be a change worth working and striving for.

For the Church, its congregations, and its publishers to view the composer not simply as a product to be peddled by any good marketer, but as a long-term asset in need of careful nurture and support, and to whom is given ongoing commitment, would be real change. And that would be a change from which both the composer and the Church today would benefit, and in which both would find not only a challenge but an opportunity of boundless dimension.

Notes

1. Carl Schalk, *God's Song in a New Land: Lutheran Hymnals in America* (St. Louis: Concordia, 1995), 13.
2. This discussion focuses on the combination of words and music. Instrumental music, apart from text-related melodies, is another subject, but not the concern here.
3. Carl Schalk, *Luther on Music: Paradigms of Praise* (St. Louis: Concordia, 1998), 49.
4. See Robert W. Jenson, *Systematic Theology*, vol. 1, *The Triune God* (New York: Oxford University Press, 1997), 5.
5. Schalk, *Luther on Music*, 37.
6. Ibid., 38.
7. Jenson, 134.
8. Schalk, *Luther on Music*, 39.
9. From the *Witness*, a publication of the Biblical Witness Fellowship, a renewal movement within the United Church of Christ, quoted in *First Things* 99 (August/September 1999): 97–98.
10. Erik Routley, *Church Music and Theology* (London: SCM, 1959), 31.

V

Meditations and Homilies

A Lament for Resounding Praise

And I will stop the music of your songs.
—Ezek. 26:13

Both the sixteenth-century Protestant Reformation and the twentieth-century Vatican II, it is widely observed, set God's people free to sing their praises in psalms and hymns. Through the ages, a variety of spiritual canticles has constituted the people's unique liturgy of song. In our time, the sound of singing congregations has traditionally characterized much of both Protestant and Catholic worship.

But today, congregational song is in serious trouble. It is being strangled by the good—though often ill-informed—intentions of some architects, pastors, church building committees, and church musicians who simply haven't done their homework.

Having literally been sold a bill of goods by church furnishing houses, architects, and others who should know better, many parishes have allowed their church buildings to become surrogate living rooms with wall-to-wall carpet, cushioned seats, and an aura of comfy coziness. Worshipping at the altar of "dry" (i.e., dead) sound, architects and church interior designers continue building and furnishing monuments to lackluster liturgy and stifled song. The symbol of the movement: the padded pew. Its marching song: "Sit Down, O People of God."

The result, of course, is an abominable acoustical environment. In church after church, the song of the faithful—in fact, the total sound of worship—is muffled and hushed, the victim of an environment that inhibits and represses, that stifles and suppresses the best efforts of congregations to lift up their voices as one in praise and adoration.

Originally published in *The Christian Century* (March 23-30, 1983).

The designers' goal seems to be the creation of a hushed funeral parlor atmosphere in which no sound can be allowed to disturb the private meditation of the people. If not the funeral parlor, the model must be the radio studio. The watchword concerning sound is "Absorb! Absorb!" Where the voices of worshippers should be buoyed up, reinforced, and made ever more vital as they "do their liturgy," they are more likely to be smothered by ubiquitous carpet, omnipresent acoustical tile, porous brick walls, and thick drapes.

In recent months I visited several middle-western churches. I had the opportunity to experience again the agony and the ecstasy of both good and bad acoustical environments and their effect on the vitality of worship. Two examples stand out. They are undoubtedly typical of hundreds of other similar churches throughout the nation. Both church buildings were small- to medium-sized, seating perhaps 200 to 300. Both were comfortably full when I attended, though not jammed to capacity. The people reflected what I suppose to be a fairly normal mixture of children, teenagers, young couples with children, the middle-aged, and the elderly. The hymns sung were familiar to the people. But there, at least as far as the singing and general participation in worship was concerned, the similarity ended. The two churches were as different as night and day.

In the first church—a modest-sized, suburban St. Louis A-frame with tile floor, plaster walls, and wooden ceiling—the participation in worship and song was thrilling. Full-throated and exuberant, the singing was led by a modest-sized pipe organ which sounded fuller and larger than its 25 ranks of pipes suggested it could. Young and old joined together in songs of praise which almost raised the roof. The resonance of the building encouraged even the recalcitrant and those who could only drone along an octave below the prescribed pitch to join in. It didn't matter. When we sang "Hallelujah! Let Praises Ring!" to Philip Nicolai's majestic tune, the praises really rang. Even those songs of a more subdued and quietly reverent nature were haloed and made vibrant by the rich reverberation of the building.

The song was the voice of God's people at prayer. The building was the instrument upon which that song was played. And the sound of the building reinforced, amplified, and unified our individual contributions, enabling us to sound as one. The congregation that morning hardly seemed to notice the special sound of their building. They were used to it and what it meant for their common prayer. To this visitor, however, it was evident that it was the physical character of the building which facilitated such a vital and lively response of the people in word and song.

The second church building—in another city—was depressing indeed. It was as though we were singing into a giant sponge which sopped up the sound as soon as it was out of our mouths. I could hear only myself and the two people closest by. Others were singing, but our song was a gray mumble. The organ which accompanied us was larger than the first church's—a relatively new instrument designed and built, I was told, especially with congregational singing in mind. But strangled by the oppressive deadness of the building, it was forced to play full out most of the time simply to be heard.

We sang the Venerable Bede's great American text "A hymn of glory let us sing, new songs through the world shall ring," but the ringing was largely in my mind. As I sang what passes for my own full-throated sound, I realized that people were staring, wondering who this stranger was who presumed to lead the singing all by himself. I tempered my voice, retreating to a more subdued sound. The listless and lifeless sound of worship spread like a contagious infection, effectively muting every other aspect of the church's gathering that morning.

It was the building that prevented us from actualizing all that we knew was true: that we were the *people* of God gathered together for *common* prayer. Instead we were forced to fight the depressing acoustics. The building won.

The prodigal use of the sound-deadening material has been aided and abetted by several basic misconceptions about what corporate worship is and how it is most effectively done.

A renewed understanding of the Church as the people of God and the liturgy as their work suggests that not only is the arrangement of the worship space important but an acoustical environment which enables the people to do their work is crucial.

For much of American Protestantism, the Sunday gathering for worship has become primarily the time for a private moment with God. It is too often a time that is personalistic and without reference to those about us. But if we have been listening at all to the shapers of liturgical renewal, worship is first of all the *corporate* response of God's people. Together we offer our common prayer, praise, and supplication. For many Roman Catholics, the realization following Vatican II that the people were to participate actively and corporately came as a shock. The Mass had been something that others did while the people simultaneously carried on their private devotional exercises. Protestants have their own parallels to that privatistic tradition.

A bright, lively, and reinforcing acoustical environment is important, therefore, primarily for the sake of the congregation. Certainly a live acoustical situation has much to do with the success or failure of much choral and organ music, particularly where the resources are modest, the singers few and the organ weak. Church musicians will be the first to affirm that fact. The building itself is an instrument which must be designed so that the praise of God—whether spoken or sung, whether with voices or instruments—is a thing of beauty, lifting the spirits, bringing God's people together in a unified whole, encouraging and reinforcing their song, rather than draining its vocal energy as it attempts its praise and prayer.

A second misconception is the idea that live acoustics are possible only in large, cavernous interiors. Even the most cursory visits will reveal that some of the finest acoustical environments for congregational song are to be found in church buildings of modest size where care has been taken to ensure that hard, reflecting surfaces of walls, ceilings, and floors predominate. Ironically, a whole new industry has developed which attempts to introduce—through elaborate and expensive sound systems—artificial reverberation into a building whose natural resonance has been destroyed.

A third misconception mistakenly pits the spoken word against congregational song. Such alternatives are often set against each other, as though one must win, the other lose. There are, of course, parishes in which the sermon is the single focus. Where that is so, congregational participation in worship is largely ancillary and subordinate.

What is often overlooked where choices between singing and speaking are suggested, however, is that a worship space sufficiently reverberant for spirited singing can easily be made suitable for public speaking. But a worship space designed only with the speaking voice in mind has effectively been ruined for the music-making of congregation, choir, and organ. Since the people's song—whether hymns, psalms, or liturgy—is such an important and vital ingredient in worship, it is not only natural but imperative that the public speaking voice accommodate itself to an environment that is sufficiently live for effective congregational song.

Recapturing a vital sound for congregational song will mean, among other things, the recovery of the congregation's awareness of its role as chief "actor" in worship, a refusal by parishes with smaller buildings to acquiesce to a cathedral complex that suggests that good acoustics are possible only in large interior spaces, and a realization that vibrant acoustics are not incompatible with the needs of public speech.

All this may mean ridding buildings of all those sound-deadening furnishings with which so many are burdened. It may mean a return to the simple integrity of slate or tile instead of carpet, and wooden ceilings uncluttered and unencumbered with acoustical tile. It may mean installing or uncovering hard surfaces for walls and ceilings.

If congregations ever become seriously exercised about the "sound of worship" and its importance for their corporate praise and prayer, there is no telling what might happen. Worship spaces might once again come to life with the canticles of the faithful. Organs might once again speak out bright and clear. Churches might once again become halls of resounding praise. Even heretofore recalcitrant singers might be enticed into joining the song.

Such a joyful noise would certainly make glad the heart of Isaac Watts, were he here to enjoy it. His paraphrase of Psalm 100 said it well:

> We'll crowd thy gates with thankful songs,
> High as the heav'ns our voices raise;
> And earth, with all its thousand tongues,
> Shall fill thy courts with sounding praise.
>
> (*Lutheran Worship*, #454)

The only honest—though not very attractive—alternative seems to be a respectful silence.

A Song for Silent Praise

There was silence in heaven about the space of half an hour.
—Rev. 8:1

Americans are a noisy people, and ours is a noisy culture. Our lives are filled with unremitting racket. Whether we live in a bustling city or the idyllic countryside, whatever our social standing or economic station, Americans seem obsessed by the need for unending sound to accompany their waking hours.

We awaken to the buzzing of the alarm clock. At day's end, we are lulled to sleep by machines simulating rain, ocean waves, or other continuous humming. And in between, our days are filled with ceaseless sound.

Places roaring overhead shake our walls and crack our plaster. The rumbling of cars and trucks reverberates throughout our houses. In the streets our ears are assaulted by oversized portable radios, and at home the stereo devotee demonstrates enthusiasm for his or her equipment by turning up the volume to the limits of human endurance. At work, "white noise" machines drown out other sounds. At play, solitary joggers need personal stereos to help them persevere. Despite the best efforts of those who bemoan its effects on the environment and attempt to contain it, incessant noise accompanies our lives from morning to night.

Indeed, silence is usually seen as an anomaly, a digression from the norm, some kind of deviant behavior. "He is so quiet," we say, suggesting something must be wrong, that it is perhaps a symptom of illness.

Church worship leaders have not escaped this frenetic drive to avoid silence. They believe that there must always be some sort of sound. Or-

---
Originally published in *The Christian Century* (March 23-30, 1988).

ganists, egged on by pastors and parishioners from the "no dead spots" school of worship learn to "doodle" until the next sounds can begin. The famous organist E. Power Biggs, once exhorted by a pastor to "play a few chords while I go from here to there," suggested that if he wanted simply some kind of perfunctory noise, the pastor need merely "mumble a few words."

Many consider silence in worship a breach of etiquette, to be avoided at all costs. Certainly no one would actually plan for moments in which nothing is really happening! And should such moments occur, they are certainly unintentional: the pastor has lost her place, the organist can't find the right hymn, or someone has expired in the choir loft. From such a perspective, worship becomes continual noise, noise, noise—to be sure, often carefully orchestrated noise, but noise nevertheless. The only exception to this rule is the "moment of prayer," the briefer the better, and best accompanied by soft chords from the organ.

Traditional liturgy leads us in a different direction. In the past, silence played a significant role in Christian worship. Today, despite the general attitude described above, some worshippers, of various denominations, are beginning to recover moments of silence as an important and integral part of gathering to hear the Word and celebrate the sacrament. Periods of silence for quiet meditation on psalms, lessons, or sermons are sometimes finding a place in worship. Silence following confession and absolution, as part of community prayers and in connection with the breaking of bread, is appearing as a meaningful part of some parish liturgies.

Many of us, uncomfortable with such silence, fidget in our pews, shuffle our bulletins, or page through the hymnal, not knowing quite what to do or what is expected of us. But we can learn.

We can learn that if a psalm has been well sung, a lesson effectively read, or a sermon preached with power and authority, we benefit from quietly pondering its meaning for our lives.

We can learn that it takes time for real silence to settle in on a worshipping community, and that for silence to be most effective, it must be ample, giving us sufficient opportunity to ponder the significance of what we have heard.

Pastors and worship leaders can learn that it takes effort and patience to help people understand how profitably to use periods of silence. To help their congregations experience the riches inherent in silence, worship leaders must carefully prepare and sensitively introduce it in services.

But most of all, worshipping communities can discover the richness and blessing of reflection and contemplation—opportunities denied by the view of worship services as something to be rushed through or as a form of entertainment.

Silence in worship slows the frantic pace of contemporary worship—and contemporary life. It allows the community to contemplate and reflect, or provides time for individual prayer in the midst of communal prayer.

To be sure, there is a time for resounding praise, for pulling out all the stops, for making a joyful noise. But there is also a time to "be still and know that I am God," for quietly pondering God's goodness and the meaning of the Word, for the song of silent praise.

Brief Meditations on the "Great O Antiphons" of Advent

Introduction

Advent is a time for watching and waiting, two things in our culture we have almost forgotten how to do. We are impatient people. Waiting is not part of our vocabulary. We want everything yesterday, or at least "as soon as possible." Yet the psalmist encourages us to "Wait for the Lord; be strong, and let our heart take courage; yea, wait for the Lord" (Ps. 27:14). But not waiting in a passive sense: a waiting that has us on our tiptoes, in eager anticipation of what is to come.

In Advent we are to wait like the ten virgins with our lamps trimmed and burning, watching, yearning, for the bridegroom to appear. We are to be like the watchman on the watchtower waiting for that first glimmer of light, a signal that the day is breaking and the night is over.

The Church's liturgy has given us the matchless gift of seven brief prayers to assist us and to help focus our waiting and watching, remembering him who once came as a little child, who comes to us daily in Word and sacrament, and who will come again at the end of the ages.

As the days of Advent draw to a close, as the light grows shorter and the darkness grows longer, let these antiphons help us to focus our waiting and watching for he is surely coming soon.

Written for use at Grace Lutheran Church, River Forest, Ill. (Advent 2003).

O Wisdom, proceeding from the mouth of the Most High, pervading and permeating all creation, mightily ordering all things: Come and teach us the way of prudence.

Here are two words we rarely hear in our day: wisdom and prudence. We live, we are told, in an "information age" where we know so much, where knowledge is king, and yet where we don't know what to do with all that knowledge. Wisdom, the dictionary tells us, is the understanding of what is true, right, or lasting. The wisdom of which this antiphon speaks is that wisdom which "proceeds from the mouth of the Most High": the Word which is the wisdom which pervades and permeates all creation, the Word which was in the beginning with God, the Word which in the fullness of time the Father sent into this world, the Word made flesh who dwelt and dwells among us.

Prudence implies not simply self-control and cautiousness, but good judgment, common sense, the capacity for judging in advance the probable results of one's action. But we are imprudent people. So often we not only do not judge what the results of our actions might be, we hardly care.

In the midst of this imprudent and unwise world, we can only pray: O Wisdom, come and teach us the way of prudence.

O Adonai and ruler of the house of Israel, who appeared to Moses in the burning bush and gave him the Law on Sinai: Come with an outstretched arm and redeem us.

This prayer addresses Adonai as the one who appeared to his people in two specific circumstances. First, to Moses in the burning bush, that numinous moment when the Lord said to Moses, "Take off your shoes from your feet for the place where you are standing is holy ground" (Exod. 3:5). Second, the Lord is addressed as the one who "gave the law" on Mount Sinai. When someone needs correcting or set on the right path, we say we need to "lay down the law," set that person straight, tell that person what they should or should not do.

That is what the law does. It shows us that we have deviated from the right path. It shows us that no matter how hard we may try, we have not done what we should have done, or we have done what we should not have done. In short, we are alienated from God, we are in bondage to sin; we cannot free ourselves.

But in the petition that follows, Adonai is pictured in quite a different way, as one with outstretched arms, as a loving father who beckons us with open arms to embrace us and be reconciled to him. In the mystery of the Holy Trinity, the very same Lord who has "laid down the law" has fulfilled it on our behalf in his life of perfect obedience to the will of the Father.

The good news of Advent is that even while we were in bondage to sin and unable to fulfill God's law, God reached out to us. God's only begotten Son became like us in every way, took our place and in our stead perfectly fulfilled the Law on our behalf, and by his death and resurrection redeemed us. As we await his coming, we can only pray: O Adonai, who gave the law on Sinai, come with outstretched arms and redeem us.

O Root of Jesse, standing as an ensign before the peoples, before whom all kings are mute, to whom the nations will do homage: Come quickly to deliver us.

We have a tree in our yard that we have been trying to get rid of for as long as I can remember. We have repeatedly cut it down, leaving only a stump in the ground. But no matter how hard we try, no matter how much we ignore it, new shoots keep coming back. We have learned that no matter how dead we think that stump may be, new life can still spring forth.

When the fortunes of Israel had reached bottom, Isaiah foretold that the savior would come forth as a shoot from the dead stump of Jesse's lineage, and as a flower of the branch that shall grow out of his roots. The familiar sixteenth-century German hymn proclaimed:

> Lo, how a Rose e'er blooming, from tender stem hath sprung!
> Of Jesse's lineage coming as prophets long have sung,
> It came, a floweret bright, amid the cold of winter, when half-spent was the night.
>
> (*Lutheran Service Book*, #359)

This improbable shoot from the stump of Jesse—this Rose blooming in the dead of winter—stands as an ensign before the people, a sign which comes to us in the cold and darkness of our lives to be a sure signal that God has not forsaken us, a seal of God's promise that amid all the trials and troubles of this life, this "True man, yet very God from sin and death now saves us, and shares our every load."

O Root of Jesse, to whom all the nations will one day pay homage, come quickly to deliver us.

O Key of David and scepter of the house of Israel, you open and no one can close, you close and no one can open: Come and rescue the prisoners who are in darkness and the shadow of death.

There is nothing a prisoner desires more than a key which can open the door to the cell in which he finds himself, a key which brings rescue and freedom from bondage. By our very nature as human beings we are all in bondage to something. We are all prisoners, captives of our own appetites and desires. The one whose coming we await, Jesus the Christ, is the Key of the line of David, the Savior for which we long, who opens the prison doors of our captivity.

Each week in the church's liturgy we confess "that we are in bondage to sin and cannot free ourselves." *We cannot free ourselves!* Yet in our darkness and in our mistaken understanding, how hard we try. Yet the harder we try the more we realize that we have "sinned by what we have done and by what we have left undone. We have not loved you with our whole heart; we have not loved our neighbors as ourselves". (*Lutheran Book of Worship*, Brief Order for Confession and Forgiveness, p. 56.)

We yearn for someone to come and save us from our sin. We look for someone to come and free us from our captivity and from the darkness in which we live our lives of quiet desperation. That one is the Key of David, the one who is to rule Israel, his people, Christ the Savior. From the depth of our bondage to sin, we can only pray: You, who open the door of our prison and no one can close it, come and rescue us who sit in darkness and in the shadow of death.

O Dayspring, splendor of light everlasting: Come and enlighten those who sit in darkness and in the shadow of death.

We sit in darkness and in the shadow of death. We cry with the Psalmist, "How long, O Lord?" We are like those depicted in the old Finnish hymn:

> Lost in the night do the people yet languish
> Longing for morning the darkness to vanquish,
> Plaintively heaving a sign full of anguish.
> Will not day come soon? Will not day come soon?
> *(Lutheran Book of Worship, #394)*

Is there one of us here today that does not stumble in the darkness of our own making? Is there one of us here today who does not dwell in the shadow of death?

Yet the good news of Advent is that no matter how dark the night, no matter how lost we are, the darkness will soon give way to light. The message of Advent is that "The people who walked in darkness have seen a great light" (Is. 9:2). That light is the Dayspring from on high who comes into the darkness of our lives to bring light and life and healing on his wings.

It is that light which enlightens us all who sit in darkness and in the shadow of death. It is the light for which the watchman on the towers are waiting, watching for that first glimpse of light, the promise of the coming of the light everlasting. It is the light spoken of in the final stanza of that same Finnish hymn:

> Light o'er the land of the needy is beaming;
> Rivers of life through its deserts are streaming,
> Bringing all peoples a Savior redeeming.

It is that light for which we pray: come and enlighten those who sit in darkness and in the shadow of death.

O King of the nations, a ruler they long for, the cornerstone uniting all people: Come and save us all, whom you formed out of clay.

He who came into the world, who comes to us in Word and Sacrament, and who will come again at the end of time: he is the cornerstone who unites all people. No building is complete and unified until the cornerstone has been put into place. And just as a cornerstone unites the intersecting walls of a building, Christ is the cornerstone who unites, unifies, and brings together all things.

This King of the nations, this ruler we long for, this cornerstone which connects and brings together what was disconnected and torn asunder, this one who has created us all out of clay, is the One who has become clay like us, who has taken on human form that we who have been alienated and disconnected from the Father might be once again restored and united with him. This King of all the nations is the One who has come, who still comes among us, and who will come at the last day to unite us and all who believe in him, and bring us and all creation to eternal glory, and into the reconciled relationship which was God's original intent for us all.

You, who formed us out of clay, come and save us.

O Emmanuel, our king and our lawgiver, the anointed of the nations and their Savior: Come and save us, O Lord our God.

Emmanuel! It is the name given in Isaiah's prophecy: "Behold a virgin shall conceive and bear a son, and shall call his name Emmanuel." (Isaiah 7:14) It means "God is with us." It is the name of our King and Lawgiver, the Anointed of the nations, the name of the one who is our Savior, as the familiar hymn reminds us.

> Christ, by highest heav'n adored, Christ, the everlasting Lord,
> Late in time behold him come, offspring of the virgin's womb.
> Veiled in flesh the Godhead see! Hail, incarnate deity!
> Pleased as man with us to dwell, Jesus, our Emmanuel!

Here is the scandal of the Gospel: that God took on human form to be like us, to take upon himself our guilt, to suffer, to die, and be raised from the dead by the glory of the Father. The message of Advent and Christmas is that God came into the world to die. When we separate the incarnation, God's coming in the flesh, from the death and resurrection of our Lord, we trivialize and sentimentalize both. Advent helps us understand that they belong together, that God came into the world to die—for us.

And so we watch and we wait for his coming. Like the sentinel on the high tower we strain to see the first glimpse of the Dayspring from on high. Like the watching virgins we await the coming of the Bridegroom who will take us to the banquet hall where we will celebrate the feast that has no end. John's Revelation gives us Jesus simply and directly: "Surely I am coming soon" (Rev. 22:20). He *is* coming soon. Come and save us, O Lord our God.

Mary and the Pound of Spikenard

A Homily for Monday in Holy Week

John 12:1-8

In the name of the Father, the Son, and the Holy Spirit.

Lent, we say, is a time of quiet introspection and thoughtful self-examination. We take stock of our lives to see where we have done what we should not have done, and where we have not done what we should have done. Many Christians "give something up" for Lent. Many embark on particular Lenten disciplines in their personal lives. And this self-examination intensifies during what Christians have long called "Holy Week" as we look with special emphasis on the suffering and death of our Lord.

But today's Gospel reading strikes a note that seems somehow dissonant with all of that. The story is a familiar one.

Just a few days before the Passover, Jesus travels to Bethany to the house of Mary and Martha and Lazarus, whom he had sometime earlier raised from the dead. While at dinner, Mary takes a pound of spikenard, a very expensive ointment, a kind of perfume, and anoints Jesus' feet, wiping his feet with her hair. Judas, the treasurer of the disciples, like many treasurers, questions the sheer lavishness of this display. "Why waste money on something like this," we can hear him say. (We hear echoes of Judas's question even in our own day: "The money this spikenard cost could certainly be put to better use. Give it to missions, the poor, or use it for the new boiler that needs replacing.") Jesus finally rebukes Judas saying, "Let her observe it now against the day of my burial," a day which he knew was coming all too soon.

Two comments. First, here, as elsewhere in Scripture, we see the clear connection between Jesus' incarnation and his suffering and death. Jesus was born to die. As Jesus connects Mary's use of ointment and his burial, it reminds us of an earlier and similar association we have heard in connection with Jesus' birth. Of the three gifts of the Wise Men (gold, frankincense, and myrrh), myrrh, in the words of the Epiphany hymn, was the last prophetic sign: "with myrrh they shadow forth his sepulcher." A lesser-known Christmas carol text anticipates Jesus' death in these words: "When he is King they will clothe him in grave sheets, myrrh for embalming and wood for a crown." And now, just a few days before he goes to Jerusalem to suffer and die, Mary shows us this sign of her extravagant and unselfconscious love with another indication of this connection between his birth and his death.

Second, Mary's action was extravagant in the extreme. She took the most precious thing she possessed and spent it all on Jesus. "Love," William Barclay reminds us, "is not love if it nicely calculates the cost. It gives its all and its only regret is that it has not still more to give."

But even Mary's extravagant gift pales in comparison with the gift our Lord gives us and which we remember this and every Holy Week: the gift of himself for our salvation. And it is a gift we receive each and every time we come to the Lord's table and receive, not a symbol, a memory, or some sort of "spiritual" gift, but the very body and blood of our Lord spilled out for us in his passion and death. "This is my body given for you." "This is my blood shed for you."

Was it a coincidence that it was in the context of a meal that Mary showed her extravagant love for her Savior? Is it a coincidence that Jesus shows his great love for us also in a meal? No hymn writer has captured both the lavish love which Christ expended for us and the making of himself available to us in the bread and wine as well as Martin Franzmann's great text "O kingly love." His second stanza, written for the 450th anniversary of the Reformation, rings as true today as the day it was written.

> O lavish Love, that didst prepare a table bounteous as thy heart,
> That men might leave their puny care and taste and see how good thou art,
> This day we raise our song of praise, adoring thee,

> That in the days when alien sound had all but drowned
> Thine ancient, true, and constant melody,
>
> Thy mighty hand did make a trumpet none could silence or mistake,
>
> Thy living breath did blow for all the world to hear, living and clear:
>
> The feast is ready. Come to the feast, the good and the bad. Come and be glad! Greatest and least, come to the feast!
>
> ("O Kingly Love, That Faithfully," *Lutheran Worship* #346; Copyright © 1969 Concordia Publishing House)

John adds this comment to Mary's anointing of Jesus' feet: he says "and the house was filed with the perfume of the ointment." There are two meanings here: the factual and obvious one which lies on the surface, the smell of the ointment filled the room, and a second, the suggestion that the whole Church was filled with the sweet memory of Mary's action. One lovely deed becomes the possession of the whole Church.

Like the house of Mary and Martha, this house of Grace is also filled with the sweet smell of God's lavish goodness: in the sweet-smelling oil with which those baptized are sealed with the Spirit, in the smell of wine which permeates this house at Holy Communion, in the incense at Evening Prayer as the prayers of the faithful ascend to the throne of God. Let this house always be filled with the sweet smell of God's lavish goodness to us and the sweet smell of our response to his goodness to us.

Member, Dismember, and Remember

A Homily for Good Friday

John 17:20-26/Psalm 22:1-23

In these words from John's Gospel, often referred to as the high priestly prayer, Jesus prays to his Father on behalf of his disciples. He prays that they may be one—that they, and we his disciples, might be one with the Father as he, Jesus, was one with the Father, and that as disciples, they and we might be one with each other.

As this Lenten journey comes to its climax in these three most holy days, three words seem to capture what this journey is all about.

The first word is *"members."* Scripture reminds us that we are members of one body, the Church. Our membership comes by virtue of our baptism when we were washed of our sins, sealed with the Holy Spirit, and marked by the cross of Christ forever. It is that cross we remember especially today. As Christians, we live our lives from birth to death under the sign of the cross, the first sign made upon our foreheads when we entered into His Church at baptism, and the last sign which will be made over our bodies as we are laid into the grave. Under this baptismal sign we were "membered" into Christ's body, the Church.

The second word is *"dismembered."* So often we seem not to be members of that Church, but dismembered, removed, cut off. The Latin prefix *dis-* means "apart"—or the opposite of what follows the prefix. If we are dysfunctional, we are the opposite of functional. If we have a

---

Preached at Grace Lutheran Church, River Forest, Ill., March 29, 2002.

disease, we are the opposite of a body at "ease." If we are dismembered, we are pulled or torn apart from the body to which we should belong. In the creeds of the Church we confess that "I believe in one, holy, catholic, and apostolic Church." We believe in it, because its holiness, its catholicity, its apostolic character, and certainly its oneness are often so hard to see. Because of sin, our brokenness—the dismemberment in our individual lives as well as in our life together in the Church—is all too evident as we strive each day to live the life of faith. We are, as Luther phrased it, at the same time, both saints and sinners. Yet we are still members of Christ's body, we say, and so we are, in the face of all the evidence to the contrary. Lent calls us, with Luther, to say with courage, conviction, and sure confidence when faced with trials, temptations, and the troubles of this life, in the face of our dismemberment as sinners, "I am baptized." It is in our baptism that we have the seal that neither life, nor death, nor anything else can keep us from the love of God in Christ Jesus.

But if the season of Lent, and especially this week we call "Holy," is about anything, it is about the third word, about *"remembering."* To remember certainly means to recall, but it also means to "member again," to join what was disjoined, to bring together what was torn apart. It means to become ever more firmly attached to the body of Christ, as members of his Church, and as members of one another. We remember first God's promise to us in our baptism. As we walk this Lenten season with those preparing to be baptized tomorrow at the Vigil of Easter, we affirm with them our oneness in baptism. There is no doubt. We stand firm in God's baptismal promise.

And with the echo of Maundy Thursday still ringing in our ears, "This is my body, this is my blood given and shed for you for the forgiveness of your sins," our Lord reminds us that we are to do this "in remembrance" of him. To remember in this sense is not simply to mentally recall that sometime long ago something happened, but in a far deeper sense, to become members once again, to become part of that story and to have it become for us a part of our living present. To remember, in this sense, is to graft us ever more strongly into the body of Christ, to "remember" us into the Church.

Was the dying thief, who cried out to our Lord on the cross saying,

"Jesus, remember me when you come into your kingly power," just keeping his options open, hedging his bets, or was he saying more than just "Keep me in mind when you come into your kingdom?" Or was he in reality asking that he be grafted into the vine which was Christ? We cannot know for certain. What we can know for certain is that through our baptism God has made us members of his body, the Church. That amid all the trials, troubles, and temptations of life that would tear us from his grasp, that would dismember us from his body, his promise is certain and sure. That as we share his body and blood in Holy Communion in remembrance of him, that promise is renewed again and again as we are "remembered" into Christ's body, the Church.

What we know for certain is that amid the grief and sorrows of life, we remember how it all turned out some 2000 years ago, how sorrow and sadness was turned to joy, how death was conquered on a cross. What we know for certain is that in spite of whatever the world may throw our way, in spite of hopelessness and despair which can so easily beset us, we stand firm in the sure knowledge of the hope of the resurrection of the dead, and that we can indeed, with Christians everywhere, call this Friday "Good."

In Jesus' name, Amen.

New Year: It's about Time

> But when the time had fully come, God sent forth his Son, born of a woman, born under the law, to redeem those who were under the law, so that we might receive adoption as sons. And because you are sons, God has sent the Spirit of his Son into our hearts, crying, "Abba! Father!" So through God you are no longer a slave, but a son, and if a son, then an heir.
>
> (Gal. 4:3-7)

Janus was the god of transitions. He was one of the many gods in the Roman pantheon of gods, the god of gates and doorways. He was two-faced, not in the sense in which we tend to use the word. He had two faces. One face resolutely looked backward to the past, the other face looked forward to the future. His festival month was January.

It is not unlike what most of us do at this time of year—and in today's cantata—in which we look back in time and give thanks to God for the blessings of the past year and look forward

in time with hope for God's continued grace toward us in the year ahead.

Janus was all about time. And in so many ways our lives too are wrapped up with time. How often don't we hear the complaint: "I just don't have enough time to do everything that needs to be done." For others, time hangs heavy in their lives. Young people want to be older and older people, in so many ways, try to recapture their youth. Young people can't wait until they are old enough to get their driver's license. Others dread the day the mail carrier brings them news that they are now

---

First preached for a Vespers service with a Bach cantata—*Gottlob! nun geht das Jahr zu Ende* ("Praise God! The Year Now Draws to a Close," BWV 28)—at Grace Lutheran Church, River Forest, Ill., January 28, 2007.

eligible for membership in AARP. We worry about "wasting" time. We worry about how we "spend" our time.

We live and die by the clock. We are constantly checking our watches. And if one watch is not enough you can buy a watch with two dials so you can keep track of time in at least two time zones or continents. And if that is not enough, some watches can supply you with the day of the week, the month of the year, the phases of the moon, and a stopwatch as well.

Take a trip in the car with children and their first questions are "Are we there yet?" "How much longer will it take?" And as we grow older we being to ask ourselves in the quiet of our hearts, "How much time do I have left?"

So what about time? Does God really care about our obsession with time? Does God live in some timeless existence and look down with bemused detachment at our obsession with time? Or is it that as Albert Einstein once remarked, "The only reason for time is so that everything doesn't happen at once."

The Apostle Paul in today's lesson gives us a clue. "When the fullness of time had come, God sent forth his son, born of a woman, born under the law, to redeem those who were under the law, so that we might receive adoption as sons." God, when the time was full, when the time was right, when in God's economy of time everything was ready, God broke into our world of time and space, took upon himself our bondage to sin, our worries and concerns, our obsession with time and all that goes with it. Here is the scandal of the good news of the Gospel: that God takes on our human form, becomes like us in every way except that he was sinless. This was the "great exchange" of which the sixteenth-century Lutheran poet wrote:

> [God] undertakes a great exchange,
> Puts on our human frame,
> And in return gives us his realm, his glory and his name.
>
> ("Let All Together Praise Our God,"
> *Lutheran Book of* Worship #47, st. 4)

Christ gives us his name as adopted sons and daughters of the Father. And as adopted sons and daughters we are heirs, inheritors of his kingdom prepared for us from the foundation of the world, a kingdom which will be made manifest to all the world when he comes at the last day. We now live "between the times": between the time when Christ broke into our world as a baby at Bethlehem and the time when he will come again as he promised to draw all people to himself.

This is the gift we celebrate in this cantata this afternoon, the gift we celebrate with voices and instruments: that God who has brought us this far by faith will never abandon us but will continue to be with us and bless us in the days ahead in ways that we cannot yet imagine. But along with the joys and delights of life we will surely experience heartaches, sorrow, and disappointments. God does not promise immunity from all of that. But God does provide a way through them all and promises to be with us whatever may come. In Christ's death and resurrection we have the assurance that the victory is already ours. That nothing, neither life nor death, nor angels, nor principalities, nor powers, nor things present, nor things to come will be able to separate us from the love of God in Christ Jesus won for us at the cross. That is God's promise.

And so we live our lives under the sign of the cross: that sign first traced on our foreheads and breast at our baptism with the words "You are sealed with the cross of Christ forever" and the last sign to be made over us as we are laid into the ground. And in between we live our lives under that sign, the sign with which Luther in his Small Catechism encouraged us to begin and end each day.

But to live under the cross is not to live for ourselves, but first and foremost to live for the sake of the world. Is it possible, as Gerald Schlabach reminds us, for us to imagine "a church . . . that cannot sing without feeding the poor, a church that cannot feed the poor without nourishment from the Eucharist, a church that cannot pass the peace without living peaceably in the world, a church that cannot be peacemakers without depending on prayer, nor pray without joining in robust song"?[1] That is both the vision before us and the task we are given to do.

Nothing says it quite as well as the sixteenth-century Slovak hymn which calls us to place our trust in God whatever the future may bring and which we shall sing at the close of this service.

God, my Lord, my strength, my place of hiding
and confiding in all needs by night and day;
    Though foes surround me,
    and Satan mark his prey,
        God shall have his way.

Christ in me, and I am freed for living
and forgiving, heart of flesh for lifeless stone,
    Now bold to serve him,
    now cheered his love to own,
        nevermore alone.

Up, weak knees and spirit bowed in sorrow!
No tomorrow shall arise to beat you down;
    God goes before you
    and angels all around:
        on your head a crown!

                      (*Lutheran Book of Worship* #484)

As we look back over the past year with thanks to God who has brought us this far by faith, through both joys and sorrows, and as we look forward to the days ahead with all the unknowns that will surely face us, we can rest assured that God will keep his promise to be with us all the way. "No tomorrow shall arise to beat you down; God goes before you and angels all around."

No matter what tomorrow may bring, we can rest secure in the promise of God's presence. God will have his way. God surely will!

In Jesus' name.

Notes

[1] Gerald W. Schlabach, "Statement upon Confirmation in the Catholic Church," blog post (May 29, 2004).

Now Thank We All Our God . . . with Hands

Like an awkward adolescent, most of us just don't know what to do with our hands. Hands often get in the way, which is why we depict someone who is clumsy as "unhandy." Hands easily get us into trouble, which is why parents tell their children to "fold their hands" when praying. We all learn early on that "idle hands are the devil's workshop."

Martin Rinkart, for one, knew what to do with his hands. Use them, he suggests in his seventeenth-century text, to thank God for the wondrous things he has done.

> Now thank we all our God
> with hearts and *hands* and voices (emphasis mine).
> (*Lutheran Book of Worship* #533, #534)

But how does one do that? How does one thank God with one's hands? At certain times and places we thank and praise God with hands raised in prayer or with hands folded in supplication. But we also thank and praise God by using our hands to do our daily work—whatever it may be—to the very best of our ability, whether that work be carpenter, parent, farmer, architect, social worker, or computer programmer.

But who really works with their hands anymore? When was the last time you tried to find a good carpenter to do some necessary repair work, a capable plumber to work on your bathroom, or a reliable mechanic to fix your car?

In today's world we often denigrate those who earn their daily bread through manual labor, placing greater value on the work people do with their brains. "It's getting more and more difficult," we say, "to find people who can really work with their hands." We lament the fact that craftsmen who build and shape are increasingly difficult to find, and we worry that the world is poorer for it.

God worked with his hands and we work with ours. The creation account reminds us that we are God's "handiwork"—the result of God working with his hands. God "formed man of dust," shaping and molding the raw material of the earth, breathing into its nostrils, and man became a living being. In our daily work we, in turn, shape, mold, and form the raw materials of this world —brick and steel, wood and earth, words and notes—into works in which God is praised and glorified through the material stuff of creation.

Our privilege and responsibility as Christians, as faithful stewards and custodians of God's creation, of the gifts and talents God has placed into our hands, is to be the best carpenter, the best farmer, the best poet, the best parent, the best musician of which we are capable. In the honing of our talents and skills in whatever work has been given us to do, we strive always for the best of which we are capable. And in bringing the firstfruits of our talents and abilities and placing them in the service of him who did and still does wondrous things, we are making a profound witness to the world, pointing to the creator of all things who first made us, who first formed us out of the earth. In Richard Mowbray's words,

> Poet, painter, music maker, all your treasures bring;
> Craftsman, actor, graceful dancer, make your offering;
> Join your hands in celebration! let creation shout and sing!
>
> ("Come to Us, Creative Spirit," st. 2)

But even if the modern world too often depreciates "manual labor," we cannot escape the vocabulary of work, labor, and creation. The very words we use to describe our lives and activities remind us that it is through the work of our hands that God is praised and thanked. Parents and teachers "mold" young lives; heredity and environment, we say, "shape" our attitudes; artists "create and form"; we "build" a family; we "carve out" our careers. The vocabulary of laboring with our hands is always with us.

Into such a world of thought Martin Rinckart's hymn bursts in to remind us that the wondrous things we do with our hands—our "handiwork"—is a way of thanking and praising God who has first done wondrous things. This is our vocation as Christians: that we use our talents, great or small, wherever God places us—as parents, as teachers, as musicians, as laborers—and that we use them to the best of our ability, that the work of our hands may be a labor of thanks and praise to the God for all the wondrous things he has done for us.

When we do that we are surely thanking God with our hands. When we do that we are joining the song of the psalmist:

> Let the favor of the Lord our God be upon us, and
> establish thou the work of our hands upon us;
> yea the work of our hands establish thou it.

(Psalm 90:17)

St. Michael and All Angels

Now war arose in heaven, Michael and his angels fighting against the dragon, and the dragon and his angels fought, but they were defeated and there was no longer any place for them in heaven.

And the great dragon was thrown down, that ancient serpent, who is called the Devil and Satan, the deceiver of the whole world—he was thrown down to the earth, and his angels were thrown down with him.

And I heard a loud voice in heaven, saying, "Now the salvation and the power and the kingdom of our God and the authority of his Christ have come, for the accuser of our brethren has been thrown down, who accuses them day and night before our God. And they have conquered him by the blood of the Lamb and by the word of their testimony, for they loved not their lives even unto death.

Rejoice then, O heaven and you that dwell therein! But woe to you, O earth and sea, for the devil has come down to you in great wrath, because he knows that his time is short!"

(Rev.12:7-12)

Today's lesson, the appointed Second Lesson for the Feast of St. Michael and All Angels, tells the story of war in heaven, of angels and Satan, the great deceiver. Michael and his angels battle Satan—the Devil, the deceiver of the world—and he and his angels are thrown out of heaven, thrown down to earth. So watch out, the lesson warns us, Satan and

---

First preached for a Vespers service with a Bach cantata—*Herr Gott, dich loben alle wir* ("Lord God, We All Praise Thee, BWV 130—at Grace Lutheran Church, River Forest, Ill., September 29, 2001.

his minions are angry, and, as 1 Peter reminds us, he prowls around like a roaring lion, looking to see whom he may devour —because his time is short.

Part of my problem—and I suspect yours, as well—is that I have never seen an angel. But I am reasonably certain that the angels that appeared to Daniel, to Zechariah, to Mary, to the shepherds, and to the women at the tomb, did not look like the baroque cherubs or the wispy figures that adorn our greeting cards. Today's culture surrounds with angels. But in poet laureate Billy Collins' book of poems *Questions about Angels*, he notes that

> Of all the questions [we] might want to ask about angels,
> the only one you ever hear is how many can dance on the
>   head of a pin.
>
> No curiosity about how they pass the eternal time
> besides circling the throng chanting in Latin
>
> or delivering a crust of bread to a hermit on earth
> or guiding a boy and girl across a rickety wooden bridge.

I typed the word "angels" into my computer's search engine. The result? Forty-four categories and over twelve hundred sites for angels. If you want to shop for angels, there are over nine hundred sites. If you want to buy one, gift shops and hobby shops will accommodate you. Do you want to tell someone special they're an angel? Hallmark cards will help you out. And if you want to be touched by one, turn to Channel 38, Monday or Wednesday evenings at 8 o'clock. New Age bookstores offer workshops on "angel channeling." And then we have someone's remark that an angel is simply a pedestrian who forgot to jump.

Our culture has trivialized angels beyond recognition. But as Kathleen Norris reminds us in her book, *Angels in the House*, these angels that we encounter in today's culture are not God's angels. Rather they "have become our angels, shaped and fashioned not by God's design and purpose, by our own thoughts and hopes and desires."

And then there is a war. After the events of recent days, it should be clear that words like sin and Satan can no longer be understood simply as metaphors describing humanity's bad side. To think that way simply does not reflect the all-too-stark reality of evil, the demonic, and the diabolical we see all around us. Yet September 11th is simply one example of the battles which rage around us every day. The quiet, desperate wars—in our world, in our homes, within families, between spouses, at work—all testify to the pervasive reality of sin and evil in our lives.

It is into just such a world of quiet desperation that God sends his angels to do his bidding. But God's angels are not the sentimental, effeminate cherubs on the greeting cards. The Christian tradition looks at angels in quite a different light. God's angels are God's messengers, pointing us to Christ. And to a world that before September 11th seemed afraid of nothing, and after September 11th seems afraid of everything, God sends his angels with the same message proclaimed in Luke's Gospel: "Fear not! Don't be afraid." Not simply, "Don't worry, things will look better after a good night's sleep." That is the message of the deceiver of the world. The message of God's angels is to "fear not" because God's final victory in Christ is certain; that Satan —the Devil, the great dragon, the great deceiver—has been conquered. While he prowls around in our lives and in our world, his power is gone; he has already lost the battle.

That has always been the testimony of the Church's song. That great hymn of Fortunatus, written over 1500 years ago and still regularly sung by this congregation at the service of the Veneration of the Cross on Good Friday, begins with the words

> Sing, my tongue, the glorious battle; sing the ending of the fray.
> Now above the cross, the trophy, sound the loud triumphant lay:
> Tell how Christ, the world's redeemer, as a victim won the day.
> (*Lutheran Book of Worship*, #118)

Appointed as the Hymn of the Day for Good Friday, this hymn points us, in the midst of the dark day of Christ's crucifixion, to Easter. It reminds us that Good Friday was not God's final word. That the song we sing, even in the bleakness and blackness of Good Friday, is ultimately the song of triumph and victory. "Sound the loud triumphant lay: tell how Christ, the world's redeemer, as a victim won the day." And the very next day at the Easter Vigil, this congregation reaffirms that message as it signs our loud and clear, in Martin Luther's words, that

> It was a strange and dreadful strife
>   when death with life contended;
> The victory remained with life,
>   the reign of death was ended;
> Holy Scripture plainly says that death
>   is swallowed up by death,
> its sting is lost forever.
>
> ("Christ Jesus Lay in Death's Strong Bands,"
> *Lutheran Book of Worship* #134, st. 4)

No wispy sentimental spirituality here. Just the plain unvarnished truth that though the devil still prowls around, he has lost the battle. The outcome is certain. Life has overcome death. Hope triumphs over despair. Satan's sting is lost forever.

But angels do more than just announce the good news of Christ's triumph over sin, death, and the devil. I vividly recall that in the Lutheran elementary school which I attended, there was a picture that I am certain graced the halls of many Lutheran schools. It was the one referred to in Billy Collins' poem. It pictured two young children walking over a rickety bridge. Hovering in the background was an angel, wings outspread, ready to protect the children from any evil. It was called simply "Guardian Angel." Whatever its artistic merits, the picture echoed the words of The Morning and Evening Blessings from Luther's Small Catechism which we are encouraged to say at the beginning and close of each day: "Let your holy angel be with me, so that the wicked foe may have no power over me." Even our Lord accepted the comfort and ministrations of angels. After Christ's temptations in the wilderness, Matthew's Gospel says: "Then the devil left him, and behold, angels came and ministered to him" (Mt. 4:11). And they minister to us as well, watching over us, shielding us, guarding, and protecting us.

Angels have yet one more task. At our last hour they take us—in the words of today's cantata— to Abraham's bosom, to be with God eternally. Listen to the tenor aria in which, while the solo voice sings "Stay with me, allay my fears, guide me, keep my feet from straying," the solo trumpet plays the simple unadorned melody from the sixteenth-century hymn—"Herzlich lieb hab ich dich, O Herr"—which Bach's congregation knew and which this congregation knows so well. Listen for that melody in the trumpet, and sing along in your hearts the words of the hymn:

> Lord, let at last thine angels come,
> To Abr'ham's bosom bear me home,
> > that I may die unfearing;
> And in its narrow chamber keep
> My body safe in peaceful sleep
> > until Thy reappearing
> And then from death awaken me,
> That these mine eyes with joy may see,
> > O Son of God, thy glorious face,
> > my Savior and my fount of grace.
> Lord Jesus Christ,
> My prayer attend, my prayer attend,
> > and I will praise thee without end!
>
> ("Lord, Thee I Love with All My Heart,"
> *Lutheran Book of Worship* #325, st. 3)

The tenor also asks the angels to help us sing "Holy, holy, holy." Henry Lyte, in his familiar hymn "Praise, My Soul, the King of Heaven" (*Lutheran Book of Worship* #549) wrote, "Angels help us to adore him" This is not a prayer or a plea—as in "angels [comma] help us to adore him"—but a simple statement of fact—"angels [do indeed] help us to adore him." This is, of course, an echo of the words we hear at each celebration of Holy Communion: "Therefore with angels and archangels and all the company of heaven, we laud and magnify your glorious name, ever praising you and singing: Holy, holy, holy." Our song is joined by Michael, Gabriel, Raphael, all the angels, and the entire company of heaven. Perhaps it would better be said that the angels and all the company of heaven are continually singing God's praise before the throne, and we in our little corner of River Forest are privileged to sing along, to join the Church's song which continues from age to age and into eternity.

Some years ago at another Bach cantata service in this church, Rev. Ralph van Loon spoke of a little Swedish country church. He described the altar, set back a bit from the wall, and in front of it a semicircular altar rail at which the parish would gather for communion. He described a church that many of us have seen or know from childhood. But, he reminded us, that half-circle was only half of the circle. The other invisible half of the circle continues around and behind the altar and encompasses all the saints who have gone before, who, together with the angels and archangels, join us in one communion. We need to remember that picture the next time we gather at the altar for Holy Communion. Whether your altar rail is semicircular or straight, completing the circle, which our eyes cannot see, are all the company of heaven, angels, archangels, and all those who have gone before us in the faith—our mothers and fathers, our grandfathers and grandmothers, our sisters, brothers, friends, neighbors, and sometimes even our children—who join with us in celebrating and singing our "Holy, holy, holies."

Now they celebrate with the angels the fullness of joy which we can only anticipate in the Eucharist. "For now we see in a mirror dimly," St. Paul reminds us, "but then face to face" (1 Cor. 13:12). As we press toward that goal, may our prayer be that of the final words of the cantata:

> Lord,
>> Let thine angels not forsake me.
>> But to Thee, when life shall cease,
>> May Elijah's chariot take me
>> There, like Lazarus, in peace.
>> Let me rest in Thine embrace,
>> Fill my heart with joy and grace,
>> When my days on earth are ended,
>> May my soul with Thine be blended.

In Jesus' name. Amen.

www.ingramcontent.com/pod-product-compliance
Lightning Source LLC
Chambersburg PA
CBHW070045230426
43661CB00005B/773